THE CHINESE LANGUAGE TODAY

Modern Languages and Literature

Languages Editor
R. AUTY
M.A., DR.PHIL.(MÜNSTER)
Professor of Comparative Slavonic Philology
in the University of Oxford

THE CHINESE
LANGUAGE TODAY

FEATURES OF AN EMERGING STANDARD

Paul Kratochvíl

Lecturer in Modern Chinese
in the University of Cambridge

HUTCHINSON UNIVERSITY LIBRARY
LONDON

HUTCHINSON & CO (*Publishers*) LTD
178–202 Great Portland Street, London W1

London Melbourne Sydney
Auckland Bombay Toronto
Johannesburg New York

First published 1968

*This book has been set in Times, printed in Great Britain
on Smooth Wove paper by William Clowes and Sons, Limited,
London and Beccles, and bound by Wm. Brendon, of Tiptree, Essex*

TO LAURA

CONTENTS

V. THE NORM

FIGURES

PREFACE

The purpose of this book is to describe the main features of the standard variant of Chinese spoken at present in Mainland China, and also to point out some of the major general issues reflected in the process of its formation. Although the book roughly outlines the system of the standard form of Modern Chinese, it is not a textbook or a grammar; neither is it primarily concerned with writing or the overall historical development of Chinese, and comments in these respects are made only where they are of some importance to the main topic.

One of the major problems which arise when a language like Chinese is discussed is a certain lack of a general frame of reference: relatively little of what has now become universally taken for granted about the more familiar languages appears valid for Chinese, or at least valid without reservations. On the other hand, the Chinese language has acquired an unfortunate position among the kind of exotic phenomena about which various myths and misconceptions persevere with surprising tenacity in the West. On the whole, this means that any attempt at a serious discussion of any aspect of Chinese tends to be directed towards elementary matters rather than delicate points. This book is intended to be such an attempt, and the preceding statement should perhaps partly explain the author's awareness of its obvious shortcomings.

The greater part of this book is based on lectures given by the author at Cambridge University in the years 1963–1966. The informal atmosphere of small classes substantially contributed to the final result, and the author wishes to express his gratitude to all his students whose arguments and suggestions have made them *de facto* co-authors of the book. For reasons determined by the range of its subject, it was necessary to rely on the results of the work of others in many respects. The bibliography on pp. 183–8 contains several books and articles without which many sections of the book would have been impossible to write. The writings of two prominent scholars in particular, Yuen Ren Chao and Charles F. Hockett, have been a constant source of inspiration to the author, and the mark of their ideas is obvious throughout the whole book. Among other publications which have been constantly referred to, the series *Studies in Chinese Communist Terminology* has to be pointed out in particular. Needless to say, the author is solely responsible for any statements which distort or misrepresent what others have written elsewhere. A special word of thanks is directed to the Modern Languages editor of Hutchinson University Library, Professor Robert Auty, for his patience and kind help.

The use of a considerable amount of general linguistic terminology could not be avoided in a book of this kind. Some of the terms and the categories they represent are explained in the text itself, especially those which are applied in a consciously idiosyncratic manner. Others are briefly described in the *List of linguistic terms* on pp. 171–82. The Chinese material in the book is transcribed in the system known as Pinyin, with the exception of some proper names which are presented in the form customarily appearing in current English and American publications. Transcriptions of these proper names are distinguished by the lack of tone diacritics. The Pinyin transcription is indirectly described in Sections 1 and 2 of Chapter II; those readers who are better acquainted with another common system of transcribing Chinese will perhaps find it necessary to use conversion tables accessible in other publications. A conversion table of the Wade-Giles, Pinyin, and Yale transcriptions is contained in the textbook *Beginning Chinese* by John DeFrancis, and also in the 1966 edition of the *Dictionary of Spoken Chinese*. Similar conversion tables including the Gwoyeu Romatzyh system are in W. Simon's *A Beginner's Chinese-English Dictionary*.

P. KRATOCHVÍL

CHAPTER I

INTRODUCTION

I. AFFILIATION AND DIALECTS OF CHINESE

The position of Chinese in relation to the languages of neighbouring communities is a subject of great controversy among scholars.
At present, most languages spoken on Chinese territory, in east
and southeast Asia, as well as in parts of northern India share a
number of more or less similar features. It is not established, however, which of these similarities are distinctive signs of linguistic
affiliation and which are the consequences of many centuries of
coexistence in one cultural area. Another problem arises from the
fact that although many of the languages in question have been
described and studied for many years, others are practically
unknown. Differences in classification are also caused by different
theories about the historical development of the individual
languages and the relationships between them. According to the
most widely accepted opinion Chinese belongs to what are commonly called Sino-Tibetan languages which consist of four main
groups: Chinese, Miao-Yao (a number of languages spoken by
tribes in the mountainous parts of Indochina, northern Burma and
southwestern China), Kam-Thai (Thai, Lao, Shan, and other
languages of southeast Asia), and Tibeto-Burman (spoken in
Tibet, Burma, other parts of south and southeast Asia, and some
areas in northern India). Altogether, several hundred languages
are included within these four groups with an uncertain number
of speakers, possibly as many as 800 million. There are other languages spoken in countries neighbouring on China which show a
great deal of superficial similarity to Chinese, particularly, but

not only, in vocabulary, although their basic structural features clearly show that they are not linguistically related to Chinese. These are in particular Korean and Japanese, and perhaps also Vietnamese. The affiliation of these three languages (Vietnamese is sometimes included in the Sino-Tibetan languages) is unknown and the similarities to Chinese are due to China's long-lasting cultural influence exercised through the intermediary of various Chinese dialects.

The linguistic situation within the area where Chinese is spoken is rather similar to the situation in the larger area of Sino-Tibetan languages in the sense that features of linguistic affiliation are often mixed with features resulting from a long period of cultural co-existence. To deal with the question of Chinese dialects fully it would be necessary to venture into their history, the study of which is one of the main topics of traditional sinology. This, how-ever, would not prove very helpful for describing the present-day situation. The two questions concerning Chinese dialects raised by people interested in Chinese: 'Are Chinese dialects actual dialects or rather different languages?' and 'What is the degree of differ-ence between Chinese dialects?' can perhaps be better elucidated, if not answered, by a closer identification of the term 'language' in relation to dialects and by observing similar language-versus-dialects situations in culturally more familiar areas.

The term 'language' when used in this context has not a purely linguistic meaning. It denotes a variety of forms of oral and some-times also written communication which, on the one hand, share common but not necessarily distinctive linguistic features, and, on the other hand, are used within a culturally, politically, and other-wise socially defined community. When we consider Bavarian and Thuringian two dialects of one language, German, and Dutch a different language, our primary criterion is the latter: while Bavarian and Thuringian are spoken in Germany, Dutch is spoken in the Netherlands. This is not only a consideration of political boundaries. Beside other things, we know that speakers of Bavar-ian and Thuringian have a common cultural and political (in the broad sense) tradition which is reflected in their form of oral communication, and in what they feel and think about this form, and which is not shared by speakers of Dutch; we also know that educated speakers of Bavarian and Thuringian have a common standard, both oral and written, form of communication used in defined social situations, while educated speakers of Dutch use another form in similar situations. The fact that Bavarian, Thuringian and Dutch all share common linguistic features, that it would be difficult to find a set of linguistic features which would draw a clear line between Bavarian and Thuringian on one hand and Dutch on the other, and that it would, actually, be difficult to draw any lines between the three forms at all, because they are linked by chains of communities between which one form of communication gradually merges into another, does not stop us from considering Bavarian and Thuringian as two dialects of one language and Dutch another language.

Transitional links which make the drawing of clear linguistic borderlines next to impossible can be observed in many other cases, for example most of the Romance languages. Although we consider Portuguese, Spanish, French, and Italian as four separate languages, they are connected by chains of groups of speakers in approximately the same way as the above-mentioned dialects of German and Dutch. Our criterion is again non-linguistic: the division into four languages rather than four dialects of a single language is based on traditional cultural, political, and other social considerations.

When we speak of Chinese as a language distinctly different from the languages of neighbouring communities, we are approaching it on grounds not too different from those on which we drew a line between Dutch on the one hand and Bavarian and Thuringian on the other. Irrespective of linguistic evidence, speakers of what is called Chinese share a common cultural heritage which is reflected in many aspects of their life including their language behaviour and which makes them different from speakers of Tibetan, Burmese, Thai, and other languages. Their common standard form of communication represents an important part of this cultural heritage. The Chinese language community is, however, substantially different from the language community to which Bavarian and Thuringian belong, because (among other features) it has so very many more members. We should perhaps be closer to a proportional depiction of the internal composition of Chinese and of the mutual relationship between Chinese dialects if we compared Chinese to a group of related European languages. If, for example, a great number of historical events had not taken place in Europe and if speakers of Portuguese, Spanish, French, and Italian coexisted at the moment in a single political unit, if they had been using Latin as their common written form of communication up to the twentieth century, and if they considered, say, French as spoken in Paris as the most

proper means of oral communication, they could be, although
with a rather large pinch of salt, compared to the speakers of four
large dialectal areas in China.

There are some controversies among scholars as to the classification of modern Chinese dialects. This is partly due to the fact
that a thorough dialectal investigation has not yet been carried
out on the whole Chinese territory and partly to the introduction
of historical criteria into the discussion which makes it necessarily
very complicated and often rather subjective. From the narrow
point of view of the present situation, which will be sufficient for
our purposes, and on the basis of accessible data, Chinese can be
divided into the following seven large groups of dialects (see
Fig. 1)[1]:

(1) Northern Chinese or Mandarin dialects with about 387
million speakers, spoken north of the Yangtze River and also in
large areas south of the river in southwestern China. They are
further divided into four subgroups: the Northern dialects spoken
in Hopeh (including Peking), Shantung, Honan, the northwestern
parts of Anhwei and Kiangsu, the three northeastern provinces
Liaoning, Kirin, and Heilungkiang, and by Chinese speakers
living in the eastern part of Inner Mongolia; the Northwestern
dialects spoken in Shansi, Shensi, and by Chinese speakers living
in Kansu, Tsinghai, the western part of Inner Mongolia, and
further to the northwest; the Southwestern dialects spoken in the
greater part of Hupeh, the northwestern part of Hunan and Kwangsi, in Szechwan, Kweichow, Yunnan, and by Chinese speakers further to the southwest; the River dialects spoken in central Kiangsu
and Anhwei, in southeastern Hupeh and northern Kiangsi.

(2) Wú dialects with about 46 million speakers, spoken in
southern Kiangsu (including Shanghai), southeastern Anhwei,
and by the majority in Chekiang.

(3) Xiāng or Hunanese dialects with about 26 million speakers,
spoken in the greater part of Hunan.

(4) Gàn or Kiangsi dialects with about 13 million speakers,

---

[1] The data on modern Chinese dialects presented here were drawn from the
latest summary of dialectal investigation carried out in Mainland China in the years
1955–1958: Yuán Jiāhuá and others, *Hànyǔ fāngyán gàiyào* 'A Survey of Chinese
Dialects', Peking 1960. The numbers of speakers given in this survey are now, of
course, out of date, and they are valid only in their mutual proportions. When the
survey was published, the total number of Chinese speakers in Mainland China
(that is not including non-Chinese national minorities such as Tibetans, Mongols,
Miao, etc.) was estimated at over 540 million.

spoken in most of Kiangsi, southern Anhwei, and southeastern Hupeh.

(5) Kèjiā or Hakka dialects with about 20 million speakers, spoken in large scattered areas in eastern and southwestern Kwangsi, and in northern Kwangtung.

(6) Yuè or Cantonese dialects with about 27 million speakers, spoken in southeastern Kwangsi and the greater part of Kwangtung (including Canton and Hong Kong).

(7) Mín or Fukienese dialects (further divided into Northern and Southern Mín dialects) with about 22 million speakers,[1] spoken in Fukien, southern Chekiang, northeastern Kwangtung, and also in Hainan and Taiwan.

Chinese dialects share many important features on all structural levels. A relatively simple syllable structure and the occurrence of tone phonemes as parts of syllables are characteristic for all Chinese dialects. The great majority of morphemes in all Chinese dialects are monosyllabic and there is a large common stock of morphemes, although there are differences in the frequency and distribution of the individual member morphemes of this common stock in different dialects. The distribution of morphemes, however, again follows similar general lines: there is practically no formal paradigmatic patterning, and word-formative morphology is limited to a few types of constructions which occur in all dialects. Indistinct borderlines between morphology and syntax, resulting from the fact that a large number of independent syntactic units consist of single morphemes and enter into constructions which are often similar to constructions of morphemes within the smallest syntactic units, are typical for all Chinese dialects. Also typical is probably the most important syntactic feature of all —the occurrence in syntactic constructions of many formal elements or markers whose presence is not always obligatory.

We could find many other common features and it would also be possible to establish on all structural levels (not only on the phonemic level, or 'pronunciation', and in vocabulary, as is commonly believed) features distinctive for individual Chinese dialects. It would, on the other hand, be rather difficult to do so in detail. This is partly due to the lack of complete data which was mentioned above, but primarily to the complex internal composition of individual dialects which makes comparative statements rather

[1] This number does not include Chinese settlers outside China in southeast Asia most of whom are Mín speakers.

2—C.L.T.

problematic. As will be seen later, there has never been in China until relatively recently a strictly defined standard language used by educated speakers in the whole country in oral contact, and the traditional written form of communication was of such a kind that it did not always have to be directly connected with any of the dialects, or in other words, it could be used, to a certain extent, by all educated people without their having to master a standard language form different from their own dialect. This led to a situation quite unlike that in European language communities where the difference between the standard language and dialects is marked by a different degree of sophistication: the standard language is commonly the only basis of the written style and with minor exceptions it is usually the only form of oral communication between educated speakers; dialects are usually not reflected in writing for systematic communicational purposes and within their realm each one maintains a high degree of uniformity irrespective of the social position and educational background of its speakers. In China, this kind of, so to speak, vertical differentiation took place within the dialects themselves, or at least in each of the large groups of dialects. Thus, there are today great differences, particularly in vocabulary, but also on other levels, between various language forms within each dialectal area in China, connected with the social position and mainly the educational background of individual speakers. These differences range from forms used only by uneducated speakers up to the rather strange local variants of language forms associated with units in the traditional written style and usually used only in the sophisticated milieu of literary discussions among intellectuals. If differences between Chinese dialects were to be described in detail, it would have to be done for each of the socially and educationally conditioned variants separately. It will, perhaps, be sufficient for our purposes to state that the differences vary in degree: they are much greater in the 'lower' (forms of oral communication used only by uneducated speakers) than in the 'higher' position. It is mainly in vocabulary where the differences between individual dialects become markedly smaller the 'higher' the position in question: educated speakers of all dialects tend to refer to a common set of vocabulary items and to avoid those which occur only in their dialect. Because of various historical and cultural factors, the Northern Chinese or Mandarin dialects carry more weight in this situation, so that, for example, in the case of vocabulary, the common set of items represents proportionally more of the vocab-

ulary of Mandarin dialects than that of others. This tendency
grows weaker in the relatively 'lower' positions. The possibility of
oral communication between speakers of different Chinese dialects
has to be understood in these terms. It is relatively easier for
educated speakers of different dialects to establish oral contact or
to adapt their speech behaviour to this purpose, while oral communication between uneducated people from different dialectal
areas is difficult or even impossible, mainly in proportion to the
degree of geographical separation, without special training.

2. MODERN STANDARD CHINESE

Perhaps the most unusual feature of Modern Standard Chinese
(MSC), the subject of this book, is that it does not exist at present
as a common tangible fact in the way that, say, Modern Standard
English does in the English-speaking world. By this we do not
mean to say that there is no such thing as Modern Standard
Chinese. The overwhelming majority of educated speakers of all
Chinese dialects share a feeling that some forms, namely those
used by educated speakers of Peking dialect, are 'better' or more
'correct' than others in oral and written communication and most
of them agree on what forms these are, although they are usually
much more liberal about it than speakers of European languages.
Educated people in China very often associate individual language
and written style phenomena, for instance the speech of a Peking
Radio announcer, or the writings of a particular modern author,
such as Lu Hsün, or products of modern Chinese linguistics and
lexicography, such as the popular *Hànyǔ cídiǎn* 'Dictionary of
Chinese', with the concept of standard language forms in the same
way as an educated Englishman thinks of BBC English, E. M.
Forster, and the Oxford Dictionary. On the other hand, however,
educated people in China do not usually feel compelled to go far
beyond the recognition and passive understanding of these commonly accepted 'correct' forms in oral communication, and the
consequence is that proportionally very few people in China
actually use them or even know how to use them in oral contact
systematically. This is particularly striking in various social situations which Europeans associate with the employment of standard
language. It is very common, for example, to hear a Chinese
statesman deliver an important speech in a dialect which is not
commonly understood by speakers of MSC (neither Mao Tse-tung
nor Chiang Kai-shek can speak MSC), and the lectures of many

professors at Peking University (including Wáng Lì, the Professor
of Chinese) are known to be understood completely only by a small
number of students. These are, of course, extreme cases, but it is
generally true that most educated Chinese eliminate possible communicational barriers only by relatively minor adjustments of
their speech behaviour in favour of the 'correct' language forms,
while they prefer to consider the total of these forms, MSC, as a
symbol of national language unity or an important achievement of
modern cultural movements rather than a practical language norm.

The concept of language norm and all that comes with it has
had a long uninterrupted tradition in the sphere of European culture. It is from the point of view of the sometimes subconsciously
accepted norms of individual national European languages that
we speak of dialectal expressions, colloquialisms, archaisms, slang,
and misspellings, all opposed to very concrete features of the
normative, standard language which is described in authoritative
grammars and dictionaries, taught in schools, used in defined
social situations, and reflected in the written style. Such tradition
of language norm and a corresponding norm of writing existed in
China until relatively recent times. The classical written style
called *wényán* 'literary language' or *wénlǐ* 'literary style' represented the norm of writing, and *guānhuà* 'officials' language', also
known as Mandarin, was used, although in a much narrower
sense than European standard languages, as the norm of oral
communication. For various reasons among which the impact of
Western culture on China and the necessity to cope with this
impact played the decisive role, the old written norm began to be
gradually abandoned almost fifty years ago. As a sole means of
written communication it is used today only very exceptionally,
for example in classical poetry, although individual expressions
from the old written style and even some of its syntactic patterns
still occur frequently. In spite of remarkable efforts of at least
three generations of intellectuals the old norm has not yet been
replaced by a modern written style of similar normative standing.
During the same period of time Mandarin went through many
changes and reforms which have not brought it much nearer the
goal of a generally accepted standard language with clearly defined
features. Instead of a concrete norm there is a range of variants
both in the written style and the standard language together with
an abstract idea of unity based on past traditions and stimulated
by modern needs.

This situation has to be taken into account when speaking of

MSC, because it calls for a rather different kind of discussion than if one were dealing with a modern European language. If we aim to present a broader picture than that of an idiolect or a dialect, it is possible, in the case of a modern European language, to make rather exact relative statements on any linguistic phenomenon from the point of view of the existing norm. Corresponding statements on MSC are more like a mean value in statistics: they reflect the common features of individual variants none of which is strictly normative. Such statements are valid only when applied to great numbers of speakers of the language, and when they are applied to idiolects or dialects they often prove inaccurate or even erroneous. It is the aim of this book to present a rather broad picture of MSC and any statements made here will be of this nature. Consequently, they have to be taken with reserve when compared with detailed observations of the speech of individual speakers of MSC or of small groups of such speakers.

The term Modern Standard Chinese, or rather Modern Chinese which is the current term used with a chronological significance, may be and frequently is understood in at least two ways. Many sinologues use the term Modern Chinese in opposition to Classical Chinese: when used in this sense, the term denotes mainly the written style of modern, that is twentieth-century Chinese literature and also the similar style of earlier prose, namely the great Ming and Ch'ing novels, belonging to the sphere of the so-called popular literature which was not considered a part of the officially recognized literary production. Language is not in the centre of attention in this concept of Modern Chinese standard. It is often discussed only in relation to the written style as a kind of underlying criterion whose relative distance from the various forms of the written style serves as a means of their classification: one of the main features of medieval popular novels is that they are written in a style presumably much nearer to the contemporary language than that of the official literature of the same period. This concept of Modern Chinese standard is not linguistic in the strict sense and also not purely historical; it is based mainly on cultural considerations which are not of primary importance for the purposes of this book. The term Modern Standard Chinese will be understood here in the linguistic sense: it will denote, roughly speaking, the language used today by educated speakers of Peking dialect which most speakers of other Chinese dialects consider as the 'correct' form of oral communication and in whose favour they adjust their own speech behaviour.

The broader frame of historical reference necessary for discussing certain features and levels of MSC, particularly its vocabulary, will be the relatively recent period of time stretching slightly more than forty years back. The reason for establishing such a precise limitation in time is a matter of technical convenience. There is no known linguistic evidence according to which Chinese spoken more than fifty years ago could be considered as basically different from the present-day language, that is, as showing that the language had at that time features marking a distinct earlier stage of development. On the other hand, it would be rather difficult to prove the opposite. The problem is that until relatively recently no large-scale direct and systematic recording of the language has ever been made, and this has resulted in an almost total lack of any evidence on its earlier stages. The traditional Chinese writing system is not phonemic (although it does provide some kind of limited phonemic evidence) which makes tasks like the phonemic reconstruction of various historical stages of the language extremely difficult, and in spite of the system's ability to reflect very accurately the morphological and syntactic structure, most of the preserved written documents tell us very little about these levels of the language, because they are written in *wényán*, a highly formalized style with a world of structural patterns of its own. There are literary pieces within the realm of popular literature written in what is claimed to be a close reflection of the language of as early as the T'ang period, but their number is relatively small and they are written in a way which makes them almost useless as documents of the language. The authors of most of them had had some traditional education which included training in *wényán*, and as there had been no other generally recognized norm of writing, their style is a mixture of *wényán* and unsystematic attempts to render the language.

The period of the past forty years or so of MSC covers the time from the so-called May 4th Movement, the modern Chinese cultural revolution of 1919, since when the great majority of all published literature has been written in a more or less sophisticated reflection of the language. The accuracy of this reflection, especially in the beginning of this period, is not much greater than in pre-1919 times, but the extent of the source material permits comparisons and generalizations which could not be easily drawn for earlier periods. This is also the period of the birth of modern Chinese linguistics during which MSC has first been systematically recorded, described, and analysed by Chinese and foreign scholars.

CHAPTER II

PHONEMICS

I. SEGMENTAL FEATURES

Relatively simple syllable structure has been mentioned as one of the characteristic features shared by all Chinese dialects. The fact that this particular formulation was chosen to describe a common feature of the phonemic systems of Chinese dialects (i.e. that syllable structure was mentioned rather than the general pattern of phoneme distribution) is not coincidental. The position of the syllable in the structure of all Chinese dialects, including MSC, is, if the need is felt to introduce evaluatory concepts for the purpose of comparison, more important than might be expected from experience with European languages.

The syllable is the phonemic shape of what might be called the 'basic natural unit' in MSC. If asked to divide an utterance of his into smaller segments, an educated speaker of MSC automatically dissects it into syllables without the slightest hesitation; speakers of European languages in such a situation divide their utterances into larger units comprising one or more syllables, usually words. Many reasons could be found for this, one of them being the influence of the particular type of writing system one is accustomed to on one's feelings about the structure of one's language: while the Chinese use a writing system the basic unit of which roughly corresponds to a syllable, speakers of European languages have developed systems which do not mark borderlines between syllables unless they correspond with word boundaries. This kind of influence undoubtedly exists, but it is misleading to refer to it as the sole reason for the strange predilection for dividing utterances into syllables which is shared by speakers of all Chinese dialects. One may well ask why the Chinese writing system is so different in this respect from the writing systems used by speakers of European languages: are there not perhaps some underlying distinctive features in the structure of the given languages which are merely reflected in the characteristics of the systems of writing their speakers have adopted? Without attempting to answer this question at the moment, it is essential to point out a presumably more important clue than that of the writing system for evaluating the position of the syllable in MSC. The syllable appears as a kind of crosspoint where different levels of MSC grammar intersect: the overwhelming majority of morphemes in MSC are monosyllabic and most MSC morphemes occur as basic syntactic units (or words). It is perhaps primarily this feature which makes speakers of MSC so aware of syllable boundaries: they are usually significant markers of the limits of basic grammatical units.

On the phonemic level itself the syllable is the minimal ground within the limits of which phonemes of different types meet. The syllable in MSC may be defined as a phonemic unit consisting of at least two immediate constituents (or IC's): the specific arrangement of segmental phonemes on the one hand, and one suprasegmental phoneme of one type (or more suprasegmental phonemes of different types) on the other hand. By the latter we understand such phonemes as tones and stress, by the former the arrangement of consonants and vowels which in terms of the laws of MSC phoneme distribution may occur in conjunction with these phonemes.

The laws which govern the arrangement of consonants and vowels in MSC syllables can be summarized by the formula $(C)V(C_1)$ in which each letter symbol represents a specific set of segmental phonemes and the round brackets denote non-obligatoriness of occurrence. Thus, four types of segmental arrangements occur in MSC syllables: CVC_1, CV, VC_1, and V. C stands for the non-obligatory initial consonant, V for the obligatory medial vowel (a simple vowel, a diphthong, or a triphthong), and C_1 for the non-obligatory final consonant.

Consonants included in the following table[1] comprise the non-obligatory set C:

---

[1] For definitions of phonetic terms used in the table and later, see the *List of linguistic terms*, pp. 171–82. Individual sounds are transcribed by symbols of the International Phonetic Alphabet (the first of each pair in square brackets) and of the so-called Pinyin transcription of MSC (the second of each pair in italics).

		Bilabial	Labio-dental	Dental	Alveolar	Alveopalatal	Palatal	Velar
Stop	Unvoiced Non-aspirated	[p-] b-			[t-] d-			[k-] g-
	Unvoiced Aspirated	[p‘-] p-			[t‘-] t-			[k‘-] k-
Nasal	Voiced	[m-] m-			[n-] n-			
Fricative	Unvoiced		[f-] f-	[s-] s-		[ʂ-] sh-	[ɕ-] x-	[x-] h-
	Voiced					[ʐ-] r-		
Lateral	Voiced				[l-] l-			
Affricate	Unvoiced Non-aspirated			[ts-] z-		[tʂ-] zh-	[tɕ-] j-	
	Unvoiced Aspirated			[ts‘-] c-		[tʂ‘-] ch-	[tɕ‘-] q-	

Fig. 2 Table of initial consonants

Perhaps the most striking feature of this set is the overall occurrence of the opposition aspirated versus non-aspirated on the one hand, and the almost total lack of the opposition voiced versus unvoiced. This feature is just the opposite of the corresponding situation in English.[1] While in most dialects of English the opposition aspirated versus non-aspirated is not usually considered phonemic (non-aspirated consonants occur as variants of aspirated consonants in certain environments: [p'in] *pin*—[spin] *spin*), the opposition voiced versus unvoiced is ([p'in] *pin*—[bin] *bin*). Since all initial stops in most English dialects are, at least in slow careful speech, either unvoiced aspirated (as in [p'in] *pin* or [k'ik] *kick*) or voiced non-aspirated (as in [bin] *bin* or [geit] *gate*), speakers of English have difficulties in producing MSC unvoiced non-aspirated initial stops and tend to add either voicing or aspiration (e.g. [pīŋ] *bīng* 'soldier',[2] very often sounds like *[bīŋ] or *[p'īŋ] when coming from an English speaker). For similar reasons, speakers of English do not usually produce easily MSC aspirated unvoiced affricate initial consonants (e.g. [tʂ'á] *chá* 'tea').

As can be seen from Fig. 2, voicing is the sole distinctive feature only between two initial consonants in MSC: *sh*- and *r*-, as in *shén* 'spirit'—*rén* 'man'. In the case of pairs of consonants distinguished by aspiration (stops and affricates) voicing is not a distinctive feature and although these consonants are generally unvoiced in slow careful diction, they frequently acquire some degree of voicing (namely the non-aspirated consonants) in rapid careless speech, particularly if they occur in unstressed syllables. Thus, a word like *kànguo* 'to have seen', may occur in variants ranging from [k'ànkuo] to [k'ànguo]. There are no aspirated fricatives, laterals and nasals, and the respective consonants do

The Pinyin transcription is the only one used in the text from now on except when a relevant phonetic feature is discussed: there the IPA symbol or symbols are given as well.

[1] Some of the consonantal sounds listed in the table are utilized in various English dialects, although, needless to say, their phonemic status in English is quite different. In the following discussion, sounds which cannot be said to occur in English in this sense are dealt with in greater detail than others. However, when English is mentioned, the only purpose is to give a rough impression of the physical features of the given MSC sound and no functional equivalence or resemblance between MSC and English consonantal sounds is implied.

[2] All MSC expressions given as examples in this chapter are free morphemes. In a few cases, however, it was necessary to give a bound morpheme, since the respective free morpheme does not exist. Such bound forms are marked by a dagger, such as [ẓ̩] *rì*† 'sun'. Non-existent forms or arrangements of sounds are marked by an asterisk.

not pattern in pairs, with the above mentioned exception of *sh-* and *r-*.

The phonemic status of the palatal series in MSC (*x-*, *j-*, and *q-*) has been a source of controversy among some scholars. These three consonants occur only before certain vowels (namely [-i] -*i*, -*ü*, and diphthongs and triphthongs the first component of which is [-i-] -*i-* or -*ü-*), while the corresponding consonants of the dental series (*s-*, *z-*, and *c-*) occur preceding all other vowels. The palatal series can, therefore, with certain justification be considered a series of allophones of the dental consonants. Nevertheless, most scholars consider the palatal series a separate set of phonemes on the basis of various arguments among which the need of a simple phonemic system is probably the most important.

Like the dental series, MSC alveopalatal (*sh-*, *r-*, *zh-*, *ch-*), velar (*g-*, *k-*, *h-*) and labiodental (*f-*) consonants do not occur preceding [-i] -*i* and -*ü* (or [-i-] -*i-* and -*ü-*). Since English fricatives and affricates have a relatively narrow range of variants occurring in different environments, speakers of English usually find it difficult to distinguish and imitate the distributionally different MSC dental or alveopalatal consonants on the one hand and the palatal series on the other hand. They commonly tend to produce alveolar or alveopalatal fricatives and affricates regardless of the following vowel (correct [sān] *sān* 'three', but *[sīn] instead of [ɕīn] in *xīn* 'heart', *[tʃˈĭŋ] instead of [tɕˈĭŋ] in *qĭng* 'to ask permission', *[tʃˈá] instead of [tʂˈá] in *chá* 'tea', etc.).

Some sets of MSC initial consonants cause difficulties to speakers of English, since they do not occur in any English dialect. These are all the alveopalatal and palatal consonants, the dental affricates, and the velar fricative. MSC consonants of the alveopalatal series, unlike English alveopalatal consonants (as [ʒ] in [pleʒə] *pleasure*, [ʃ] in [ʃuː] *shoe*, [tʃ] in [tʃek] *check*, and [dʒ] in [dʒem] *gem*), are retroflex, that is they are produced with the tip of the tongue pointed sharply upwards. The resulting effect is particularly audible in the case of MSC *r-* which to many speakers of Modern Standard English seems to remind of r-sounds in some American dialects. Some perceptional resemblance may also be found between the palatal series and English alveopalatal consonants. The main difference is the more backward position of the tongue in the case of MSC. MSC dental affricates (*z-* and *c-*) have no counterparts among English consonantal sounds. They are produced with an affricate release in the same position as the fricative *s-*. The phonemic system of Modern Standard English has a corresponding opposition of sibilance versus affricate release in its alveopalatal series ([ʃ] as in [ʃuː] *shoe*, versus [tʃ] as in [tʃuː] *chew*), but not in the dental position. The MSC velar [x-] *h*- is produced by velar friction unlike the English [h] which is a glottal fricative. It is unvoiced, but similarly as many other unvoiced consonants in MSC, it acquires some degree of voicing in rapid speech mainly in unstressed syllables.

The following vowel sounds occur as individual phonemes or phoneme components (in diphthongs and triphthongs) of the obligatory set V in MSC syllables:

		Front		Central	Back	
		unrounded	rounded	—	unrounded	rounded
High	plain	[-i] -*i* [-i-] -*i*-	[-y] -*ü* [-y-] -*ü*-			[-u] -*u* [-u-] -*u*-
	retro-flex	[-ʅ] -*i*			[-ʅ] -*i*	
Mid	plain	[-e] -*e* [-e-] -*e*-		[-ə-] *e*- [-ə-] -*e*-	[ɣ] *e* [-ɣ] -*e*	[-o] -*o* [-o-] -*o*-
	retro-flex			[ɚ] *er*		
Low	plain	[a] *a* [a-] *a*- [-a] -*a* [-a-] -*a*-		[-ʌ] -*a* [-ʌ-] -*a*-	[ɑ-] *a*- [-ɑ-] -*a*-	

Fig. 3   Table of medial vowels and vowel components

As was mentioned above, V represents a simple vowel, a diphthong or a triphthong. Simple vowels occurring in the CV type of syllables are -*i*, -*ü*, -*u*, -*e*, -*o*, and -*a*. They have the following features:

(1) The vowel phoneme -*i* has three variants: [-i], [-ʅ], and [-ʅ]. The plain front unrounded variant [-i] occurs after bilabials ([pi̯] *bi* 'brush, pen', [p'i̯] *pi* 'leather', [mi̯] *mi* 'rice'), alveolars ([ti̯] *di* 'bottom', [t'i̯] *ti* 'to lift', [ni̯] *ni* 'you' [li̯] *li* 'pear'), and palatals ([ɕi̯] *xi* 'to wash', [tɕi̯] *ji* 'to send', [tɕ'i̯] *qi* 'seven'). The allophone [-ʅ], a retroflex variant produced in the same position as

[-i] with the tip of the tongue pointing upwards, occurs after dentals ([sì] *sì* 'four', [tsì] *zì* 'written character', [ts'í] *cí* 'word'). The allophone [-ʅ], also retroflex, but produced approximately in the same position as [-u] *-u*, occurs after alveopalatals ([ẓʅ] *rì*† 'sun', [ʂʅ] *shí* 'ten', [tʂʅ̌] *zhǐ* 'paper', [tʂ'ʅ] *chī* 'to eat'). None of the *-i* variants occur after *f-* and the velars.

(2) [-y] *-ü*[1] occurs only after *n-* (*nǚ*† 'female'), *l-* (*lǜ* 'green'), and the palatals (*xū* 'empty', *jù* 'a saw', *qù* 'to go').

(3) [-u] *-u* occurs after all consonants excepting the palatals (e.g. *mù* 'tomb', *fú* 'to submit', *zū* 'to rent', *tǔ* 'to spit', *lù* 'road', *shū* 'book', *hú* 'pot').

(4) [-ɤ] *-e* occurs after dentals ([sɤ̀] *sè* 'rough', [tsɤ́] *zé*† 'duty', [ts'ɤ̀] *cè*† 'policy'), *d-* ([tɤ́] *dé* 'to get'), *t-* ([t'ɤ̀] *tè*† 'special'), *l-* ([lɤ̀] *lè* 'to be happy'), the alveopalatals ([ẓɤ̀] *rè* 'to be hot' [ʂɤ́] *shé* 'snake', [tʂɤ̀] *zhè* 'this', [tʂ'ɤ̄] *chē* 'vehicle'), and velars ([kɤ̄] *gē* 'to put', [k'ɤ̀] *kè* 'guest', [xɤ̄] *hē* 'to drink').

(5) *-o* occurs only after bilabials (*bō* 'to push aside', *pò* 'to break', *mō* 'to touch'), and *f-* (*Fó* 'Buddha'). The phonemic status of *-o* is questioned by some scholars who prefer to consider it an allophone of *-e*, others consider it a variant of the diphthong *-uo*.

(6) [-a] *-a* occurs after bilabials ([pā] *bā* 'eight', [p'á] *pá* 'to crawl', [mǎ] *mǎ* 'horse'), *f-* ([fā] *fā* 'to issue'), dentals ([sǎ] *sǎ* 'spill', [tsá] *zá* 'mixed', [ts'ā] *cā* 'to wipe'), alveolars ([tà] *dà* 'to be big', [t'ā] *tā* 'he', [ná] *ná* 'to take', [lā] *lā* 'to pull'), alveopalatals ([ʂā] *shā* 'to kill', [tʂà] *zhà* 'to explode', [tʂ'á] *chá* 'tea'), and velars ([kǎ] *gǎ*† 'to be a rascal', [k'ā] *kā* in *kāfēi* 'coffee', [xā] *hā* 'to exhale').

Diphthongs and triphthongs occurring in the CV type of syllables are *-ia*, *-ie*, *-iao*, *-iu* ([-iu] or [-iou]), *-ua*, *-uo*, *-uai*, *-ui* ([-ui] or [-uei]), *-üe* or *-ue*[1], *-ou*, *-ei*, *-ai*, and *-ao*. They have the following features:

(1) Of the unrounded high and mid vowel sounds only [-i] *-i* (or [-i-] *-i-*) and [-e] *-e* (or [-e-] *-e-*) occur as components of diphthongs and triphthongs (e.g. [pēi] *bēi* 'to carry on one's back', [tɕiè] *jiè* 'to borrow').

(2) Of the low vowel sounds [-ʌ] *-a* (or [-ʌ-] *-a-*) occurs only in the diphthong [-iʌ] *-ia* and the triphthong [-iʌo-] *-iao* (e.g. [tɕiʌ̄] *jiā* 'family', [ɕiʌ̀o] *xiào* 'to laugh'). [-a] *-a* (or [-a-] *-a-*)

---

[1] In Pinyin transcription [-y] *-ü* (or [-y-] *-ü-*) can be written as *-u* (or *-u-*) after *x-*, *j-*, *q-*, and *y-* which are never followed by [-u] *-u*. Thus, *xü*, *jü*, *qü*, *yü*, etc. are commonly written as *xu*, *ju*, *qu* and *yu*.

occurs in other diphthongs and triphthongs (e.g. [kuà] *guà* 'to hang', [ʂuāi] *shuāi* 'to fall', [lái] *lái* 'to come', [māo] *māo* 'cat').

(3) The distribution of diphthongs and triphthongs in regard to the preceding consonants in the CV type of syllables roughly corresponds to the distribution of the given first component as a simple vowel. For example, the diphthong -*ia* occurs after consonants which may precede the simple vowel [-i] -*i* (some forms which could be expected to occur do not, however, exist in the MSC phonemic system, viz. *bia, *pia, *mia, *dia, *tia, and *nia) and it does not occur after consonants which do not precede this vowel. There are examples of non-occurrent forms in the case of most diphthongs and triphthongs and there are also cases of non-occurrent forms containing simple vowels, namely of the simple vowels -*o* and -*e* after consonants which occur with the diphthongs -*ou* and -*ei* (e.g. *do, but *dōu* 'all'; *zo, but *zǒu* 'to walk'; *pe, but *pèi* 'to match'; *fe, but *fēi* 'to fly', etc.).

(4) MSC diphthongs and triphthongs are complex vowels, not combinations of individual simple vowels. Very impressionistically speaking, they are produced by the shape of the oral cavity smoothly shifting in the general direction of the vowel sounds concerned, but not necessarily starting from, crossing through or reaching the target position of these sounds. In slow, careful speech the diphthongs and triphthongs of most stressed syllables approximate to these ultimate and intermediary targets; in rapid speech, however, the distance between the actual and the target positions (especially of the last component) may be relatively great. In rapid speech the shape of the oral cavity tends to shift along, so to speak, straight short lines. This can be demonstrated by two examples:

(a) *lái* 'to come' in slow careful speech sounds [lái] or even [láei]; the shape of the oral cavity is changed by the tongue moving upwards from the almost ultimate target position of [a-] through the position of [-e-], almost reaching the position of [-i] (see Fig. 4). In rapid speech the shift follows the same general direction, but it is considerably shorter (see Fig. 5). The syllable then sounds more like [láe], [léi], or even [lé].

(b) *jiù* 'to be old' in slow careful speech sounds [tɕiòu] or even [tɕiəou] (see Fig. 6). In rapid speech it sounds [tɕiù] or even [tɕiò]: the shift of shape is shorter and more straight (see Fig. 7).

The phonetic shape of diphthongs and triphthongs is considerably variable in the preceding terms. The variability is particularly perceptible in the case of -*iu* and -*ui* which commonly sound either as diphthongs or triphthongs (e.g. [kuì] or [kueì] *guì* 'to be expensive', [liù] or [lioù] *liù* 'six').

The complex character of MSC diphthongs and triphthongs is also reflected in their duration as compared with that of simple vowels. Generally speaking, diphthongs and triphthongs have slightly greater duration than simple vowels, but much smaller

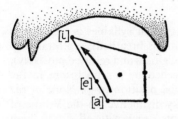

Fig. 4
Tongue shift in [lái] ~ [láei] *lái*

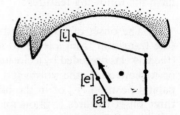

Fig. 5
Tongue shift in [láe] ~ [léi] ~ [lé] *lái*

than the combination of the durations of their components occurring as simple vowels. For example, the duration of vowels in the syllables [pà] *bà*, [pò] *bò*, and [pào] *bào* recorded by the same speaker of MSC in similar conditions was measured with

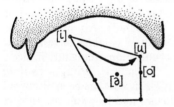

Fig. 6
Tongue shift in [tɕiòu] ~ [tɕiəou] *jiù*

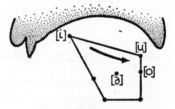

Fig. 7
Tongue shift in [tɕiù] ~ [tɕiò] *jiù*

these results: [-à] *-à* in [pà] *bà* 0·23 sec, [-ò] *-ò* in [pò] *bò* 0·22 sec, and [-ào] *-ào* in [pào] *bào* 0·28 sec. [-ào] *-ào* lasted longer than either [-à] *-à* or [-ò] *-ò* (0·28 sec:0·23 sec, 0·22 sec), but its duration was much smaller than the total of durations of [-à] *-à* and [-ò] *-ò* (0·28 sec:*0·45 sec).

This feature results in the auditive impression of MSC simple vowels being 'long' as opposed to the corresponding 'short' components of diphthongs and triphthongs. Length, however, is not

a phonemically distinctive feature in MSC, since there are no oppositions of long versus short between either simple vowels or complex
vowels themselves (e.g. *[pà:]—[pà] *bà*, *[pà:o]—[pào] *bào*).

The V type of syllables (a relatively small group) consist of a
simple vowel, a diphthong or a triphthong. They are *a, e, er, ai, ao,
ou, yi, yu, ya, ye, yao, you, yue, wu, wa, wo, wai*, and *wei*, and they
have the following features:

(1) The onset of vowels in this type of syllables is either zero
(the transition from silence to sound is breathed), a glottal stop
(the vowel is preceded by a closure of glottis and released plosively),
or a semivowel (the vowel is preceded by a semiclosure in the
palatal position [j-] or in the bilabial position [w-]). None of the
three onset features is phonemically distinctive. In the V type of
syllables, the semivowel components occur with all simple high
plain vowels and with diphthongs and triphthongs the first component of which is high plain: [j-] *y-* precedes all high front plain
sounds ([-i] -*i*—[ji] *yi* as *yī* 'one'; [-y] -*ü*—[jy] *yu* as *yǔ* 'rain';
[-iA] -*ia*—[jiA] *ya* as *yā* 'to press down'; [-ie] -*ie*—[jie] *ye* as *yě*
'wild'; [-iAo] -*iao*—[jiAo] *yao* as *yào* 'medicine'; [-iu] or [-iou] -*iu*
—[jiou] *you* as *yóu* 'oil'; [-ye] -*üe*—[jye] *yue* as *yuè* 'month'), and
[w-] *w-* precedes the high back [-u] -*u* or [-u-] -*u*- ([-u] -*u*—[wu] *wu*
as *wǔ* 'five'; [-ua] -*ua*—[wua] *wa* as *wā* 'to dig'; [-uo] -*uo*—[wuo]
wo as *wǒ* 'I'; [uai] -*uai*—[wuai] *wai* as *wāi* 'to be tilted'; [-ui] or
[-uei] -*ui*—[wuei] *wei* as *wéi* 'to surround'). All other simple
vowels, diphthongs, and triphthongs in V syllables have zero or
glottal stop onset. The glottal stop occurs more frequently in slow,
careful speech (e.g. [ʔáo] or [áo] *áo* 'to endure', [ʔòu] or [òu] *òu*
'to steep'). (The question of semivowels in MSC has been discussed
in different ways by many phonologists and it is still the subject
of controversy. The approach presented above is based more on
phonetic than phonemic considerations.)
(2) Only the front allophone [a] of the phoneme *a* and the back
allophone [ɤ] of the phoneme *e* occur as simple vowels in the V
type of syllables (e.g. [a] *a* 'Oh!', [ɤ] *è* 'to be hungry').
(3) The mid central retroflex [ɚ] *er*, produced in about the same
position as the mid central [ə] with the tip of the tongue pointing
upwards, occurs only in the V type of syllables (e.g. [ɚ] *èr* 'two').
The syllable *er* under certain conditions clusters with the preceding syllable. This phenomenon called 'erisation' or 'cacuminal
modification' is not purely phonemic, since the conditions are

morphological, and as such it will be discussed later together with other morphophonemic features of MSC.

(4) The phonetic features of diphthongs and triphthongs occurring in the V type of syllables, beside the features mentioned above, are generally the same as those of diphthongs and triphthongs occurring in the CV type. The variability of the phonetic shape of some diphthongs and triphthongs in the CV type of syllables is, however, somewhat restricted in the V type. For example, *-iu* and *-ui* which sound either as diphthongs ([-iu], [-ui]) or triphthongs ([-iou], [-uei]) in the CV type, appear in a more uniform shape of triphthongs ([jiou] *you*, [wuei] *wei*) in the V type.

Two nasal consonants *-n* ([-n], produced in the alveolar position) and *-ng* ([-ŋ], produced in the velar position) are the only members of the non-obligatory set C_1 in MSC syllables. They have the following features:

(1) Both the final nasal consonants cause a slight nasalization of the preceding simple vowel or vowel component if the vowel is a diphthong (nasal consonants do not occur after triphthongs), and the position of the preceding vowel sound is influenced by the given nasal: of the mid plain vowel sounds only [ə-] *e-* (or [-ə-] *-e-*) occurs before both *-n* and *-ng*, of the low vowel sounds [a-] *a-* (or [-a-] *-a-*) occurs before *-n* and [ɑ-] *a-* (or [-ɑ-] *-a-*) before *-ng*. The character of the production of a vowel sound followed by a nasal consonant is similar to that of the production of diphthongs and triphthongs in the gradual and smooth shift of the shape of the oral cavity. In this sense, vowels form complex sounds with the following nasal consonants. This is reflected in the duration of vowels followed by nasal consonants as compared with that of vowels in the CV and V type of syllables. The duration of vowels in the CVC_1 or VC_1 type of syllables is considerably smaller, and the duration of both the vowel and the nasal consonant is usually only slightly greater than that of the corresponding vowel in the CV or V type. For example, the durations of [-ù] *-ù* in [tù] *dù* and [-ùŋ] *-òng* in [tùŋ] *dòng* recorded in similar conditions by the same speaker of MSC were measured as 0·23 sec ([-ù] *-ù*) and 0·26 sec ([-ùŋ] *-òng*), while the duration of [-ù-] *-ù-* in [tùŋ] *dòng* alone was measured as only 0.14 sec. This feature results in the auditive impression of MSC vowels in the CV and V type of syllables being 'long' as opposed to the corresponding 'short' vowels in the CVC_1 and VC_1 types.

(2) In CVC₁ and VC₁ syllables where the nasal consonant -*n* is preceded by the simple vowel [-u-] -*u*- the shift of the tongue from the one position to the other is not always straight, but it dips slightly in the intermediary mid central position. Thus the mid central [-ə-] appears in most of these syllables between [-u-] -*u*- and the final nasal -*n*. For example, [lùn]—[luən] *lùn* 'to discuss', [wùn]—[wuən] *wèn* 'to ask'. The same happens when [-u-] -*u*- precedes the final -*ng* in the VC₁ type of syllables ([wùŋ]—[wuəŋ] *wèng* 'to sound thick'), but not in the CVC₁ type ([lúŋ] *lóng* 'dragon').

(3) In the CVC₁ type of syllables -*n* occurs after [-a-] -*a*- ([pān] *bān* 'to remove'), [-ə-] -*e*- ([tʂən] *zhēn* 'needle'), [-iə-] -*ia*- ([tɕiən] *jiàn* 'to see'), [-i-] -*i*- ([ɕīn] *xīn* 'heart'), [-ua-] -*ua*- ([kuān] *guān* 'to shut'), [-u-] or [-uə-] -*u*- ([lùn] or [luən] *lùn* 'to discuss'), [-ya-] -*üa*- ([tɕ‘yán] *quán* 'completely'), and [-y-] -*ü*- ([tɕỳn] *jùn* 'handsome'). -*ng* occurs after [-a-] -*a*- ([máŋ] *máng* 'to be busy'), [-ə-] -*e*- ([ʂəŋ] *shēng* 'to be born'), [-u-] -*o*- ([tùŋ] *dòng* 'to move'). [-ia-] -*ia*- ([tɕiăŋ] *jiǎng* 'to talk'), [-i-] -*i*- ([pīŋ] *bīng* 'soldier'), [-iu-] -*io*- ([tɕ‘iúŋ] *qióng* 'to be poor'), and [-ua-] -*ua*- ([kuāŋ] *guāng* 'light'). The occurrence of the initial consonants in this type of syllables is roughly the same as in the CV type of syllables with the same medial vowels. Among several exceptions is the occurrence of *b*-, *p*-, *m*-, and *f*- in CVC₁ syllables where the medial vowel is -*e*- (e.g. **be*, but [pən] *bèn* 'stupid'; **fe*, but [fəŋ] *fēng* 'wind').

(4) In the VC₁ type of syllables (a rather small group), the final -*n* occurs after [a-] *a*- ([àn] *àn* 'shore'), [ə-] *e*- ([ən] *ēn* 'kind act'), [jiə-] *ya*- ([jiən] *yǎn* 'eye'), [ji-] *yi*- ([jín] *yín* 'silver'), [wua-] *wa*- ([wuán] *wán* 'to be finished'), [wu-] or [wuə-] *we*- ([wùn] or [wuən] *wèn* 'to ask'), [jya-] *yua*- ([jyǎn] *yuǎn* 'to be distant'), and [jy-] *yu*- ([jỳn] *yùn* 'to iron'). -*ng* occurs after [a-] *a*- ([āŋ] *āng*† 'filthy'), [jia-] *ya*- ([jiáŋ] *yáng* 'sheep'), [ji-] *yi*- ([jīŋ] *yīng* 'eagle') [wua-] *wa*- ([wuàŋ] *wàng* 'to forget'), [wu-] or [wuə-] *we*- ([wùŋ] or [wuəŋ] *wèng* 'to sound thick'), and [jiu-] *yo*- ([jiùŋ] *yòng* 'to use').

Some scholars posit the occurrence of consonants in MSC in the C₁ position other than the two nasals, namely [-m], for example in [t‘ām] 'they'. All syllables containing such final consonants occur, however, only in rapid speech as variants of a small number of certain disyllabic constructions ([tām] or [t‘āmən] *tāmen* 'they'). It is therefore preferable to consider these final consonants as morphophonemic variants of full syllables.

2. SUPRASEGMENTAL FEATURES

The most striking suprasegmental feature of MSC syllables is the characteristic contour known as the tone. Since tones are minimal distinctive features differentiating syllables identical in segmental structure, they are phonemically distinctive features and we speak of tone phonemes (sometimes called tonemes). There are four tone phonemes in MSC: high (as in *bā* 'eight'), rising (*bá* 'to uproot'), low (*bǎ* 'to hold'), and falling (*bà* 'a harrow'). The tone phoneme is an immediate constituent of the syllable whose other IC is the given arrangement of segmental phonemes, which means that only one tone phoneme may occur in a syllable. The overwhelming majority of MSC syllables have tone phonemes as IC's, that is to say they may comprise the phonetic shape of a variant of one of the four tones, although they not always do so. These are the so-called tonic syllables. There are, however, syllables which never have a tone phoneme as their IC. Such syllables, called atonic, have certain specific segmental features (some of them, for example, have variants which are not full syllables, as the [-m] in [t'ām] which is a variant of the syllable [-mən] *-men* in *tāmen* 'they' mentioned earlier), but since they are characterized by their morphological status rather than their phonemic structure, their distinctive lack of tone belongs to the sphere of morphophonemics. They will be only occasionally mentioned in this chapter which is primarily concerned with tonic syllables.

In spite of everything that has been written and said by linguists about MSC tones, their phonetic character is still frequently misunderstood and misinterpreted, and they often cause frustration to students of MSC who are puzzled by the vast difference between the common theoretical description and the appearance of tones in neatly arranged tone combination patterns on the one hand, and the phonetic reality of tones in live speech on the other. The reason for this is mainly that MSC tones are high degree abstractions of only one of an extremely complex network of MSC suprasegmental features. All phonemic categories are, of course, abstract by nature, but a segmental unit is abstract in a slightly different sense than a suprasegmental unit. A segmental unit belongs to a set comprising a relatively large number of discrete items each of which is based on a relatively narrow range of variants; its concrete basis consists of formally different variants whose shape is influenced by environmental factors, but the individual factors are relatively easy to identify, and what is probably most important, the abstract segmental unit is usually most closely associated with only one concrete form of the most commonly occurring variant. Thus, when we speak of a segmental unit like the phoneme -*i* in MSC, we know that it is one of some fifty discrete MSC phonemes and that it is an abstraction of at least three different but relatively very similar concrete forms: the front plain variant [-i], the front retroflex variant [-ɿ], and the back retroflex variant [-ʅ]. Since the first variant occurs in most segmental environments, it may be considered as basic, a kind of concrete equivalent of the abstract phoneme, and the other variants may be treated as deviations from this basic form. The main factors influencing the occurrence of these deviations are simple and they can be identified and isolated easily: [-ɿ] occurs only after dental consonants and [-ʅ] after alveopalatal consonants in the CV type of syllables.

In comparison with this situation, such suprasegmental units as tones are abstractions of, so to speak, a much higher degree. They are derived from a closely knit pattern of various suprasegmental features each of which consists of a small number of items with numerous variants; these features almost always cluster together and their mutual relationship is extremely flexible. They can be identified and isolated by careful acoustic analysis, but it is next to impossible to separate them auditively from each other (for example, to separate tone and stress in MSC). Moreover, the abstract tone has no concrete equivalent as a segmental phoneme has, apart from some very general common tendencies shared by all its variants. It rather occurs in the form of a great number of variants whose shapes depend on the number and type of other suprasegmental features with which it clusters. It is helpful to make the abstraction and know about it, but the abstraction is practically useless—much more so than a segmental abstraction—for any but the most general approach to the language unless we know and understand what is between it and the concrete forms.

Although tones are, structurally speaking, IC's of the whole syllables, their actual physical shape is the way in which they modify the only obligatory segmental component of the syllable, that is the vowel. The modification has three acoustic dimensions: fundamental frequency, intensity level, and duration, which means that syllables, or rather the vowels of syllables with some tones are perceived as, for example, 'higher', 'louder in the beginning', and 'longer' than syllables with other tones. Of the three acoustic dimensions fundamental frequency (perceived as relative pitch) is the most easily identified and the only one usually mentioned in connection with MSC tones. The remaining two dimensions are, however, equally important; this can be observed in situations where tones can be distinguished, although fundamental frequency is excluded, as in whispering.

The general tendencies of the four tones are commonly demonstrated on isolated tonic syllables. These citation forms practically never occur in live speech, but they are useful as an illustrative starting point for a more detailed discussion on the relationship between suprasegmental abstraction and concrete shape. The four tones of such citation forms have the following phonetic shape:

(1) The high tone (marked ‾ above the vowel symbol in Pinyin, as in *bā* 'eight') has an almost level contour of pitch which is positioned in the upper third of the natural pitch range of the speaker's voice; the loudness of the respective vowel sound remains the same throughout the whole vowel, and the duration of syllables with this tone is slightly above average.

(2) The rising tone (marked ´ as in *bá* 'to uproot') has a rising pitch contour starting in about the middle of the range and ending slightly above the level of high tone; the loudness rises towards the end of the vowel, and the duration is slightly below average.

(3) The low tone (marked ˇ as in *bǎ* 'to hold') has a dipping pitch contour mildly falling in the first two thirds of the vowel, reaching almost the bottom limit of the range, and sharply rising in the last third; the loudness is generally slightly falling with a small rise at the very end of the vowel, and the duration is well above average.

(4) The falling tone (marked ` as in *bà* 'a harrow') has a falling pitch contour starting almost at the top limit of the range and reaching its lower third at the end; the loudness falls sharply towards the end of the vowel, and the duration is far below average.

The phonetic shapes of tones in citation forms can be visually summarized by diagrams such as those in Fig. 8.[1]

---

[1] The two horizontal lines in tone graphs delimit the natural range of the given speaker's voice pitch, the bottom line representing the low limit. Vertical lines delimit the relative duration (from the left to right) of the given segmental sound; since differences between the durations of consonants are irrelevant in the great part of the discussion, the space between vertical lines delimiting consonants merely suggests their position, not their relative duration. Varying thickness of the tone curve indicates increase or decrease in loudness. The tone diagrams in this chapter are based on acoustic measurements, but since it was necessary to generalize and schematize to a considerable degree, they are of a merely illustrative nature.

One of the factors which cause modifications of these general tendencies of tones in continuous speech is the influence of the tone environment of the given syllable. This is what is known as tone sandhi. The conditions under which tone sandhi affects syllables are rather complicated and not only phonemic: it does not only matter if the syllable in which some tone modification is liable to take place is immediately followed by a syllable whose tone could cause the change, but also what grammatical value

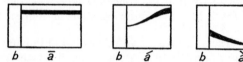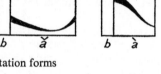

Fig. 8   Tones in citation forms

each of the syllables has, for example, whether or not both of the syllables belong to one morphological unit. The two most common modifications caused by tone sandhi affect the tendencies of the low tone and the falling tone. If a syllable with low tone is immediately followed by another syllable with low tone, the low tone of the first syllable may be modified to a variant similar to the citation form rising tone in pitch contour and duration, but retaining the fall in loudness characteristic of the first two-thirds of the citation form low tone, as, for instance, in the word *lǎozǎo* 'long ago, for a long time' (see Fig. 9). If a syllable with low tone

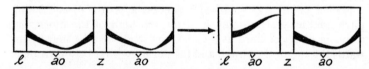

Fig. 9   Modification of low tone by tone sandhi in *lǎozǎo*

is immediately followed by a syllable with any other but low tone (or an atonic syllable), its low tone may be modified to a variant which resembles the first two-thirds of the citation form low tone pattern in all three dimensions, as in *lǎodà* 'the eldest (of brothers)' (see Fig. 10). If a syllable with falling tone is immediately followed by another syllable with falling tone, the falling tone of the first syllable may be modified to a variant which, in comparison with the citation form falling tone, starts slightly lower and drops to only about the middle of the pitch range, is of about equal duration, and has its loudness more evenly distributed while retaining the falling tendency, as in *dàlù* 'continent' (see Fig. 11). Similar modifications take place in syllables in sequences of three or more.

Beside the factor of tone sandhi, important modifications of tones are caused by the influence of concurring suprasegmental

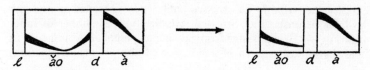

Fig. 10   Modification of low tone by tone sandhi in *lǎodà*

features of other types. This influence, since unlike tone sandhi it affects practically every syllable in continuous speech and since it also affects syllables whose tones were already modified by tone sandhi, gives tones their final phonetic shape. The suprasegmental features involved are mainly stress and intonation.

The influence of intonation, a phonemic feature of relatively large segments of speech, materializes in the modification of the pitch contour of individual tones and the general position of the

Fig. 11   Modification of falling tone by tone sandhi in *dàlù*

pitch contour between the limits of the natural range of voice pitch. Thus, for example, in a short sentence whose intonation contour is level and mildly falling towards the end (a typical intonation contour of unemphatic declarative statements), the pitch contours of the tones of all but the last syllable are somewhat levelled out and the pitch contour of the tone of the last syllable is modified by the final falling tendency of the intonation contour. Such intonation contour influence is shown in Fig. 12. The sentence in question is *tā ài huā qián*, 'He loves to spend money' (*tā*

'he', *ài* 'to love to', *huā* 'to spend', *qián* 'money'). This influence of
intonation on the phonetic shape of tones is on the one hand
extremely variable, since the number of intonation contours and
their variants is very high, but on the other hand it is very simple
in its general character, as it has only a one-dimensional effect in
modifying the pitch contour of the tone and its position. It is,
therefore, relatively easy to perceive and identify.

The similar influence of stress is much more complex. By stress
in this context we mean a feature whose presence in a syllable
marks the syllable as stressed and whose absence marks the
syllable as unstressed. Stressed syllables fulfil a number of functions in MSC which range from serving as points of prominence in
the rhythmical pattern of a sentence (a non-phonemic function)

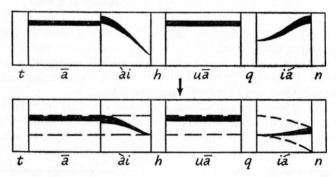

Fig. 12   Influence of intonation on tones in *tā ài huā qián*

to distinguishing members of pairs of polysyllabic constructions
identical in segmental structure and tones. Since the latter function is phonemic, stress is a phonemically distinctive feature in
MSC, although its phonemic value is not always utilized. The
situation is not unlike that in English where stress may also fulfil a
phonemic function (as, for example, in pairs like [ˈɔbdʒekt] *object*
'thing aimed at' and [əbˈdʒekt] *object* 'to express disapproval'),
but not always does. Since all occurrences of stress in MSC share
the same phonetic shape, although their grammatical function
may vary greatly, the influence of stress on tones can be discussed
in the following general manner leaving the question of stress
function aside for the moment.

Stress, like tone, is an IC of the syllable and its physical shape takes the form of the modification of the obligatory vowel. The modification has again at least three acoustic dimensions: fundamental frequency, intensity level and duration,[1] which means that some stressed syllables are perceived, for example, as 'higher', 'louder', and 'longer' than some unstressed syllables. Since the acoustic dimensions of stress and tone are the same (that is the same in quality, not in function), it is obviously difficult to discuss the phonetic shape of one without referring to the other, particularly when the two features occur together. In fact, the only reason why we speak of tone and stress rather than a single tone-and-stress system (or *accentual system*) is that the two features are subordinate in the phonemic structure of the language, tone being the condition of stress and not vice versa. There exist tonic unstressed syllables in MSC, but there are no atonic stressed syllables; in tonic stressed syllables the phonetic features of stress vary according to the syllables' tones.

The way stress modifies the vowel of a syllable can be demonstrated in the final phonetic shape of tones in constructions of two tonic syllables where no or very little tone sandhi takes place. For our purpose citation forms of such constructions will be used to exclude the influence of intonation, and we shall compare pairs of constructions of syllables identical in segmental structure and tone (that is where stress has a phonemic function, as in the abovementioned case of English ['ɔbdʒekt] versus [əb'dʒekt]).

In a pair of disyllabic constructions like ['ɕíŋli] *xíngli* 'luggage' and [ɕíŋ'lǐ] *xínglǐ* 'to perform a courtesy', the only distinctive feature is stress: in the former construction the first syllable is stressed and the second unstressed, in the latter the first syllable is unstressed and the second stressed. The modification caused by stress is shown in Fig. 13; Fig. 14 indicates stress modification in a similar pair of constructions ['tɕɕȳnʂ̩] *jūnshi* 'military affairs' and [tɕɕȳn'ʂ̩] *jūnshì* 'balance of power'. As can be seen from the respective graphs, the shape of stressed syllables differs from that of neutral syllables in isolated citation forms. However, the influence of stress is not uniform: it modifies syllables with different tones

[1] Beside these three dimensions, the characteristic formant structure which is an acoustic property of vowel quality distinguishing one vowel sound from another is also an acoustic dimension of stress: the vowels of stressed syllables are slightly different from vowels of unstressed syllables in this respect (i.e. different in the place of their production and consequently in their acoustic quality). This dimension is, however, not important in the case of tonic syllables and need not be discussed here. Some modification of vowel quality is, in fact, a dimension of tones as well, but there it is of even less importance than in the case of stress.

in a different way. This so-called positive influence of stress (modification of vowels in stressed syllables) affects syllables with different tones as follows:

(1) Vowels of stressed syllables with high tone are shorter and louder in the beginning than those of unstressed syllables, and they have a slightly falling pitch contour. (See *jūn* in citation form and in [ˈtɕȳnʂ̩], Fig. 14.)

(2) Vowels of stressed syllables with rising tone are slightly longer, less loud in the beginning and louder towards the end than those of unstressed syllables, and their pitch contour is more pronounced: it starts lower and ends higher. (See *xíng* in citation form and in [ˈɕíŋli], Fig. 13.)

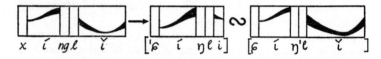

Fig. 13   Modification by stress in [ˈɕíŋli] *xínglĭ* and [ɕíŋˈlĭ] *xínglĭ*

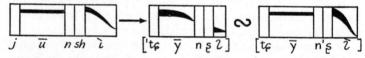

Fig. 14   Modification by stress in [ˈtɕȳnʂ̩] *jūnshì* and [tɕȳnˈʂ̩] *jūnshì*

(3) Vowels of stressed syllables with low tone are longer, louder at the beginning and at the end than those of unstressed syllables, and their pitch contour is more pronounced: it starts higher, falls lower, and ends higher. (See *lĭ* in citation form and in [ɕíŋˈlĭ], Fig. 13.)

(4) Vowels of stressed syllables with falling tone are shorter, louder in the beginning and less loud towards the end than those of unstressed syllables, and their pitch contour is more pronounced: it starts higher and ends lower. (See *shì* in citation form and in [tɕȳnˈʂ̩], Fig. 14.)

These modifications (and similar modifications of syllables affected by tone sandhi) take place in stressed syllables regardless of their stress environment, that is whether they are preceded or

followed by unstressed syllables. There are, however, considerable
differences between unstressed syllables preceding and following
stressed syllables, as can be seen from the diagrams in Figs. 13
and 14. Vowels of unstressed syllables which precede stressed
syllables do not differ from those of neutral isolated citation forms
or neutral citation forms of syllables affected by tone sandhi (see
xíng and *jūn* in citation forms and in [ɕíŋˈlǐ] and [tɕȳnˈʂɿ̀] in
Figs. 13 and 14), but vowels of unstressed syllables which follow
stressed syllables have rather different features (see *lǐ* and *shì* in
citation forms and in [ˈɕíŋli] and [ˈtɕȳnʂɿ] in Figs. 13 and 14).
The modification in the latter group of syllables is caused by the
so-called negative influence of stress, and vowels exposed to this
influence occur in a very broad range of variants. Generally
speaking, the negative influence of stress modifies vowels so that
they are shorter and less loud than vowels of neutral citation form
syllables, and their pitch contour and distribution of loudness
tend to be less pronounced. However, the degree of this modification varies greatly: at one extreme are vowels only slightly different from those of neutral citation form syllables, while at the other
extreme are very short vowels which tend towards a uniform falling shape of unpronounced pitch contour and distribution of
loudness, irrespective of their tone. (The vowels of unstressed
syllables following stressed syllables in Figs. 13 and 14 are of the
latter kind.) The actual position between these two extremes of the
vowel of a given unstressed tonic syllable negatively influenced by
stress depends on several factors of which the tempo and carefulness of diction are the most important.

The suprasegmental shape of atonic syllables is the same as that
of unstressed tonic syllables negatively influenced by stress positioned very near the lower extreme: their vowels are very short,
their loudness is very slight, and their pitch contour and distribution of loudness are unpronounced, having a uniform falling
tendency.

The position of the pitch contour and its shape in syllables with
unpronounced features, tonic or atonic, are influenced by the tonal
environment of these syllables and by the intonation of the sentence in which they occur. The position of the pitch contour
within the limits of the natural pitch range is given mainly by the
tone of the preceding syllable which is usually stressed: when the
preceding syllable is a syllable with high or falling tone, the position of the unpronounced pitch contour is relatively low, as in
-men in *tāmen* 'they', and *-ba* in *bàba* 'daddy' (see Fig. 15); when

the preceding is a syllable with rising tone, its position is around
the middle of the range, as in -*tou* in *gútou* 'bone' (see Fig. 15);
when the preceding is a syllable with low tone, its position is relatively high, as in -*hu* in *mǎhu* 'to be confused' (see Fig. 15). The
generally falling tendency of the pitch contour in syllables with
unpronounced features may be slightly influenced by the tone of
the following syllable and by the intonation contour of the sentence: it may, for example, become almost level when it occurs at

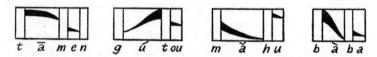

Fig. 15   Influence of tone environment in *tāmen*, *gútou*, *mǎhu*, and *bàba*

the end of a sentence with rising intonation contour or if the tone
of the following syllable begins in a relatively high position within
the range, as in -*men* in *tāmen qù* 'they'll go' (see Fig. 16). Similarly as in the case of syllables with pronounced features, the position of the pitch contour in syllables with unpronounced features
is further influenced by sentence intonation contour: it may, for
example, rise if the intonation contour is level (see the rise of the
pitch contour of -*ge* in *gēge* and of *běn* in Stage 6, Fig. 17).

Fig. 16   Influence of tone environment in *tāmen qù*

Stress not only influences the shape of vowels but also, though
to a much smaller degree, the shape of the consonants of MSC
syllables. Again, tempo and carefulness of diction are factors
important for the final shape of consonants which may vary
greatly, but very generally speaking, stress influences consonants
in the two following respects:

(1) Stops and affricates, particularly those which are non-
aspirated, are more voiced in unstressed than in stressed syllables.

The aspiration of aspirated stops and affricates is much slighter in unstressed syllables.

(2) All other consonants are shorter in unstressed than in stressed syllables. The final consonants -n and -ng are often almost imperceptible in unstressed syllables and the given syllables are distinguished more by the specific quality of their vowels than by the occurrence of the final consonants.

In the preceding discussion M S C syllables were classified according to their suprasegmental IC's as tonic, atonic, stressed or unstressed (further divided into those which are not influenced by stress and those which are negatively influenced by stress). Since all atonic syllables are unstressed, three basic types of syllables distinguished by their suprasegmental features may be established: tonic stressed syllables, tonic unstressed syllables, and atonic unstressed syllables. All syllables occurring in continuous speech belong to one of these three basic types. It follows from the discussion that some syllables may also be further modified by the negative influence of stress and their tonal environment, and all syllables may be further modified by intonation and such factors as tempo and carefulness of diction. In normal speech the final concrete shape of syllables is thus the result of the influence of numerous concurrent features and the general tendencies ascribed to abstract suprasegmental categories are commonly modified beyond recognition in the resulting final shape. The highly abstract categories of MSC suprasegmental phonemics must be understood in relation to this phonetic complexity, particularly for the applied purpose of language learning, but also in linguistic analysis and description.

The following example shows the difference between the general tendencies of tones and the concrete suprasegmental shape of syllables in a sentence, and it demonstrates the importance of knowing what lies between phonemic abstraction and phonetic reality. The individual stages indicated below do not, of course, take place in speech and they are not meant to suggest the speaker's mental process or anything of that sort; they are rather an illustration in reverse of how the abstraction is arrived at from a concrete segment of speech. The sentence in question is *gēge gěi wǒ yì běn shū* 'My elder brother gave me a book' (*gēge* 'elder brother', *gěi* 'to give', *wǒ* 'I, me', *yì* 'one', *běn* 'copy of', *shū* 'book'), spoken as an unemphatic declarative statement in casual moderately rapid conversation. The general tone tendencies of the individual syllables are shown in Fig. 17, Stage 1. Within the sentence, the tone features of the syllables *gěi*, *wǒ*, and *běn* are modified in terms of tone sandhi (see Fig. 17, Stage 2). The first two syllables of the sentence belong to a single word, a morphological construction whose second syllable is atonic (*gēge*, 'elder brother'); due to the influence of non-phonemic rhythm some syllables in the sentence are stressed, while others become unstressed. The resulting stress pattern of the sentence is then

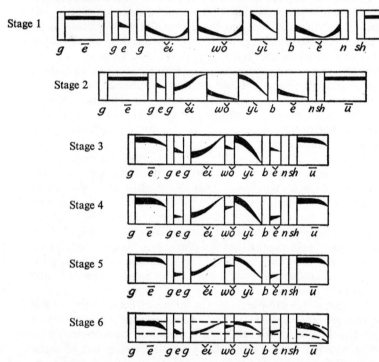

Fig. 17 Modifications of suprasegmental features in the sentence
gēge gěi wǒ yì běn shū

[ˈkɤ̄kɤˈkéiwuoˈjìpənˈʂū]; all the stressed syllables are positively influenced by stress, and since all the unstressed syllables follow stressed syllables, they are negatively influenced by stress (see Fig. 17, Stage 3). The unpronounced pitch contours of the atonic syllable and of the unstressed tonic syllables negatively influenced by stress are modified by their tonal environment (see Fig. 17,

Stage 4). In somewhat unnaturally slow and careful speech this could be the final shape of the sentence. In moderately rapid speech, however, the intermediary points of rhythm prominence ([ˈkéi] *gěi* and [ˈjì] *yì*) are weakened and the given syllables acquire the features of unstressed syllables; since these are not preceded by stressed syllables, no negative influence of stress takes place in them (see Fig. 17, Stage 5). The level-falling intonation contour of a declarative statement modifies the pitch contours of the individual syllables to their final shape (see Fig. 17, Stage 6).

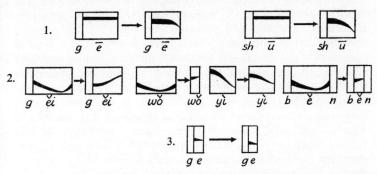

Fig. 18 Comparison of citation forms and final shape of syllables contained in the sentence *gēge gěi wǒ yì běn shū*

In Fig. 18 the final shapes of individual syllables in the given sentence are compared with the corresponding syllables in isolated citation forms. The syllables contained in the sentence belong to all three types:

(1) Tonic stressed syllables *gē* and *shū*, both of which are further influenced by intonation.

(2) Tonic unstressed syllables *gěi*, *wǒ*, *yì*, and *běn*. Of these *gěi*, *wǒ*, and *běn* are influenced by tone sandhi, *gěi* and *yì* positively by stress (this influence is, however, neutralized by the factor of rapid speech tempo), *wǒ* and *běn* negatively by stress and by their tonal environment, and all are influenced by intonation.

(3) Atonic unstressed syllable *-ge* further influenced by its tonal environment and intonation.

3. APPLIED PHONEMICS

The traditional Chinese writing system is not phonemic: that is to say, it does not consist of units representing phonemic units of the language as one-to-one relationship symbols. The Chinese partly bypassed the need for an analytical approach to the sounds of language which goes with a phonemic script, though at a price which is proving too high in the long run. The gradually growing awareness of the functional character of language sounds, which is so typical for communities using a phonemic or partly phonemic writing system, has been conspicuously weak in Chinese learned literature until very recently. This may have been one of the reasons why the European kind of linguistics with its Indian and later traditions had had no equivalent discipline in China before it was imported there during the modern European cultural invasion. Elementary phonetic and phonemic notions (like 'consonant', 'syllable', 'intonation', etc.) which have become part of general education in Europe are still commonly unknown among educated Chinese non-linguists, and the confusion of script and language is much greater among them than among Europeans with comparable educational background: for example, the difference between language units similar or identical in sound (as that, mentioned above, between [ˈɕíŋli] *xíngli* 'luggage' and [ɕíŋˈlǐ] *xínglǐ* 'to perform a courtesy') is not usually understood by educated Chinese speakers in terms of a specific sound feature or grammatical feature, but on the grounds of difference between the characters used for writing each of the units (as in this case, where a different character is used to represent -*lǐ* in each of the two words). At the present time it is also interesting to observe that educated speakers of Peking dialect with no training in linguistic theory find the new official, more or less phonemic transcription called Pinyin, which is being slowly introduced into everyday life alongside the characters, incomparably more difficult to learn than foreigners with very superficial knowledge of the dialect.

In spite of this general lack of what may be called applied phonemics in traditional Chinese culture and learning, there have been situations in the history of Chinese scholarship when the need was felt to devise a way of describing the sounds of language. The stimulus came invariably from the direction of interest in writing and interpretation of written texts rather than in the language itself: to explain the origin and the uneven paths of development of the character script usually with the aim of reaching a better understanding of ancient writings, to elucidate problems like rhyming in ancient poetry, and also for very practical purposes like the standardization of the pronunciation of script units, Chinese scholars have developed a specific way of describing the phonemic system, or rather the 'pronunciation of characters'. They have again achieved this without referring to any concrete sound values by using the non-phonemic symbols of the writing system as a means of comparison. If, for example, they wished to describe the doubtful sound value of the character *A*, they did this simply by stating that it was the same as that of character *B* which was well known. This method was, of course, sufficient only when such a character *B* existed. When it did not exist, Chinese scholars in early times referred to another character whose sound value was only similar to that of *A*. This inaccurate method which makes modern evaluation of the ancient descriptions extremely problematic was superseded sometime after 200 A.D. by the invention of a more complicated technique: the character *A* for which there was no character *B* with the same sound value was described by two characters: *C*, whose initial consonant value was the same as that of *A* (but not necessarily the other features of its sound value), and *D*, all of whose sound value features but that of its initial consonant were the same as those of *A*. For example, a character which was said to represent the syllable *lán* could be described by two characters, one of which would represent the syllable *luó* (or *là*, *lǐ*, *lē*, or any other syllable with *l-* as the initial consonant), and the other the syllable *tán* (or *pán*, *mán*, *chán*, or any other syllable which would contain the element *-án*).

The two methods of describing the sound value of a character by giving another character with the same sound value or two characters with the same initial and residual sound values are still used in many Chinese dictionaries, namely dictionaries of *wényán*. The latter method is of particular importance, since it requires some understanding of the phonemic structure of the syllable. Its introduction led to the important concept in traditional Chinese phonology of dividing the syllable into three parts: the so-called initial (initial consonant or semivowel), final (the medial vowel and the final consonant) and tone.[1] Since every syllable is in a way a combination of these three parts, the initial and tone occasionally being zero and the final reduced to a single vowel, it is to a certain degree possible to describe the phonemic system by enumerating all existing initials, finals and tones, and stating the terms of their combining. Such description is relatively simple and its principles are suitable for numerous practical purposes, as for

[1] For purposes of practical description tone is often considered as a component of the final.

example arranging syllables in dictionaries, etc. It is mainly for the reason of relative simplicity that the concept of initial, final and tone was taken over from traditional Chinese phonology by modern linguists and that it is still used both in theoretical descriptions of MSC phonemics and in practice. The concept is not, however, without disadvantages. The division of syllables into three parts is an artificial imposition which to a certain extent distorts the nature of syllable structure in MSC: the boundary between the initial and the final covers up differences between the phonemic status of sounds which happen to be grouped together on either side of it (as, for example, differences between consonants and semivowels), and the isolation of tone or its association with the final obscure the complexity of relations between various suprasegmental features on the one hand, and between suprasegmental features and the whole segmental IC of the syllable on the other.

Except for the identification and systematizing of initial consonants, tones and the residual components of syllables, and also excepting stray attempts at further more detailed classification, the first approaches to the actual phonemic description of Chinese were made only during the relatively modern era of contacts between China and the Western world by foreign scholars and Western-educated Chinese linguists. This is not so much proof of the superiority of Western scholarship (quite the contrary, as can be seen from the rather chaotic nature of the early European approach towards Chinese sounds), as it is the consequence of the very practical needs of phoneme-conscious Westerners with their particular type of writing systems. If Chinese was to be learned and taught and if names of people and places in China were to be recorded, the Westerner needed a set of symbols, preferably consisting of letters of the Latin alphabet, which he could easily use and translate into terms he was accustomed to for writing down Chinese. These were, very roughly speaking, phonemic (or rather semi-phonetic and semi-phonemic) terms, and what resulted was a kind of phonemic transcription of Chinese. Since the great majority of people who first attempted to transcribe Chinese were not linguists (and even if they were, the principles of modern phonemics were not discovered for another two centuries), their endeavour was marred by a lack of systematic approach and many contemporary European misconceptions about language. Even more than two hundred years later, during the last century, when Western specialists in Chinese, who had by that time created the discipline known as sinology, designed the early forms of the

numerous transcriptions used today, the first mistakes of enthusi-
astic missionaries, envoys and businessmen were not fully eliminated. In fact, their traces can be seen even today. Most existing
transcriptions of MSC suffer from minor inconsistencies (cases
of transcribing one phoneme in different environments by different
symbols, etc.), and many are the result of confusing historical
considerations with descriptive aims (such as using different symbols for what is a single phoneme now, but what had supposedly
been two or more different phonemes in some earlier stage).

In other respects, differences between the existing transcriptions
of MSC are of three kinds: those which result from different
phonemic solutions, those reflecting the degree to which
suprasegmental features are brought into consideration, and the
purely formal differences of using different graphic symbols for
the same phonemic features.

Different phonemic solutions influence differences between
transcriptions to a considerable degree. They reflect traditional
clashes of opinion on several points in the phonemic system of
MSC, most of which concern the structure and status of the vowel
constituents of syllables (questions like 'is [-iòu] ~ [-iù] in [liòu] ~
[liù] a triphthong or a diphthong'), but also problems like the
phonemic status of the so-called semivowels and of the palatal
consonants. The forms chosen in individual transcriptions reflect
the opinion of their authors on these questionable points. Thus,
[liòu] ~ [liù] is transcribed as *liù* by some and as *liow* by others;
[jī] as i^1 or *yī*; [sān] and [ɕīn] as *sān* and *xīn*, or *sān* and *syīn*. The
differences are often great. For example, the transcription known
as Pinyin which is the present official transcription used in Mainland China with potential aspirations of becoming the future
Chinese script, considers [-i], [-ɿ], and [-ʅ] as three allophones of
a single phoneme and transcribes them as *-i* in all environments
(thus, [pǐ] *bǐ* 'brush, pen', [ɕǐ] *xǐ* 'to wash', [sɿ] *sì* 'four', and [ʂʅ]
shí 'ten'); the most common transcription used in the English-
speaking parts of the world called the Wade-Giles system considers them as three separate phonemes and uses different symbols
for each: *-i* for [-i], *-ŭ* or only *-u* for [-ɿ], and *-ih* for [-ʅ] (thus,
[pǐ] *pi*[3] 'brush, pen', [ɕǐ] *hsi*[3] 'to wash', [sɿ] *szu*[4] 'four', and [ʂʅ]
shih[2] 'ten'). Another, less widely known English transcription of
MSC called the Yale system transcribes the three sounds in various
environments by five different symbols: *-i* or *-yi* for [-i], *-z* or zero
for [-ɿ], and *-r* for [-ʅ] (thus, [pǐ] *bǐ* 'brush, pen', [ɕǐ] *syi* 'to wash',
[sɿ] *sż* 'four' as opposed to [sān] *sān* 'three', [tsʅ] *dż* 'written

character' as opposed to [tsǎo] *dzǎu* 'early', and [ʂ̩] *shŕ* 'ten').

Transcriptions of MSC do not differ considerably in the degree to which they take suprasegmental features into consideration. Most of them have symbols for tones which many commonly omit when the given transcription is used for non-scholarly purposes, e.g. for transcribing Chinese proper names in newspapers. Some transcriptions differentiate tonic and atonic syllables simply by not giving any tone symbol in the case of atonic syllables, others do not or at least not always: thus, [tūŋɕi] 'thing', where the second syllable is atonic, is transcribed only as *dōngxi* in Pinyin, but *tung¹-hsi* or *tung¹-hsi¹* in the Wade-Giles system which uses raised numerals as tone symbols. Very few transcriptions, however, have symbols for any other suprasegmental features. One of the few existing transcriptions indicating the position of stress and thus differentiating tonic stressed syllables from tonic unstressed syllables was the now abandoned transcription used in the Chinese language courses given to U.S. Army personnel during World War II. Pairs of expressions like [ˈjiāoʂ̩] 'if' and [jiàoˈʂ̩] 'important matter', which are both transcribed as *yàoshì* in Pinyin and *yao⁴-shih⁴* in Wade-Giles, were differentiated in that transcription: ˈ*yàw-shŕ* 'if' and *yàw-*ˈ*shŕ* 'important matter'.

Formal differences between transcriptions are, of course, the most conspicuous and the most far-reaching. They are in great part the consequence of differences between the usage of the same symbols of the Latin alphabet (or other alphabets, such as Cyrillic) for different purposes in individual European national orthographies. Thus, [ʂān] 'mountain', is transcribed as *shan¹* by an Englishman, *chān* by a Frenchman, *šan¹* by a Czech, and *шань* by a Russian, although their phonemic solution of the structure of the given syllable is the same. Some of these differences are, however, the consequence of a different phonemic solution. Since, for example, Wade-Giles and Pinyin consider [s-] and [ɕ-] as two separate phonemes, they both use a different symbol for each: the former uses *s-* and *hs-*, and the latter uses *s-* and *x-*. This differentiates them formally from a transcription like Yale which uses a single symbol *s-* in both cases, since it considers [s-] and [ɕ-] as allophones of one phoneme. Still other differences are the result of arbitrary choice, particularly in cases where units and internal relationships within the MSC phonemic system cannot be associated with similar features in the phonemic systems of individual European languages. For example, the opposition of aspirated versus non-aspirated common to all MSC stops and affricates is reflected in two different ways in transcriptions: either by introducing specific symbols for aspiration which is not a phonemically distinctive feature in most European languages, or by associating the given distinction with some other opposition which is not present in the given part of the phonemic system of MSC, namely the opposition voiced versus unvoiced. Wade-Giles makes use of the former way, transcribing [tā] as ta^1 and [t'ā] as $t'a^1$; Pinyin uses the latter and transcribes [tā] as *dā* and [t'ā] as *tā*.

Because of their large number, it would be rather tiresome to present a survey of even the very widely used transcriptions of MSC. In English-speaking countries the best known is the previously mentioned Wade-Giles system, a product of gradual development the beginnings of which date from the second half of last century. This transcription is used by most sinologues and also in a modified version for transcribing Chinese expressions in non-sinological publications in Great Britain, the United States and other countries. Among English-speaking sinologues several other transcriptions are in use, mainly because their authors or supporters have applied them in textbooks, dictionaries and other widely used handbooks. These include mainly the so-called National Romanization system (also known as Gwoyeu Romatzyh or G.R.) which originated in China in the 'twenties, and the Yale transcription, noted above, which is of very recent origin. In the last few years the transcription called Pinyin also mentioned above has gained some ground among English-speaking sinologues.

Perhaps it was the spirit of pre-twentieth century linguistics which led to the often unformulated belief that there is some mysterious quality present in written symbols, some direct association with the essence of language sounds whose understanding reveals to the enlightened the secrets of language. Some of this belief can be felt in the rather sad battles over the merits of this or that transcription in the history of Western sinology. There were times, and it seems now and then that these times have not altogether disappeared, when every respectable sinologue felt it his moral duty to devise a new transcription which would presumably be better, simpler, more accurate and 'nearer to Chinese' than any other. This situation was by no means resolved when the battleground shifted to China itself at the beginning of this century: then the first large-scale attempts at replacing the traditional Chinese writing system by a phonemic script were launched and the possibility of creating an official writing system rather than a mere auxiliary transcription became the goal of scholars and, unfortunately, also of politicians. The truth is that the most widely used transcriptions of MSC differ very little in their basic character and, judging by present-day linguistic theory, they are all almost equally good (or, if this viewpoint is preferred, equally bad). Each of them is an adequate tool for elementary practical purposes of teaching and learning MSC, and of rendering the occasional Chinese expression in non-sinological writings; at the same time, none of them is sufficiently accurate in the strictest sense, since they do not account for many important details of the MSC phonemic system. The need for choice between this or that transcription will perhaps disappear if one of them eventually becomes the future Chinese script. The demand for greater accuracy, on the other hand, is not so much a question of a better transcription as of a better analysis of the MSC phonemic system. The student of Chinese who is often puzzled and frustrated by transcriptional mysteries may, in view of this, perhaps be advised to regard the existing transcriptions of MSC as a means rather than an end, and to consider them as more or less imperfect devices for the graphic recording of the matter which, after all, deserves much more of his attention: the phonetic reality and phonemic structure of MSC.

CHAPTER III

MORPHOLOGY

I. MORPHEMES AND THEIR TYPES

The speaker of MSC who automatically divides his previous utterance into syllables when asked to segment it arbitrarily, does not do so only because the segments he finds the easiest to establish happen to be the respective arrangements of segmental and suprasegmental phonemes. As mentioned earlier, his approach is motivated mainly by the common coincidence of syllables with what were called the 'basic natural units' of MSC: the smallest units which 'mean something', that is morphemes.

The definition of morphemes as the smallest meaningful units presents problems which have to be elucidated before the definition can be used for practical purposes. All these problems concentrate on the meaning of the word *meaningful*, or rather what will be understood by that word in the present discussion of MSC grammar. This is, in fact, the second time that the concept of meaning entered into the discussion: when the basic phonemic units called phonemes were established, it was done implicitly on the basis of their function as distinguishers of meaning. The phonemes *b* and *m*, for example, were set up because words like *bǐ* 'brush, pen' and *mǐ* 'rice' mean different things. In this sense, phonemes bear some relation to meaning, but since they do not convey any meaning by themselves, they will not be covered by the term *meaningful* and they will not be considered as morphemes. However, the mere decision to understand 'conveying meaning' and not 'distinguishing meaning' by the term does not solve the primary problem of how to identify the evasive thing called *meaning* itself. This problem is as old as linguistics and it would not be fruitful to tackle it here; it will, nevertheless, be necessary to state that in the further discussion of MSC, the term *meaning* will be used in a very broad sense and it will denote 'the [non-formal] feature [of a language form] common to all the situations in which it is used',[1] the linguistic form in the case of morphemes being the minimal arrangement of phonemes with which such feature can be associated. In the four MSC sentences *tā búqù* 'He will not go', *wǒ búqù* 'I shall not go', *wǒ bùmǎi* 'I shall not buy [it]', and *tā qù mǎi* 'He will go [and] buy [it]', the several common features are indicated by similarities between parts of the corresponding English sentences; the minimal arrangements of phonemes which these features can be associated with are *tā* 'he', *bú* 'not', *bù* 'not', *qù* 'go', *wǒ* 'I', and *mǎi* 'buy', while the feature indicated by 'will ~ shall' cannot be associated with anything smaller than the total of all the four sentences. With the exception of the last case which would apparently have to be investigated by bringing in evidence of further sentences, these minimal arrangements of phonemes represent morphemes, or rather specific instances of morphemes called *morphs*. Further evidence would show that each of them is a member of a group of minor variants which can all be associated with the given meaning; as members of such groups morphs are called *allomorphs* and morpheme is the term used for the abstract form representing the whole group. Thus, for example, the morphs *bú* 'not' and *bù* 'not' are two allomorphs of the morpheme *bú ~ bù* 'not'.[2] The distinction between morphs, allomorphs and mor-

---

[1] See B. Bloch and G. L. Trager, *Outline of Linguistic Analysis*, Baltimore 1942, p. 6.

[2] A morpheme may be represented by a single allomorph, and allomorphs of different morphemes may share the same phonemic shape. Both cases, and the latter in particular (hence Chinese 'homophones'), are very common in MSC. Since the concept of morphemes and allomorphs is reached by a great deal of abstracting, its application is not necessarily unambiguous. Problems arise when forms occurring in different environments are classified as 'the same form' or as 'different representations of the same form', such as *bú* 'not' and *bù* 'not' which were called two allomorphs of one morpheme, but could also be classified as representations of two different morphemes if only limited evidence such as the four sentences above were taken into account. A morph is defined as a form of unique features of phonemic structure and meaning; allomorphs, however, may differ in phonemic structure. It then becomes important to what degree difference in phonemic structure is considered as irrelevant. In this book, only the kind of difference which can be explained in phonemic terms will be considered as unimportant for establishing morphemes: thus, in terms of the present approach, [-s] in *clocks* and [-z] in *clubs* would be classified as two allomorphs of the English morpheme -*s* ([-s] ~ [-z]) 'plural suffix', but [-ən] in *oxen* would not be considered as another allomorph of this morpheme.

phemes will not be of much importance in the great part of this chapter and for the sake of simplicity the term morpheme will be used for all three, except for a few occasions when it will be necessary to distinguish morphemes from allomorphs in particular.

Several types of MSC morphemes can be established on the basis of their relation with units which either represent them or which they construct, and also according to the specific role they play in constructing other units. As mentioned earlier, the overwhelming majority of MSC morphemes correspond to single syllables; there are, however, cases of MSC morphemes which are represented by parts of syllables, or by arrangements of two or more syllables. The proportion of these cases is very small, they can be enumerated, and, as will be subsequently pointed out, each of them can be explained as the result of some process at the beginning of which a morpheme was represented by a syllable. Strictly speaking, the proposition of a one-to-one relationship between a syllable and a morpheme in MSC is thus false, but it can be accepted as roughly valid for practical purposes. In a detailed classification of MSC morphemes, three types can be established from this point of view: *monosyllabic* morphemes which correspond with single syllables, *polysyllabic* morphemes which correspond with arrangements of two or more syllables, and *subsyllabic* morphemes which are represented by parts of syllables. All the five morphemes occurring in the four sentences above (see p. 56) are monosyllabic. Polysyllabic morphemes in MSC are forms such as *pútao* 'grapes' or *Bù'ěrshíwéikè* 'Bolshevik' (none of the syllables within these forms represent meaningful units); there are only a few subsyllabic morphemes in MSC most of which share the same phonemic shape *-r*, such as *-r* 'diminutive suffix' in *dāor* 'knife' (cf. *dāo* 'knife, sword'), and *-r* 'suffix indicating short duration' in *tǎngtǎngr* 'to lie down for a while' (cf. *tǎngtǎng* 'to lie down'), and several morphemes have subsyllabic allomorphs, such as *-men* ([-mən] ~ [-m]) 'plural suffix' in *tāmen* ([t'āmən] ~ [t'ām]) 'they'. Beside these three types of morphemes, there are morphemes in MSC which are not represented by syllables or any arrangements including segmental phonemes. These are morphemes corresponding to suprasegmental features of grammatical constructions, such as intonation patterns. They may be called *suprasegmental* morphemes as opposed to *segmental* morphemes represented partly or fully by segmental phonemes.

The classification of morphemes according to their relation with the units they construct is of greater importance for MSC morphology, since it provides greater insight into the way morphemes function in the grammatical system of MSC. It is also much more difficult to classify MSC morphemes in this way, mainly because the status and borderlines of the units they construct are not always very clear. Besides, there are no, so to speak, units of a higher level in MSC which would be in the same close one-to-one correspondence with morphemes as syllables are on the phonemic level. Consequently, there is no single level at which a MSC utterance could be fully described in terms of morphemes as functionally equivalent entities. The most obvious example of this are sentences which, if we disregard suprasegmental morphemes (the given intonation patterns), consist of single morphemes, for instance, minimal answers to simple questions such as *qù* [I shall] go' (an answer to *nǐ qù búqù* 'Will you go or not?'), *hǎo* '[It] is all right' (an answer to *hǎo bùhǎo* 'Is it all right or not?'), and *wǒ* 'I [did]' (an answer to *zhè shì shéi xiě de* 'Who wrote this?'). Such sentences cannot be fully described in terms of the given segmental morphemes for the simple reason that not all segmental morphemes may constitute them. They can, however, be described in terms of units specially set up for such purposes: the units in question, the basic units operating on the level of sentences which can be tentatively called *words*, correspond to some morphemes and not to others. Morphemes themselves can be classified into those which correspond to words and those which do not: the former are known as *free* and the latter as *bound* morphemes.

The three morphemes *qù* 'go', *hǎo* 'to be all right', and *wǒ* 'I' are free, since they correspond to words in isolated sentences, such as the minimal answers above. This, however, does not mean that they are free whenever they occur in MSC. Sentences like *wǒmen* 'We [did]' (another possible answer to *zhè shì shéi xiě de* 'Who wrote this?'), *qùle* '[He] went' (an answer to *tā qùle méiyǒu* 'Did he go or not?'), and *bùhǎo* '[It] is not all right' (another answer to *hǎo bùhǎo* 'Is it all right or not?') contain these morphemes and also the morphemes *-men* 'plural suffix', *-le* 'suffix of completed actions', and *bù-* 'negative prefix' which are bound, since they never occur as isolated sentences.[1] If the morphemes *wǒ* 'I', *qù*

---

1 *bù* ~ *bū* 'no' which occurs as an isolated sentence (or separated from the rest of the sentence in which it occurs by a pause, such as *bū, wǒ búqù* 'No, I shall not go') is considered here as a different morpheme. The reason for this is contained in the concept of allomorphs as forms of similar phonemic shape and common meaning features, and in the definition of meaning used here. Since *bù* ~ *bū* 'no' and *bú* ~ *bù-*

'go', and *hǎo* 'to be all right' were considered as free in these sentences, that is as corresponding to words, the remaining parts of the sentences which are bound morphemes, by definition not corresponding to words, would call for establishing basic units of another kind operating on the level of sentences different from words. The morphemes *wǒ* 'I', *qù* 'go', and *hǎo* 'to be all right' are rather treated as bound in situations of this sort, because this is much simpler than introducing two different kinds of basic operational units. In concrete situations, the term 'free' is thus understood in the potential sense, that is as 'sometimes free' or 'sometimes bound', while the term 'bound' means 'always bound' or 'never free'. Words then correspond to free morphemes, such as *wǒ* 'I', *qù* 'go', and *hǎo* 'to be all right', or to arrangements of bound (i.e. 'sometimes bound' or 'always bound') morphemes, such as *wǒmen* 'we', *qùle* 'to have gone', and *bùhǎo* 'not to be all right'.

It therefore follows that the relations between morphemes and the basic operational units called words are much more complex than those between morphemes and syllables. The morphological structure of MSC words can be described only partly by stating whether a word is represented by a single free morpheme or by an arrangement of bound morphemes: since bound morphemes are either 'always bound' (such as -*men* 'plural suffix') or 'sometimes bound' (such as *wǒ*- in *wǒmen* 'we'), it is further necessary to state which of the two kinds the bound morphemes constructing the given word (that is, a word morphologically represented by more than one morpheme, or a so-called *polymorphemic word*) belong to. The words *wǒmen* 'we', *qùle* 'to have gone', and *bùhǎo* 'not to be all right' are each represented by one 'sometimes bound' and one 'always bound' morpheme. There are, however, many polymorphemic words in MSC which are not constructed in this way. For example, the word *mùliào* 'timber' is represented by two 'always bound' morphemes (*mù* 'wood' and *liào* 'material'), so is the word *mùtou* 'wood' (the meaning of the morpheme -*tou* cannot be described by a single English equivalent; it is a suffix the main function of which is to form a certain type of words together with other morphemes), and many words like *huǒchē* 'train' are represented by two 'sometimes bound' morphemes (*huǒ* 'fire' and *chē* 'vehicle'). If words represented by more than two morphemes were further taken into account, the range of combinatory

'not' share one part of their meaning features ('negative'), but differ in others ('negative-general' versus 'negative-specific'), they are not understood as allomorphs of the same morpheme.

possibilities would increase many times: a word like *huǒchēzhàn* 'railway station' is represented by three 'sometimes bound' morphemes (*huǒ* 'fire', *chē* 'vehicle', and *zhàn* 'station)', while the partial arrangements *huǒchē* 'train' and *chēzhàn* 'railway station or bus stop' are also 'sometimes bound', and a word like *gāoxìngqilaile* 'to have cheered up' is represented by an arrangement of one 'sometimes bound' (*gāo* 'to be high') and four 'always bound' morphemes (*xìng* 'interest', *-qi* 'suffix of actions directed upwards', *-lai* 'suffix of actions directed towards the speaker', and *-le* 'suffix of completed actions') whose mutual relations are even more complicated than those between the components of *huǒchēzhàn* 'railway station'.

To describe the ways in which MSC can be represented morphologically, it is obviously necessary to classify morphemes in greater detail than only by distinguishing between free and bound: the more delicate classification can be achieved by observing how individual morphemes generally behave in the arrangements which represent words. For analysing the general behaviour of morphemes in words, much more evidence than that of several examples would be required; however, even a few examples such as those given above can be used as a small sample of the overall features of MSC morpheme behaviour.

First of all, some of the morphemes which were described as 'always bound' are distinguished from all others by various aspects one of which is the lack of the characteristic features of tone. These atonic bound morphemes always occupy certain specific positions in words (e.g. *-le* 'suffix of completed actions' and *-men* 'plural suffix' which always occur at the end of words); they occur in many more words than other morphemes, and their meaning is generally of a different kind than that of most of the tonic morphemes: it is much less specific (usually difficult to describe by simple English equivalents), and it tends to modify the meaning of the remaining morpheme or morphemes within the given words rather than combine with it. There are also 'always bound' morphemes which, although tonic, share the remaining properties of atonic morphemes, such as *bú-* ~ *bù-* 'negative prefix'. All such morphemes constitute a morphological subtype of bound morphemes which will be called *affixes*, as opposed to *root morphemes*, that is all other bound morphemes and also free morphemes. A word is represented either by a single root morpheme (e.g. *wǒ* 'I' and *qù* 'go'), or by an arrangement of root morphemes (e.g. *mùliào* 'timber' and *huǒchē* 'train'), or by an arrangement of root morphemes and affixes (e.g. *wǒmen* 'we' and *bùhǎo* 'not to be all right'). It will be noticed that a word always contains at least one root morpheme.

Further, once the subtype called affixes is established, it is possible to subdivide it into morphemes which constitute words with 'always bound' root morphemes (e.g. *-tou* in *mùtou* 'wood'), and morphemes which constitute words with 'sometimes bound' root morphemes (e.g. *-le* in *qùle* 'to have gone').[1] The former will be called *word-formative affixes* and the latter *grammatical affixes*.

Before a discussion on how MSC morphemes belonging to different types and subtypes function in morphological constructions, that is arrangements of morphemes corresponding to words, it is necessary to point out that the classification of morphemes is, in fact, a much more intricate affair than it might seem from what has been said until now. On the one hand, it is very difficult to establish a firm borderline between free and bound morphemes: it is not always reliable to adopt the criterion of the isolated sentence (also known as the *absolute position*), since many units which can be considered words from other points of view, mainly that of operational features within larger constructions, never occur as isolated sentences (to give just one typical example: the word *tài* 'too much' never occurs as an isolated sentence), and it largely depends on what other additional criteria are used to place such morphemes on either side of the dividing line. On the other hand, the borderline between root morphemes and affixes is equally uncertain. Most affixes occur very frequently in a great many morphological constructions (such as *-le* 'suffix of completed actions' and *bú-~bù-* 'negative prefix'), they have a relatively constant characteristic phonemic shape (they are usually unstressed and atonic), and their meaning is of the typical 'nonspecific' kind. They are so obviously distinct in all respects from root morphemes that their identification is easy and unproblematic. There are, however, affixes whose features are not as distinct, or at least not always. The affix *-qi* 'outward expression of an inner quality', for example, which occurs in about sixty common MSC words (such as *lìqi* 'strength', *héqi* 'to be affable', and *nùqi* 'anger'), is usually atonic, but in some words it has a tonic variant

---

[1] If the given word contains more than one root morpheme, the fact whether the given arrangement of root morphemes itself is 'always bound' or 'sometimes bound' is important: for example, *gāoxìng* which occurs in *gāoxìngqilaile* 'to have cheered up' is a 'sometimes free' arrangement (meaning 'to be happy'), and this is more important in the given situation than the fact that *xìng* 'interest' is an 'always bound' morpheme.

in many idiolects (e.g. *nùqi~nùqì* 'anger'), and its meaning is generally not as 'non-specific' as that of an affix like *-le*. It is somewhat problematic to classify such morphemes as affixes; it would, in fact, be possible to speak of a gradual transition between root morphemes and affixes with the majority of bound morphemes clearly on either side of the borderline, but with a small minority in the no-man's-land in its vicinity.

Indistinct borderlines between grammatical entities in general are not a specific feature of MSC. The situation in other better known languages is not much different. However, the clarity of the borderlines is supported there by the norm: when the norm is as weak as it is in MSC, and the feeling of what is 'correct' and what is not among the speakers of the language does not extend to the delicate details, the basic nature of language as a living organism becomes more apparent. While the concept of units like words and morphemes and the concept of types of morphemes are useful and appropriate tools for the description of MSC, they are, after all, part of an abstract static frame applied to a system in motion. Like all abstractions, they are not wholly true, and it should be remembered throughout the following sections of this chapter that the edges in the living language called MSC are not as clear-cut as presented in the outline of its morphological structure. This is not an excuse for wrong or unsuitable concepts, but an expression of the belief that concepts of this kind can be better or worse, but never absolutely good, and that the realization of their limits is of greater importance for the understanding of how language works than a total acceptance or total rejection of the static tool.

2. MORPHOLOGICAL CONSTRUCTIONS

The distribution of MSC morphemes of different types within morphological constructions reflects in its variety the complex relationship between morphemes and words. Very roughly speaking, MSC morphological constructions are of two kinds: those which contain a single root morpheme and those which comprise an arrangement of two or more root morphemes. Since morphological constructions correspond largely to words,[1] it is possible to

---

[1] Morphological constructions represent the structural composition of words similarly as the arrangements of phonemes called syllables represent morphemes; strictly speaking, this does not mean that 'morphological construction' is synonymous with 'word': there is more to a word than a morphological construction, as there is more to a morpheme than a syllable. However, when the discussion is limited to the structural aspect of MSC words, the two terms are interchangeable.

speak of one-root and two-or-more-root words. In the following outline of the basic morphological constructions in MSC the former will be called *simple words* and the latter *compounds*.[1]

Since compounds always contain at least two morphemes, they are, from the viewpoint of the number of morphemes within them, *polymorphemic constructions*; simple words, on the other hand, are not always *monomorphemic constructions*, as they may (like compounds) contain one or more affixes beside the root morpheme (or root morphemes in the case of compounds). Finally, because the relationship between morphemes and syllables is not completely one-to-one, it is profitable to introduce a further distinction of *monosyllabic* versus *polysyllabic constructions*. The three aspects of morphological constructions are summarized in the following table of the structural types of MSC words:

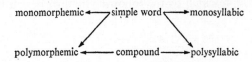

Fig. 19   Table of the structural types of MSC words

The basic types of MSC morphological constructions are thus:

(1) Simple monomorphemic monosyllabic words,
(2) Simple monomorphemic polysyllabic words,
(3) Simple polymorphemic polysyllabic words,
(4) Simple polymorphemic monosyllabic words,
(5) Compounds (all polymorphemic polysyllabic).

A more detailed classification of compounds may be reached by specifying the relationship between the given root morphemes, as will be shown later.

Before giving examples of the types of MSC morphological

[1] It should be stressed that what follows is only a very rough outline of the basic MSC morphological constructions: some of the rare types of constructions were not included, as well as constructions of constructions. Moreover, the concept that 'a morphological construction always contains at least one root morpheme' will be corrected later when it will be shown that the syntactic units called markers are often represented by single bound morphemes which are not root morphemes. The description of morphological constructions in this chapter thus deals only with the structure of plain MSC words.

constructions and attempting to establish subtypes among some of them, compounds in particular, it is important to point out that the actual number and frequency of MSC words belonging to different morphological types are not proportional to the space the individual types are given in the outline. It would be next to impossible to say even approximately what the number and frequency of MSC words of different morphological types are without a large scale analysis of the problem,[1] but perhaps an example based on a random selection of three passages from recorded speech each of which consisted of one thousand words will give at least an idea of what the proportions are like. The three passages in question came from A, a casual dialogue on everyday matters between two speakers of MSC; B, a story narrated by a single speaker; and C, a political speech broadcast by Peking Radio Station. The five basic types of morphological constructions were represented by the following number of words in each passage:

	A	B	C
1.	492	476	107
2.	3	6	5
3.	143	203	269
4.	62	34	4
5.	300	281	615

Fig. 20   Frequency of MSC words of different types

This is, of course, the kind of table from which many false impressionistic conclusions could be drawn. The numbers would most likely be different for different passages, different speakers, and different styles. Without further data on the recurrence of the given words within the individual passages (in this respect, recurrences among words of the type 1 were much more common than among the remaining words), they are not very significant. Nevertheless, it will be noted that instances of type 2 are generally

---

[1] This kind of analysis would, however, be neither easy nor profitable in the present situation: at the moment, it cannot be specified exactly what belongs to MSC and what does not. Moreover, the morphological types are not always separated by clear borderlines. The resulting generalizations would thus be dubious and of little value for appreciating the respective ways in which morphological patterning is utilized in the language. As in other similar situations, it is felt that exact static techniques cannot be applied to the kind of language phenomena whose nature is not precise in the static sense.

rare and that there are also relatively few instances of type 4, while at least in some styles (namely *A* and *B*) instances of type 1 cover as much as one half of all occurring words, and constructions of type 5 appear to be more common than type 3.

1. *Simple monomorphemic monosyllabic words*

This is probably the largest group of MSC words. Its size is one of the features which have brought about the popular notion that Chinese is a 'monosyllabic language'. For examples see the section on segmental phonemes in the preceding chapter where all the given instances of syllables represent such words unless they are specifically marked as bound morphemes.

2. *Simple monomorphemic polysyllabic words*

A relatively small group of morphological constructions some of which occur very frequently in MSC. The feature shared by most of these constructions is that they are of non-Chinese origin. They fall roughly into two main subgroups more or less historically defined.

The first subgroup comprises words which came into Chinese so long ago that the origin of many of them is either unknown or hypothetical. These are words like *pípa* 'a four-stringed plucked instrument' and its homophone *pípa* 'loquat tree', *zhīzhū* 'spider', *qīngtíng* 'dragon-fly', *húdié* 'butterfly', *gǎnlǎn* 'an olive', *pútao* 'grapes', *gēda* 'a boil', *Púsà* 'Bodhisattva', *héshang* '[Buddhist] priest', and the more common *bōli* 'glass', *hútong* 'lane', *páihuái* 'to move back and forth', *luōsuo* 'to chatter', and *hútu* 'to be muddled'. Most of these constructions are disyllabic with stress on the first syllable (the second syllable of many words belonging to this group is atonic).

The second subgroup contains words which are relatively recent borrowings from other, mainly European languages, such as *tǎnkè* 'tank', *shāfā* 'sofa', *yōumò* 'humour', *kāfēi* 'coffee', *lúbù* 'rouble', *bālěi* 'ballet', *Fǎxīsī* 'Fascist', *Sūwéi'āi* 'Soviet', and *Bù'ěrshíwéikè* 'Bolshevik'. Most proper names of non-Chinese persons and places belong to this subgroup: *Lúndūn* 'London', *Bùyínuòsī'àilìsī* 'Buenos Aires', *Shāshìbǐyà* 'Shakespeare', *Bèiduō-fēn* 'Beethoven', etc. Unlike the first subgroup, many of these words consist of three or more syllables, usually all tonic.

It is important to remember the overall one-to-one relationship between MSC syllables and morphemes in order to realize the specific character of words belonging to the latter subgroup. This can perhaps be best elucidated by outlining the process through which non-Chinese expressions enter into MSC. There are three main ways of coining new words in MSC on the basis of non-Chinese expressions and concepts: either a new word is constructed out of existing MSC morphemes (e.g. *dǎodàn* 'guided missile': *dǎo* 'to guide', a bound morpheme, and *dàn* 'bullet', a free morpheme) disregarding the phonetic shape and often, but not always, the morphological structure of the model expression in the given foreign language as well, or it is built according to the phonetic shape of the given foreign expression interpreted in terms of MSC phonemic system (such as all the words given as examples in the preceding paragraph), or the two approaches are combined (e.g. *kǎchē* 'freight automobile' where the first syllable indicates the model English expression *car* and the second syllable represents the morpheme *chē* 'vehicle'). The second way of coining new words in MSC which is the only one relevant to this discussion includes the important element of interpreting the phonetic shape of non-Chinese expressions in the terms of MSC phonemic system. The foreign sequence of sounds is, so to speak, mentally segmented into quasi-syllables which are then substituted by actual phonetically similar MSC syllables; since every MSC syllable may represent a morpheme, it is subsequently easy to establish an artificial relationship between the originally meaningless sequence of sounds and actual MSC morphemes. This possibility is further supported by the need of writing foreign borrowings down: the character writing system is a morphemic script and an arrangement of syllables has to represent morphemes before it can be written in characters. It is mainly for this reason that the syllables of borrowings are deliberately assigned morphemic values (and also tones). The assignment is limited by certain rules, because a specific set of morphemes (and the corresponding characters) was selected for the purpose of rendering foreign expressions; consequently, the way in which foreign expressions are transposed into quasi-polymorphemic MSC constructions has become so stereotype that speakers of MSC do not normally associate the individual syllables with the meaning features of the morphemes they otherwise represent (thus, *tǎnkè* is automatically understood as 'tank', or at least as 'some foreign word', rather than as *tǎn* 'to be flat' and *kè* 'to overcome'). Nevertheless, this process has created a kind of polymorphemic substructure of each of such monomorphemic words which gives them the specific properties borrowings in other languages could hardly achieve to a corresponding degree. One aspect of this is that these words are a standard source of amusement: every now and then a speaker of MSC will point out jokingly what a word like *Lìmǎ* 'Lima' really means (*lì* 'keen', *mǎ* 'horse'), to give a very mild example.

Even more involved are cases of words taken over from languages whose speakers use or used the symbols of the Chinese writing system as their script, primarily Japanese. For example, the MSC word *fúwù* 'to serve' is a borrowing from Japanese, the Japanese model expression being *fukumu* 'term of service'. Unlike expressions taken over from European languages, this and other Japanese words did not come to China through oral communication, but through writing[1]: the Chinese have borrowed the expression as it was written by two Chinese characters to each of which they assigned the normal MSC phonemic representation irrespective of what the two characters represented to the Japanese (who had originally borrowed the characters from the Chinese writing system assigning to them a specific Japanese phonemic representation). The question here is, however, that most expressions of this kind are morphologically close to Chinese (*fúwù* 'to serve' reinterpreted in MSC morphological terms, that is *fú* 'to yield', a free morpheme, and *wù* 'affair', a bound morpheme, is a word closely resembling in structure non-borrowings like *fúzuì* 'to accept punishment', that is *fú* 'to yield', a free morpheme, and *zuì* 'crime', a free morpheme) to such a degree that their foreign origin is not normally felt by speakers of MSC and they are operated with as polymorphemic rather than monomorphemic constructions. Consequently, most of such constructions do not fall within the latter subgroup of simple monomorphemic polysyllabic words in the synchronous system of MSC.

Beside the two main historically defined subgroups, simple monomorphemic polysyllabic words include a relatively large separate subgroup of constructions which represent conventionalized imitations of sounds. These are expressions like *huālā* 'to make a crashing sound', *jījī* 'to make a squeaking or creaking sound', *gūlū* 'to make a bubbling sound', and *dīngdāng* 'to tinkle'.

---

[1] This is made possible by the morphemic nature of the script. Since every character represents a morpheme, that is usually a syllable plus the respective element of meaning, characters can be used for purposes of limited communication even with the exclusion of the phonemic component (the respective syllable), or they can be assigned different phonemic components by speakers of another language. This situation is in a sense similar to that of Arabic numerals used by speakers of different languages.

3. Simple polymorphemic polysyllabic words

This very large group contains morphological constructions of one
root morpheme and one or more affixes. For the sake of simplicity, the discussion will be limited here to words comprising one
monosyllabic root morpheme and one monosyllabic affix; the
structure of more complex MSC words of this type follows similar
patterns as those described below. Simple dimorphemic disyllabic
words fall into two subgroups according to the type of morphemes
which construct them: words with word-formative affixes and
words with grammatical affixes.

The largest set of words belonging to the former subgroup and
perhaps the largest homogeneous set among MSC morphological
constructions[1] are words comprising the word-formative suffix
-z,[2] such as bíz 'nose', màoz 'hat', míngz 'name', fángz 'house',
dāoz 'knife', dànz 'bullet', lúz 'stove', kùz 'trousers', kuàiz 'chopsticks', háiz 'child', jiǎnz 'scissors', zhuōz 'table', chóngz 'insect',
shīz 'lion', lǐz 'plum', shǎz 'dimwit', sūnz 'grandchild', érz 'son',
yǐz 'chair', yāz 'duck', yàngz 'appearance', wénz 'mosquito', etc.
Other suffixes commonly occurring in words of this subgroup[3] are:

-tou 'word-formative suffix': mùtou 'wood', gútou 'bone', shétou
    'tongue', yātou 'maid', lǐtou 'inside';
-qi 'outward expression of an inner quality'; nùqi 'anger', lìqi
    'strength', píqi 'temper', kèqi 'to be polite', yǒngqi 'courage';
-ren 'person': nánren 'man', nǚren 'woman', gōngren 'worker',
    díren 'enemy', kèren 'guest';
-li 'power, energy': yǎnli 'vision', shìli 'influence', mǎli 'horse-
    power, hp';

---

[1] Zhāng Xúnrú's comprehensive Běijīnghuà qīngshēng cíhuì 'List of Words in
Peking Dialect Containing Atonic Syllables', Peking 1957, includes 685 of these
words.

[2] This suffix, similarly as the following -tou and others, has an additional grammatical function related with the concept of word classes. This function which will
be discussed later is disregarded here, as it is not essential for explaining the
morphological structure of the words in question. The meaning of the individual
word-formative affixes is indicated by an English equivalent only when the given
affix has some identifiable meaning beside its grammatical meaning; when it does
not, it is merely labelled as a 'word-formative affix'. It will be noticed that the most
common word-formative affixes have more or less only a grammatical meaning:
the lack of lexical meaning is an indication of the high degree of grammatical formalization some affixes have reached, and it is one of the extreme expressions of
the distinction between root morphemes and word-formative affixes in MSC.

[3] Běijīnghuà qīngshēng cíhuì lists 20 or more words in the case of each of these
suffixes.

-dao 'institutionalized way of doing things': *gōngdao* 'to be just', *hòudao* 'to be generous', *bàdao* 'to be aggressive';

-shi 'affair, matter': *gùshi* 'story', *gōngshi* 'public matter', *xīnshi* 'a worry';

-du 'degree': *chángdu* 'length', *chéngdu* 'degree', *rèdu* 'temperature';

-xing 'nature, feature': *jìxing* 'memory', *rénxing* '[human] nature', *tèxing* 'individuality';

-shi 'to be solid': *jiēshi* 'to be tough', *zhuàngshi* 'to be strong', *lǎoshi* 'to be honest'.

Beside the relatively frequent suffixes a great number of word-formative suffixes constitute small sets of MSC words. These usually have a more specific meaning and they stand closer to the borderline between affixes and root morphemes. They occur in words like *mùjiang* 'carpenter' and *tiějiang* 'blacksmith' (*-jiang* 'craftsman'), *zhànshi* 'warrior' and *hùshi* 'nurse' (*-shi* 'member of a respected social group'), *dòngwu* 'animal' and *huòwu* 'goods' (*-wu* 'things'), etc.

There are no words with word-formative infixes in MSC and very few with word-formative prefixes. Instances of the latter are *āyí* 'aunt', *āgē* 'brother', and *āmèi* 'sister' (*ā-* 'prefix in kinship terms used mainly in direct addressing'), *lǎoshī* 'teacher', *lǎobǎn* 'boss'. and *lǎohǔ* 'tiger' (*lǎo-* 'familiar prefix').

A special case of constructions with word-formative suffixes are words like *māma* 'mother', *gēge* 'elder brother', *mèimei* 'younger sister', *shúshu* 'uncle', and *nǎinai* 'grandmother'; these words contain a root morpheme (usually bound and represented by a stressed syllable) and a suffix which has the same segmental shape as the given root morpheme and a grammatical meaning similar with that of the most common word-formative affixes. The overwhelming majority of such words are kinship terms, but there are also a few others like *wáwa* 'doll', *bǎobao* 'darling [of a baby]', and *bōbo* '[a kind of] cake'. Perhaps the most important common feature of all these words is that they belong to the level of language shared by adults and children.

The latter subgroup of simple polymorphemic polysyllabic words, that is words with grammatical affixes, differ from the preceding subgroup in many respects, but their main distinctive feature is that they are not a limited set of words. Unlike word-formative affixes, the occurrence of grammatical affixes in morphological constructions is predictable and it can be described in general terms: it is possible to say that all free forms which may fulfil certain syntactic functions (for example, the function of a *verbal nucleus*, such as *lái* 'to come' in *tā lái* 'He will come') may occur in morphological constructions with certain grammatical affixes (in the case of free forms functioning as verbal nuclei the negative prefix *bù- ~ bú-*, for example, as in *bùlái* 'not to come'). Since the specific applications of this general statement are potentially valid for any new free form in MSC, the set of the specific morphological constructions is not limited. The close relation between particular syntactic functions and the distribution of particular grammatical affixes differs from the similar relation between syntactic function and the occurrence of some word-formative affixes in the *direction* in which valid predictions can be made: while the syntactic functioning of a word containing a certain word-formative affix can often be predicted (this is related with the 'additional grammatical function' of word-formative affixes mentioned in footnote 2 on p. 68; for example, words containing the suffix -*z* usually function as *nominal referents*, such as *háiz* 'child' in *háiz bùlái* 'The child will not come'), the occurrence of a word-formative affix in a word cannot be predicted from its syntactic functioning. In the case of grammatical affixes, valid predictions can be made in both directions: all free forms, for example, which function as verbal nuclei may occur with the negative prefix *bú- ~ bù-*, and all morphological constructions containing this negative prefix may function as verbal nuclei. In this sense, the function of grammatical affixes reaches beyond the arrangement of morphemes within the morphological constructions in which they occur. Another reflection of the main distinctive feature of grammatical affixes (as components of the general operational rules of the language as well as constituents of morphological constructions representing units governed by these rules) is their separability from other bound morphemes: in comparison with word-formative affixes, grammatical affixes constitute a more clearly delimited group and their total number is much smaller.

Most MSC grammatical affixes are suffixes falling into five main groups. The plural suffix -*men* mentioned earlier constitutes a group on its own; it occurs in words denoting groups of persons, such as *tāmen* 'they' (*tā* 'he, she, it') and *rénmen* 'people, everybody' (*rén* 'man'). The majority of morphological constructions in which it occurs, however, are structurally more complex than the kind at present under discussion. The second group contains several so-called *verbal suffixes*: the three most common members of this group are -*le* 'suffix of completed actions', -*guo* 'suffix of actions which have taken place once in the past', and -*zhe* 'suffix of actions of relatively long duration', which occur in constructions like *zǒule* 'to have gone', *zǒuguo* 'to have gone once', *zǒuzhe* 'to be going' (*zǒu* 'to go, to walk'), *mǎile* 'to have bought', *mǎiguo* 'to have bought once', *mǎizhe* 'to be buying' (*mǎi* 'to buy'), *shuōle* 'to have said', *shuōguo* 'to have said once', *shuōzhe* 'to be saying' (*shuō* 'to say'), etc. The third group which is in certain respects related with the preceding group contains what are known as *directional suffixes*, for example -*lai* 'suffix of actions directed towards the speaker' as in *nálai* 'to bring' (*ná* 'to take') and *xiàlai* 'to come down' (*xià* 'to descend'), -*qu* 'suffix of actions directed away from the speaker' as in *náqu* 'to take away' and *xiàqu* 'to go down', -*xia* 'suffix of actions directed downwards' as in *zuòxia* 'to sit down' (*zuò* 'to sit'), -*qi* 'suffix of actions directed upwards' as in *náqi* 'to pick up', and several other suffixes. Finally, there are two groups of suffixes which occur in placewords and timewords: the so-called *positional suffixes*, such as -*li* 'suffix indicating the position inside' in *jiāli* 'at home' (*jiā* 'home') and *shuǐli* 'in the water' (*shuǐ* 'water'), and -*shang* 'suffix indicating the position on the top or surface' in *dìshang* 'on the ground' (*dì* 'the ground') and *liǎnshang* 'on the face' (*liǎn* 'face'), and *temporal suffixes*, such as -*shang* 'suffix indicating a point of time' in *wǎnshang* 'in the evening' (*wǎn* 'to be late') and *zǎoshang* 'in the morning' (*zǎo* 'to be early').

There are very few grammatical prefixes in MSC, of which the negative prefix *bú-* ~ *bù-* is the most common. Another frequently occurring negative prefix is *méi-* ~ *méiyou-* which indicates that the given action has not taken place in the past, as in *méiqù* 'not to have gone' (*qù* 'to go'), *méiyoumǎi* 'not to have bought' (*mǎi* 'to buy'), and *méishuō* 'not to have said' (*shuō* 'to say'). There are two grammatical infixes in MSC, but neither of them occurs in simple words.[1]

4. Simple polymorphemic[2] monosyllabic words

From the point of view of their morphological structure, constructions belonging to this type have no distinctive features. Their

---

[1] These are -*de*- 'infix indicating that the given action can be completed' and -*bu*- 'infix indicating that the given action cannot be completed', both of which occur in complex morphological constructions whose remaining constituents are compounds like *kànjian* 'to see': *kàndejiàn* 'to be able to see' and *kànbujiàn* 'to be unable to see'.

[2] Practically all these words are dimorphemic.

characteristic feature is phonemic or rather morphophonemic: their morpheme constituents are represented by subsyllabic arrangements of phonemes, a single syllable being the phonemic shape of the whole construction.

Morphological constructions of this type are of two kinds: those which have free disyllabic variants, such as *duōr ~ duōshao* 'how much?', *tām ~ tāmen* 'they', and *tād ~ tā de* 'his', and those which have no such variants, such as *huār* 'flower', *māor* '[a small] cat', and *jīr* '[a small] chicken'. The structure of the monosyllabic variants of the former is difficult to describe in general morphological terms, since the morphological features of their final subsyllabic components are not clear without the evidence of the disyllabic variants. It is much more profitable to describe them morphologically in the terms of their disyllabic variants and state additionally the conditions under which they occur. Thus, words like the first three examples above will be excluded from the present discussion on simple polymorphemic monosyllabic words, because their disyllabic variants do not belong to this type (*duōshao* 'how much?' is a compound, *tāmen* 'they' is a simple polymorphemic polysyllabic word, and *tā de* 'his' is not a morphological construction). The respective conditions under which the monosyllabic variants occur will be mentioned later in this chapter.

Simple polymorphemic monosyllabic words proper are thus restricted here to those which have no polysyllabic variants. The final subsyllabic component of all such words is -*r* which represents several morphemes, mostly word-formative suffixes. The most commonly occurring suffixes which share this phonemic shape are -*r* 'suffix of words not denoting an action or a state' (for example, *chàngr* 'song'—*chàng* 'to sing', *huàr* 'picture'—*huà* 'to draw, to paint', *liàngr* 'light'—*liàng* 'to be bright'; this suffix stands on the borderline between word-formative and grammatical affixes: it occurs only with free morphemes but its occurrence is not predictable from the syntactic functioning of the given words), -*r* 'word-formative suffix' (for example, *huār* 'flower', *dānr* 'list, bill', *wèir* 'taste, flavour'), and -*r* 'diminutive suffix' (for example, *māor* '[a small] cat—*māo* 'cat', *jīr* '[a small] chicken'—*jī* 'chicken', *mǎr* '[a small] horse'—*mǎ* 'horse'; this suffix has the same borderline features as the first -*r*).

From the mere viewpoint of their morphological structure, words with the -*r* suffixes can be considered a subtype of simple polymorphemic polysyllabic constructions. Beside their distinctive morphophonemic feature, there is, however, still another reason for treating them separately; namely, it is not certain at the moment how many of these words will be included in the MSC norm. The -*r* suffixation is a morphophonemic device utilized in various different ways and to different degrees in individual Mandarin dialects and their styles (it is often said that this device known as *érhuà* 'erisation' is much more widespread in certain styles of Peking dialect than in any other Mandarin dialect); since MSC is in a sense conceived as the common denominator of Mandarin dialects, the norm will have to specify to what degree and what kind of 'erisation' it will include. As the norm is at present weaker in this point than in others, it is more suitable to set 'erisated' words aside from morphologically similar constructions.

5. *Compounds*

This is perhaps the second largest group of MSC morphological constructions. As in the previous cases, only the simplest compounds, that is constructions of two root morphemes will be discussed. Even with this limitation, however, dimorphemic compounds as a whole represent such a wide variety of constructions according to differences in the mutual relationship between the two root morphemes, that a further classification is necessary.

Similarly, but perhaps even to a greater extent than in most other languages, the arrangement of root morphemes within MSC compounds is a reflection of the arrangement of words in simple syntactic constructions.[1] This close structural resemblance gives the possibility of classifying compounds in quasi-syntactic terms: it is, for example, possible to classify words like *huǒchē* 'train' (*huǒ* 'fire', and *chē* 'vehicle') and *hēibǎn* 'blackboard' (*hēi* 'black', and *bǎn* 'board') as *attribute-head* constructions, because their constituents are mutually related in a similar way as the word constituents of syntactic attribute-head constructions like *Zhōngguó rénmín* 'the Chinese people' (*Zhōngguó* 'China' and *rénmín* 'the people') and *gāodà lǐxiǎng* 'lofty ideal' (*gāodà* 'to be big, to be lofty' and *lǐxiǎng* 'ideal'). Two points should, however, be remembered when MSC compounds are classified in this manner. First, that 'structural resemblance' refers to grammatical structure

---

[1] Although this is outside the scope of the present rough description of MSC in synchronic terms, it can be noted that MSC morphology is up to a point petrified earlier syntax: there is a syntactic construction somewhere in the history of most morphological constructions.

rather than mere meaning relationship (which is only one part of grammatical structure), and, second, that 'structural resemblance' does not mean 'structural identity'. These two points are of great importance for the concept of the borderline between MSC morphology and syntax which is often made even less distinct than it really is by substituting meaning for the total of grammatical features and by disregarding differences in favour of similarities.

What we actually have in mind when we classify a word like *huǒchē* 'train' as an attribute-head compound goes beyond the mere realization of the meaning of the constituent morphemes and the meaning relation between them (*huǒ* 'fire' and *chē* 'vehicle', that is 'the kind of vehicle whose chief characteristic is the association with fire'). Although not always consciously, we take into consideration much broader evidence: the realization of the meaning of the constituent morphemes itself is based on the knowledge of how the given morphemes are used in other MSC environments (e.g. *lúli yǒu huǒ* 'There is fire in the stove', *yǒu chē méiyǒu* 'Is there a car available?', *shānshan huǒ* 'to stir up the fire by fanning', *shàng chē* 'to get into a car', etc.) rather than on the comprehension of some kind of superimposed meaning not necessarily related to concrete language forms. The realization of the meaning relationship within the given construction is further based on the experience with the given kind of MSC grammatical patterning which can be briefly and somewhat inaccurately summarized as 'in a construction of two MSC meaningful units the latter is often the grammatical core of the construction and the former is grammatically subordinate to it' (cf. the examples *Zhōngguó rénmín* 'the Chinese people' and *gāodà lǐxiǎng* 'lofty ideal' mentioned above), and part of which is the meaning relationship 'specifying-specified'. On the other hand, there is a different kind of evidence which can be used to distinguish degrees of structural closeness in constructions related by these common overall grammatical features including meaning. For example, the grammatical relationship between the morphemes *huǒ* 'fire' and *chē* 'vehicle' in the word *huǒchē* 'train' is indicated partly by what kind of morphemes they are and partly by features of their arrangement: the order in which they occur in the word but also several other features like the rigidity of this order which does not permit the separation of the morphemes or insertion of other morphemes between them without breaking the grammatical relationship. The grammatical relationship between the words *Zhōngguó* 'China' and *rénmín* 'the people' in *Zhōngguó rénmín* 'the Chinese people' is also indicated by such features of kind and arrangement, but the features are not all the same as in the case of *huǒchē* 'train': the arrangement is far less rigid and its order may be broken without damaging the basic grammatical relationship (e.g. *Zhōngguó qīyì rénmín* 'the seven-hundred-million Chinese people'). What is even more important, the grammatical relationship may be further specifically indicated by formal marking (*Zhōngguó de rénmín* 'the Chinese people', *de* being the formal marker of subordinate grammatical relationship in syntactic constructions) which is never possible in the case of words like *huǒchē* 'train'.

The subsequent classification of compounds is based on this concept of structural resemblance. In its terms the following main subgroups of MSC compounds may be established.

(a) Coordinate compounds

These are compounds bearing structural resemblance with co-ordinate syntactic constructions like *wǒ hé nǐ* 'I and you' and *yòu piàoliang yòu cōngming* 'to be pretty as well as clever'. In most cases the two root morphemes within the given word have a similar meaning and the meaning of the whole word is again similar to the meaning of both of the constituent morphemes: *chéngshì* 'town' (*chéng* 'town wall, walled town', a free morpheme, and *shì* 'market, market town', also a free morpheme), *péngyou* 'friend' (*péng* 'friend', a bound morpheme, and *yǒu* 'friend', also a bound morpheme), *jiěfàng* 'to liberate' (*jiě* 'to untie', a free morpheme, and *fàng* 'to release', also a free morpheme), *xiūxi* 'to rest' (*xiū* 'to rest', a bound morpheme, and *xí* 'to rest', also a bound morpheme), *zhòngyào* 'to be important' (*zhòng* 'to be weighty', a free morpheme, and *yào* 'important', a bound morpheme), *měilì* 'to be beautiful' (*měi* 'to be beautiful', a free morpheme, and *lì* 'beautiful', a bound morpheme), etc. A special subgroup of coordinate compounds are *appositional constructions* of root morphemes whose meaning relationship is even more similar to that of co-ordinate syntactic constructions. These are words like *máodùn* 'contradiction' (*máo* 'a lance', a free morpheme, and *dùn* 'a shield', a bound morpheme), *jiāotōng* 'communication' (*jiāo* 'to establish contact', a free morpheme, and *tōng* 'to go through', also a free morpheme), *dàxiǎo* 'size' (*dà* 'to be large', a free morpheme, and *xiǎo* 'to be small', also a free morpheme), and *qībā* 'about seven or eight' (*qī* 'seven', a free morpheme, and *bā* 'eight', also a free morpheme).

(b) Subordinate compounds

Words belonging to this subgroup of compounds[1] are of several structural types characterized by the specific grammatical relationship between the constituent morphemes. The most common are words of the attribute-head type mentioned earlier. Further examples of such words are *jūnshì* 'military affairs' (*jūn* 'armed force', a bound morpheme, and *shì* 'a matter', a free morpheme), *fēijī* 'aircraft' (*fēi* 'to fly', a free morpheme, and *jī* 'machine', a bound morpheme), *báicài* 'cabbage' (*bái* 'white', a free morpheme, and *cài* 'vegetable', also a free morpheme), *bǐzhí* 'to be perfectly straight' (*bǐ* 'brush, pen', a free morpheme, and *zhí* 'to be straight', also a free morpheme), and *shēnlán* 'dark blue' (*shēn* 'to be of a dark shade', a free morpheme, and *lán* 'blue', also a free morpheme). A rather special case of attribute-head compounds are words parts of which are foreign borrowings[2]: for example, *kǎpiàn* 'card' (*kǎ* indicates the English model word *card*, *piàn* 'slice, card' is a bound morpheme), *píjiǔ* 'beer' (*pí* indicates the model English word *beer*, *jiǔ* 'alcoholic beverage' is a free morpheme), and *jiǔbà* 'bar' (*jiǔ* 'alcoholic beverage', and *bà* which indicates the model English word *bar*).

Among other structural types of subordinate compounds none of which is represented by a very large group of words the most prominent are the *head-referent*, the *head-modifier*, and the *head-measure* types. The head-referent type resembling syntactic constructions of verbal heads and nominal referents ('objects'), such as *dǎ tā* 'to beat him' or *mǎi shū* 'to buy books', comprises words like *fāyán* 'to make a speech' (*fā* 'to issue', a free morpheme, and *yán* 'speech', a bound morpheme), *gémìng* 'to make a revolution' (*gé* 'to remove', a free morpheme, *mìng* 'The Heavenly Mandate', a bound morpheme), and *bàochóu* 'to avenge' (*bào* 'to recompense', a bound morpheme, and *chóu* 'enmity', also a bound morpheme). There is a *referent-head* variant of this type which rather resembles syntactic constructions of nominal referents ('subjects') and verbal heads, such as *tā lái* 'He will come' or *shān hěn gāo* 'The mountain is high': *zìdòng* 'automatic, automatically'

---

[1] This is the largest subgroup of compounds. Lù Zhìwéi's *Hànyǔ de gòucífǎ* 'Word-formation in Chinese', Peking 1957, p. 19, states that out of the more than 30,000 items listed in the dictionary *Guóyǔ cídiǎn* 'Dictionary of the National Language' (the first large dictionary of MSC of semi-normative standing) as many as 33 per cent belong to dimorphemic compounds of the attribute-head type which is the most typical structural type of subordinate compounds.

[2] See pp. 65–67.

(*zì* 'oneself', a bound morpheme, and *dòng* 'to move', a free morpheme), *kǒuhóng* 'lipstick' (*kǒu* 'mouth', a bound morpheme, and *hóng* 'red', a free morpheme), and *niánqīng* 'to be young' (*nián* 'year', a free morpheme, and *qīng* 'to be light', also a free morpheme). Words of the head-modifier type which resemble syntactic constructions of verbal heads and resultative modifiers, such as *pǎo de yì-shēn-chū-hàn* 'to run so [fast] that one becomes all sweated up' or *lái de tài zǎo* 'to come too early', can be exemplified by *kànjian* 'to see' (*kàn* 'to look', a free morpheme, and *jiàn* 'to see', also a free morpheme), *shuōmíng* 'to explain' (*shuō* 'to say', a free morpheme, and *míng* 'clear', a bound morpheme), and *dǎkāi* 'to open' (*dǎ* 'to strike', a free morpheme, and *kāi* 'to open', also a free morpheme). The head-measure type which vaguely resembles the respective part of the syntactic constructions number-measure-nominal head (such as *yì jīn chá* 'a pound of tea' or *yì lǐ lù* 'a one-mile journey'), but which has no closer correspondence with any MSC syntactic constructions,[1] is represented by a small group of words like *zhǐzhāng* 'paper [in sheets]' (*zhǐ* 'paper', a free morpheme, and *zhāng* 'a sheet of', a bound morpheme), *fángjiān* 'a room [as a unit of space within a building]' (*fáng* 'a room', a bound morpheme, and *jiān* 'the space of', also a bound morpheme), and *mǎpǐ* 'horses [as a kind or part of live-stock]' (*mǎ* 'horse', a free morpheme, and *pǐ* 'unit measure used for counting horses', a bound morpheme).

Even the few examples of subordinate compounds of various structural types presented here suggest the difficulty of drawing a clear borderline between some syntactic and morphological constructions in MSC. Since the 'degree of structural closeness' and other similar features are difficult to describe in precise terms, there are many areas between MSC morphological and syntactic constructions where it is perhaps more suitable to speak of a gradual transition rather than a clear-cut division. One such typical area is between the syntactic and morphological constructions of the head-referent type: it is somewhat difficult to place constructions like *zǒulù* (or perhaps *zǒu lù*) 'to walk' (*zǒu* 'to walk', a free morpheme, and *lù* 'road', also a free morpheme) or *chīfàn* (or perhaps *chī fàn*) 'to eat' (*chī* 'to eat', a free morpheme, and *fàn* 'cooked rice, food', also a free morpheme) on either side of the dividing line, mainly because they behave as single words in some

---

[1] Syntactic constructions of the type nominal head-(number)-measure do not normally occur in MSC, but they are common in earlier historical stages of Chinese.

cases and as constructions of words in others. It is perhaps worth pointing out again here that indistinct borderlines between grammatical categories are primarily the result of our inability to approach language as a living organism rather than a static system or a set of unrelated developing features. The indistinct borderline between MSC morphology and syntax could be conceived as a reflection of processes in progress but even this concept does not indicate how the cuts could be made. It is not possible to go beyond this statement at the moment: however, perhaps the most important point in this context is the realization that not all language phenomena, in fact not more than very few, are of the either–or kind, and that the lack of such either–or phenomena is a natural property of the system called language.

(c) Reduplicated compounds

The difference between reduplicated compounds and simple polymorphemic polysyllabic words like *māma* 'mother' (see p. 69) is partly in the type and status of the constituent morphemes and partly in the respective function of the morphological device called reduplication. In the case of simple words, the constituent morphemes are usually bound, their status is that of a root morpheme and a suffix, and the function of reduplication is simply word-formative; reduplicated compounds usually consist of free morphemes each of which has the status of a root morpheme (the second morpheme is tonic in many of these constructions), and the function of reduplication in their case is grammatical (grammatical in the same sense as in the case of grammatical affixes, that is as opposed to word-formative). It is somewhat difficult to describe the grammatical function of reduplication in general terms, and perhaps the following examples of various kinds of reduplicated compounds will suggest its overall features. As in the preceding passages, the discussion will be limited to dimorphemic constructions among which three main kinds may be distinguished. The first kind are words like *rénrén* 'everybody, each person' (*rén* 'man', a free morpheme), *tiāntiān* 'every day' (*tiān* 'day', a free morpheme), and *jiājiā* 'every family, each home' (*jiā* 'family, home', a free morpheme); the second kind is represented by *hǎohǎo* 'very good, very well' (*hǎo* 'to be good', a free morpheme), *gāogāo* 'very high, very tall' (*gāo* 'to be high, to be tall', a free morpheme), and *zúzú* 'fully, completely' (*zú* 'to be sufficient', a free morpheme); the third kind comprises words such as *kànkan* 'to take a look' (*kàn* 'to look', a free morpheme), *tántan* 'to have a chat' (*tán* 'to chat', a free morpheme), and *xiǎngxiang* 'to give a thought' (*xiǎng* 'to think', a free morpheme). Several other kinds could be found among reduplicated compounds containing more than two morphemes.

(d) Stump compounds

This group contains words the structure of which could be described in the terms of one of the preceding groups of compounds; their distinctive feature is, however, that they have variants of syntactic constructions of two or more words. They are, in fact, deliberately constructed shortenings of these larger constructions, roughly equivalent to certain kinds of abbreviations in European languages, such as NATO in English or rather as *kolchoz* in Russian (from *kollektivnoje chozjajstvo* 'collective farm'). One of the reasons for setting these words apart as a separate kind of compounds is their relatively high number in MSC, particularly since 1949; another is that they are not as easily distinguishable from words of other kinds as are abbreviations in European languages: the constituents of such MSC words are always morphemes. They are words like *tǔgǎi* 'land reform' (from *tǔdì gǎigé* 'land reform'), *kàngzhàn* 'The War of Resistance' (from *kàng-Rì zhànzhēng* 'The Anti-Japanese War [of Resistance]'), *jūnshǔ* 'army dependants' (from *jūnren jiāshǔ* 'members of servicemen's families'), *wàizhǎng* 'Foreign Minister' (from *wàijiāobù bùzhǎng* 'Minister of Foreign Affairs'), and *Sūlián* 'USSR' (from *Sūwéi'āi shèhuìzhǔyì gònghéguó liánméng* 'The Union of Soviet Socialist Republics').

This elementary outline of the types of MSC morphological constructions roughly covers only constructions of the most frequently occurring size, that is monomorphemic and dimorphemic words. Some constructions comprising more than two morphemes could be fitted within the outline, but new types would have to be set up for many others. These new types could, however, invariably be described as arrangements of the simple types. For example, a word like *àiguózhǔyì* 'patriotism' could be described as a simple polymorphemic polysyllabic word consisting of a root (*àiguó* 'to be patriotic') and a word-formative suffix (*-zhǔyì* '-ism') in the first instance, and further in terms of compounds in the case of each of the constituents: *àiguó* 'to be patriotic' as a head-referent compound (*ài* 'to love', a free morpheme, and *guó* 'country', also a free morpheme), and *-zhǔyì* '-ism' as an attribute-head compound (*zhǔ* 'main', a bound morpheme', and *yì* 'principle', also a bound morpheme). Similarly, *zhànqilaile* 'to have stood up', for example, could be described in terms of a simple polymorphemic polysyllabic word, that is a root (*zhànqilai* 'to stand up') and a grammatical suffix (*-le* 'suffix of past completed actions') in the first instance, and its first constituent further as a simple polymorphemic polysyllabic construction of a root morpheme (*zhàn* 'to be standing', a free morpheme) and a disyllabic directional suffix (*-qilai* 'suffix of actions directed upwards and towards the speaker') which itself could perhaps be still further described as a coordinate compound of two directional suffixes (*-qi* 'suffix of actions directed upwards', and *-lai* 'suffix of actions directed towards the speaker'). A word like *kǎolùkǎolù* 'to give consideration' could be described as a reduplicated compound (from *kǎolù* 'to consider'), the reduplicated constituent being itself a compound of the coordinate type (*kǎo* 'to examine', a free morpheme, and *lù* 'to be concerned', a bound morpheme). Although this kind of description would be considerably more complicated in many other cases, and often undoubtedly questionable, not many new concepts beside those mentioned earlier would have to be introduced. Perhaps the only important new concept would be that of infixes (see footnote [1] on p. 71).

There are, however, features of MSC morphology outside the scope of the preceding discussion which have to be mentioned at this point. First of all, the tacit implication of the discussion that continuity is a distinctive feature of MSC morphological constructions should be elucidated, since it is not altogether correct: while continuity is a typical overall feature of MSC morphology, there are also cases of discontinuous morphological constructions. The most common example of constructions which may occur in discontinuous form are words containing directional suffixes, such as *shuōqi . . . lai* 'to have started saying' (*shuō* 'to say', a free morpheme, and *-qilai* 'suffix of actions directed upwards and towards the speaker, or actions the beginning of which was completed') in *shuōqi yí jù huà lai* 'to have started saying a sentence', or *náxia . . . qu* 'to take down' (*ná* 'to take', a free morpheme, and *-xiaqu* 'suffix of actions directed downwards and away from the speaker') in *náxia jǐ běn shū qu* 'to take down a few books'. Another important point here is that under certain conditions bound morphemes in MSC may occur in immediate environments of forms with which they are not in morphological construction, such as the suffix *-lai* occurring after *yí jù huà* 'a sentence', and the suffix *-qu* occurring after *jǐ běn shū* 'a few books'. From this viewpoint similar, although otherwise unrelated, are bound morphemes which actually never occur in morphological constructions at all. These are the so-called markers whose status in MSC grammar will be discussed at a later point. The most common marker in MSC is the bound morpheme *de* 'marker of subordinate syntactic constructions' (see p. 75 and p. 77) which occurs in many different environments, such as *hěn hǎo de péngyou* 'a very good friend' (*hěn* 'very', *hǎo* 'to be good', and *péngyou* 'friend'), *pǎo de màn* 'to run slowly' (*pǎo* 'to run', and *màn* 'to be slow'), and *tā lái de shíhou* 'when he comes' (*tā* 'he', *lái* 'to come', *shíhou* 'time'), constituting morphological constructions with none of them.

The last feature of MSC morphology which has to be at least briefly noted in this context concerns the very common occurrence, both in speech and in writing, of phrases and expressions taken over from earlier stages of Chinese, classical written Chinese style in particular, or newly coined along such lines. The problem of such phrases and expressions is that they represent, morphologically speaking, inorganic elements in MSC. Since they are constructed according to the grammatical patterns of old Chinese, their constituents and their structure cannot be described by using the categories of MSC morphology. They rather have to be treated separately as single morphological units and their structure has to be described, if necessary, in terms of old Chinese. The most common case of this kind are the so-called *chéngyǔ* 'established phrases' whose character and function will perhaps be best shown in the following two examples. In the sentence *tā zǒumǎ-guānhuā de kànle yí kàn* 'He looked [at it] hastily' the expression translated as 'hastily' is the phrase *zǒumǎ-guānhuā* which in old Chinese means 'to observe (*guān*) flowers (*huā*) [while] riding (*zǒu*) a horse (*mǎ*)', and which functions as an attribute to the following expression *kànle yí kàn* 'to have taken a look', their relationship being marked by *de*. In another sentence *wǒmen wànzhòng-yìxīn* 'We are all united in spirit' which happens to occur in the Communist Chinese national anthem, the expression *wànzhòng-yìxīn* 'to be all united in spirit' meaning in old Chinese 'ten thousand (*wàn*) people (*zhòng*) [have] a single (*yì*) heart (*xīn*)', functions as the verbal nucleus of the sentence and the verbal head of the nominal referent *wǒmen* 'we'. It will be noted that these expressions represent single units not only in morphological structure, but also in meaning and syntactic function. It is difficult to compare them with any similar phenomenon in European languages; the nearest would probably be Latin phrases like *prima facie* used in modern

English, but Chinese phrases and expressions of this kind are incomparably more common, for they are not limited to the speech and writing of intellectuals (on the contrary, they often carry the connotation of earthiness and working-class flavour), and their patterning is still to a certain degree productively exploited for coining new expressions.

3. MORPHOPHONEMICS

Morphophonemics is the study of the phonemic shape of morphemes in general and phonemic features conditioned by morphological factors in particular. In an earlier part of this book (see Chapter II, PHONEMICS) the segmental and suprasegmental phonemes of MSC were discussed in terms of their minimal distributional frame, that is in terms of the syllable; since the syllable is in a sense the phonemic shape of most MSC morphemes, many features which are, strictly speaking, morphophonemic rather than phonemic, have already been mentioned. The attention will now be directed towards important MSC morphophonemic features connected with the occurrence of morphemes in morphological constructions and with the variants of the phonemic shape of certain morphemes.

Perhaps the most important single phonemic feature common to all polysyllabic morphological constructions in MSC relevant to this discussion is that they contain at least one unstressed syllable. This feature is somewhat difficult to explain without introducing highly involved concepts based on both physiological and linguistic considerations. In oversimplified terms it could be pointed out that it is physiologically very difficult to produce in close sequence two or more stressed MSC syllables without at least a slight pause between them, and, although it is not altogether an obligatory rule in MSC, continuous morphological constructions occurring in normal MSC speech are never interrupted by such 'physiological pauses'.[1] Polysyllabic morphological constructions

---

[1] It would perhaps be suitable to mention here the phonemic feature known as *juncture* which is related with what is called pause in this context. Juncture is the way in which syllables are linked in speech, and in many languages different kinds of such linking are utilized to distinguish forms otherwise identical or very similar in phonemic shape (such as the English *night rate* and *nitrate*). The status of juncture in MSC is, however, questionable, and it is not certain whether it is profitable to set it up at all in the description of MSC phonemics. Moreover, the underlying phonetic phenomena are largely unexplored and it would not be possible to present more than very tentative suggestions in this respect. The category and the term of

are thus, from the point of view of stressing, either successive arrangements of alternating stressed and unstressed syllables, or arrangements of unstressed syllables, or arrangements of these arrangements. The simplest and most common case which can be used as an example, are disyllabic morphological constructions. These constructions consist either of two syllables of which the first or the second are stressed, or of two unstressed syllables. In their case, we can thus speak of three *stress patterns*: stressed-unstressed (su), unstressed-stressed (us), and unstressed-unstressed (uu). Two examples of the us-versus-su stress pattern opposition were given in Chapter II ([ˈɕíŋli] *xíngli* 'luggage'—[ɕíŋˈli] *xíngli* 'to perform a ceremony', and [ˈtɕȳnʂʅ] *jūnshì* 'military affairs'— [tɕȳnˈʂʅ] *jūnshì* 'balance of power'); oppositions of the uu pattern versus either su or us are relatively rare, for example [ˈtūŋɕi] *dōngxi* 'thing'—[tūŋɕī] *dōng-xī* 'east and west'. As was also shown in Chapter II, stress is a phonemic feature in msc; alternatively, it can be said that the respective stress pattern is the phonemic feature of the given polysyllabic morphological construction. The stress pattern of most polysyllabic morphological constructions in msc is relatively stable (although it may be modified in certain ways by various factors operating on sentence level, as will be shown later), and the choice between one stress pattern or another is often influenced by the morphological structure of the given construction. It was pointed out in Chapter II that the most drastic changes in the phonetic shape of syllables brought about by stress take place in unstressed syllables following stressed syllables, that is in syllables which are negatively influenced by stress. The relationship between the shape of syllables and the morphological structure of constructions in which they occur can thus be most clearly demonstrated, in the case of disyllabic constructions, on constructions characterized by the phonemic feature of the su stress pattern.

Unstressed syllables which occur in su constructions share much fewer common features of phonetic shape than all stressed syllables on the one hand, and unstressed syllables occurring in us and uu constructions on the other hand. There is one group of syllables among them, however, which are relatively homogeneous in the sense that all their variants (that is variants conditioned by

junction are, therefore, not made use of in the present discussion. For a description of the phonemic status of juncture in msc see C. F. Hockett, 'Peiping Phonology', *Journal of the American Oriental Society*, 67, 253–267, and C. F. Hockett, 'Peiping Morphophonemics', *Language*, 26, 63–85.

differences in the tempo of speech, carefulness of diction, and other similar factors) tend to be limited to a very narrow area: whenever they occur, they always lack the characteristic features of tone, their vowels are very short in duration (if they are diphthongs or triphthongs, they are very 'short and straight' in terms of tongue shift, see p. 30), and their consonants invariably have one of the non-distinctive features like additional voicing, partial loss of aspiration, or very short duration. There is nothing in their phonemic structure that could help define this group of syllables (which have been called atonic because of their most conspicuous and consistent feature), but when morphological evidence is taken into account, it becomes possible to make the respective statement: all such syllables represent either affixes, non-morphemes (syllables in monomorphemic polysyllabic words), or constituents of very frequently occurring compounds. The reverse is not altogether true, since not all syllables occurring in SU constructions and representing affixes, non-morphemes, and constituents of common compounds are atonic, but even there, especially in the first case, this is valid to a great extent. It would, however, be better to speak of a core of all these forms partly characterized by atonic syllable representation. The word 'partly' is meant here to indicate that the statement is not circular, that is, atonic syllables being defined by what they represent morphologically which is again defined by atonic syllable representation: the main underlying factor is morphological, since all the respective forms share what may be called a *high degree of grammatical formalization*. It could be shown on examples of markers and other MSC formal grammatical elements not included in the present discussion that atonicity is, in fact, the regular phonemic feature of this high degree of formalization. The mere possibility of distinguishing different degrees of formalization in MSC by confronting concrete morphological and phonemic evidence has far-reaching consequences, *inter alia* for refuting the traditional concept of Chinese as a 'language without grammar' where all units operate on a single level.

The narrow area of the phonetic shape of atonic syllables is shared by other unstressed syllables negatively influenced by stress under the conditions of high tempo of speech and other factors, although these syllables have variants outside this area under other conditions. To give at least one example: in rapid careless speech the final syllables in *dōngxi* 'thing' and *fēnxī* 'to analyse' which represent two different morphemes (in both constructions the first syllable is stressed) have the same shape [ɕi]; in slow careful speech the shape of *-xi* in *dōngxi* is not considerably different, while *-xī* in *fēnxī* becomes tonic [ɕī]. Within the narrow area itself, however, atonic syllables and other unstressed syllables negatively affected by stress alike acquire not only common suprasegmental, but sometimes also specific segmental features. This aspect of MSC morphophonemics has not yet been fully described and it is not possible to go beyond giving an example of a typical case: the final syllables in *shuāishuai* 'to smash to pieces' and *gānshuǐ* 'water from washing rice' (in both constructions the first syllable is stressed) not only lose their tonic features in rapid speech (or rather *-shuǐ* in *gānshuǐ* does, *-shuai* in *shuāishuai* is an atonic syllable), but also acquire the common segmental shape [ʂui]. The implications of this phenomenon not only for the description of MSC, but potentially also for the historical analysis of Chinese are perhaps obvious.

Several MSC morphemes which have, so to speak, reached the highest degree of formalization (such as the most common word-formative suffix *-z*, the grammatical suffix *-le* 'suffix of completed actions', and the marker *de*) are represented by atonic syllables whose phonetic shape is specific only to them and which is irregular from the viewpoint of the general rules of the phonetic shape of MSC syllables. Thus, for example, the shape of the syllables representing the grammatical suffix *-le* and the marker *de* is [lə] and [tə] rather than [lɤ] and [tɤ]. In the case of some of these morphemes the shape of the atonic syllables representing them has still further specific features. On the one hand, there are a few cases of morphemes occurring as final sentence particles (their function is to complement the intonation contour of sentences) which are represented by several allomorphs, the choice between them being governed by the phonemic shape of the immediately preceding syllable. Thus, for instance, the morpheme *a* 'final sentence particle indicating exclamations' occurs in at least three variants: [a] as in [ʂʅˈnǐa] *shì nǐ a* 'It's you!', [wua] as in [ˈxǎowua] *hǎo a* 'All right!', and [jiA] as in [ˈwuǒjiA] *wǒ a* 'Me?'. On the other hand, in several morphemes the vowel (and also the final consonant) of the atonic syllables representing them often does not occur at all, and the initial consonant clusters with the immediately preceding syllable as its quasi-final consonant. This is the familiar case of the suffix *-men* in words like *tāmen* 'they' which occurs in variants ranging from [ˈtʰāmən] to [tʰām], or the suffix *-me* 'suffix of question words' in words like *shénme* 'what' whose variants range from [ˈʂə́nmə] to [ʂə́m], but also of the word-formative suffix *-z* as in *yĭz* 'chair' with variants ranging from ['jĭts₁] to [jĭts]. A special and most conspicuous case of similar clustering is the 'erisation' mentioned earlier in a different context (see mainly pp. 72–73). The word-formative suffix -*r*[1] (or rather the various suffixes sharing this shape) in fact never occurs in the shape of a separate syllable, but always clusters with the preceding syllable, such as in [tāoɚ] *dāor* 'knife' ([tāo] *dāo* 'knife, sword') or [mə́ɚ] *ménr* 'door' ([mə́n] *mén* 'door, gate'). The second of these two examples shows how this clustering affects the structure of the preceding syllable (also cf. [ʂə́m] which is a cluster variant of ['ʂə́nmə] *shénme* 'what'). 'Erisation' is not, however, limited only to cases where the final component represents one of the suffixes -*r*; it often takes place, at least in Peking dialect, in rapid speech with all final unstressed syllables whose initial consonant is retroflex, such as in *duōshao* 'how much?' which has variants ranging from ['tuōʂao] to [tuōɚ], in *jīnrì* 'contemporary' ranging from ['tɕīnzɻ̩] to [tɕīɚ], and in *kànzhe* 'to be looking' ranging from ['k'àntʂə] to [k'àɚ].

A somewhat different case of morphophonemic variants are the syllables representing several morphemes which usually occur in other than the final position in morphological constructions. The morphemes in question have allomorphs differentiated by features of tone and the respective choice is governed by the tone of the immediately following syllable. For example, the most common negative prefix has the variants *bú-* and *bù-*; the former occurs when the tone of the following syllable is falling, such as in *búqù* 'not to go' and *búxiè* 'not to thank', and the latter occurs when the tone of the following syllable is other than falling, such as in *bùshāng* 'not to injure', *bùlái* 'not to come', and *bùxiě* 'not to write'. Similarly, the morpheme *yì~yí~yī* 'one' has three allomorphs: one with falling tone which precedes syllables with other than falling tone, on with rising tone which precedes syllables with falling tone, and one with high tone which occurs when the morpheme is in the final position, as in *shíyī* 'eleven', or when it is emphasized, as in *yīyuè* '[it was in] January [, not in any other month]'.

To conclude this brief discussion of morphologically conditioned phonemic phenomena in MSC, the controversial case of the morphemes *liǎ* 'two [of]' and *sā* 'three [of]' will demonstrate the richness of the variety of such phenomena. These two morphemes

---

[1] It may have been noticed that the Pinyin transcription reflects, although inconsistently, morphophonemic phenomena: thus, it transcribes the respective suffixes as -*z* rather than -*zi*, and -*r* rather than -*er*.

occur in Peking dialect as variants of the constructions *liǎng ge* 'two [of]' and *sān ge* [three [of]', as in *liǎng ge rén ~ liǎ rén* 'two people', and *sān ge rén ~ sā rén* 'three people'. Most scholars consider the forms *liǎ* and *sā* as cluster variants of the longer constructions: although this is a justified conclusion, this kind of clustering is rather difficult to explain in view of the more common MSC evidence.

MSC morphophonemic phenomena were discussed here as the specific phonemic features of specific morphological constructions or specific morphemes. It remains to pose the question whether there are any features of this kind which would themselves have a morphological status, or in other words, if there are in MSC morphemes whose representation would be morphophonemic rather than phonemic. This is a very important question, primarily for the study of the historical development of Chinese. At least two types of cases can be identified in MSC which might be taken as clues for an affirmative answer. On the one hand, it seems that certain stress patterns, of those mentioned above the UU pattern, function as morphemes. The UU pattern, for example, could with some justification be considered as a morpheme meaning 'two items of a group, or two items symbolizing a collective concept', as it occurs almost only with constructions like *dōng-xī* 'east and west' (*dōng* 'east', and *xī* 'west'), *huācǎo* 'vegetation' (*huā* 'flower', and *cǎo* 'grass'), *fù-mǔ* 'parents' (*fù* 'father', and *mǔ* 'mother'), and *chēmǎ* 'toys' (*chē* 'vehicle', and *mǎ* 'horse'). On the other hand, there are cases of pairs of morphemes whose members occur in different environments but which are strikingly similar in their phonemic shape and share a common basis of meaning.[1] For example, *hǎo* 'to be good', as in *tā hěn hǎo* 'He is good', and *hào* 'to be fond of', as in *tā hào hējiǔ* 'He is fond of drinking'; *zhǒng* 'seed', a bound morpheme which occurs in words like *zhǒngz* 'seed', and *zhòng* 'to plant, to cultivate, to grow', as in *zhònghuā* 'to plant flowers, to grow flowers', or *zhòng yì mǔ dì* 'to cultivate one *mou* of land'; *nà* 'that', as in *nàli* 'there', and *nǎ* 'which', as in *nǎli* 'where'; *zhǎng* 'to grow', as in *zhǎngqilaile* 'to have grown up', and *cháng* 'to be long', as in *cháng shéngz* 'long [piece of] string'; *chuán* 'to pass on', as in *chuán jìshù* 'to pass on know-how', and *zhuàn* 'biography', as in *zuò zhuàn* 'to write a biography'. However, there are relatively very few such cases, and their small number makes it difficult to

---

[1] Most of these pairs of morphemes are written with the same characters.

answer the question in either way. Although the significance of
these cases may in the future be emphasized by further historical
evidence, their number and importance within the total framework
of MSC are negligible, and they are easier to treat as unrelated
morphemes.

CHAPTER IV

SYNTAX

I. WORDS

One of the crucial problems of describing and understanding a language, particularly an unfamiliar language the general features of which do not always correspond to the categories of our linguistic experience, is finding a foothold in the mass of its utterances. Above all, this means finding out if and how the utterances can be segmented into small recurrent elements which could be enumerated and whose behaviour in conjunction with other similar elements could be described in general terms. There are basically two tasks which have to be carried out in this respect: first, it has to be ascertained that the segmentation of utterances of the given language is at all possible, and ways of segmenting the utterances have to be designed; secondly, it has to be decided how far the segmentation should proceed and where it is profitable to stop it.

Carrying out the first task when MSC is approached is not simple and it touches upon such very general matters as the universal nature of languages and the preference of this or that linguistic school of thought. In this book the possibility of segmenting MSC utterances will not be doubted: it could be shown that recurrent elements justifying the segmentation appear on all levels of MSC structure, and many discussions in the preceding and following sections serve as proof of this. As for the general principles underlying the ways in which MSC utterances will be segmented here, it will be attempted, as in the preceding sections, to avoid those which are directly associated with any particular linguistic school.

This is, of course, possible only up to a point. In general, it will perhaps be apparent that the approach used here is roughly based on the principles which are common to the majority of the numerous trends in what is known as modern descriptive or structural linguistics, their modification being more biased towards the needs of handling the specific MSC material than towards the idiosyncrasies of individual general methods and techniques.

The second task depends on the purpose of segmentation: language material can be segmented on different levels for different purposes. The phonemic and morphological segmentation of MSC outlined earlier in this book exemplifies two such possible levels. There is, however, a kind of basic borderline in every language which divides elements the speakers of the language consciously operate with from elements of these elements which speakers of the language are not normally fully aware of and which they simply accept as the natural mechanical components of language communication. Such elements as phonemes and morphemes belong to the latter, while units discussed in the further sections of this book are elements of the former kind. The problem, as far as MSC is concerned, is, then, where precisely is the dividing line between the two kinds of elements, or in other words, what is the smallest unit speakers of MSC consciously and consistently operate with when they communicate with each other. Or, to give still another formulation of the problem, is there a unit in MSC comparable to what is called a *word* in other languages.

In the preceding chapter, word in MSC has been posited rather than defined. The concept of this unit calls for a more detailed discussion at this point. This is important because the possibility and need to establish this unit in MSC have been questioned by many scholars, both Western and Chinese, and also because the existence of words (that is, 'the sort of thing we all know words are') in MSC has been considered a matter of course by others.

It has been pointed out earlier that it is often felt necessary to establish units of a different kind from morphemes when MSC sentences are used as the starting point for arriving at small recurrent elements in speech, that is the kind of units represented by some morphemes and not by others (see p. 58). The need is felt strongly in certain situations, such as that of sentences represented by single morphemes, but it is not always so obviously acute. Moreover, it could be argued that setting up minimal grammatical units of a different kind from morphemes in MSC (or whatever else they may be called: when sinologues speak of 'syllables', 'monosyllables', 'characters', or 'words', they often refer to what are called morphemes here; the terms themselves are arbitrary and largely irrelevant, the categories are important) is a matter of descriptive convenience, a mere means to cover up gaps in a systematic pattern, rather than a reflection of actual features of MSC structure. It still remains to be demonstrated that speakers of MSC really operate with (or 'think in') units different from morphemes in normal speech.

On the other hand, it is in a way rather uncommon to question the need to set up words in MSC. To the Westerner with common secondary school education and no specialized training in general linguistics, the unit called word is, rather than morpheme, a *sine qua non*: a language without words is simply nonsense. Not only any kind of words but units rather precisely conceived, with presumably universal characteristic features of size, shape, and general behaviour, or to be more down-to-earth, the kind of units which occur as items in dictionaries, in lists within individual lessons of foreign language textbooks, and which are marked by spaces on both sides in texts. There is just one step from this to assuming that MSC not only must have such units, but also that they must be in some way equivalent to Latin, English, and French words in these supposedly universal features. The problem is that units with such features are difficult, if not almost impossible to find in MSC. The quest for words in MSC based on the argument that being a language MSC must have words, that is 'our kind of words', and that these must be found if the language is to be properly described, has never been very successful: it has either led to establishing words in MSC according to arbitrary sets of criteria which, in fact, served as *ex post* justifications for setting up units equivalent with words in European languages (needless to say, MSC words conceived in this manner have not proved very useful for either theoretical or practical purposes), or it has resulted in the rejection of the concept of word in MSC altogether. The few existing grammars of MSC invariably reflect one or the other tendency.

There are, however, surprisingly many possible ways of establishing small operational units, or words, in MSC without referring to the concept of 'universal words', although it is generally difficult to establish these units according to a single viewpoint without ambiguity in detail. Moreover, evidence from all levels of MSC structure shows that this is not only possible but also necessary if the structure is to be fully described. The following example will perhaps make this necessity clear, and at the same time it will show one of the ways by which MSC words can be established and defined in terms of MSC itself.

The example below is based on several presumptions about universal language behaviour which can be briefly summarized in the following points:

(1) In most or perhaps even all speech conditions, an utterance of any size is practically never isolated from the general situation, or *context*, in which it occurs; this context consists either of other utterances (by the same speaker or by other speakers), or of some non-language environmental situation, or of both.

(2) The same context often elicits the same utterances (such as the context of a morning encounter will usually elicit the utterance *Good morning* from a speaker of English), but it does not always do so: choice and variability of responses to the same contexts is one of the specific features of language as opposed to most other systems of communication.

(3) In terms of component language elements (that is, disregarding variability in the idiosyncratic features of the speech of individuals, such as the typical mumbling way in which Mr Watt the caretaker utters his *'morning*), the number of utterances which may occur in the same context is limited; among them, some may differ in all formal respects (such as *Good morning* and *Lovely weather*, each uttered with a different intonation), others only in some (such as *Good morning* uttered with two different intonations, or *'morning, Good morning*, and *A very good morning to you, my dear*). If we decide to ignore such suprasegmental features as intonation in this discussion, we can establish groups of utterances used in the same context in the given language which share a common segmental feature; or, in other words, we can find groups of utterances used in the same context in the given language within each of which one utterance contains all the other utterances. We can then decide to call such an utterance the *maximal utterance* of the given group (this is the utterance which is the largest in size, such as *A very good morning to you, my dear*), the utterance which is contained in all the utterances of the group the *minimal utterance* (the smallest in size, such as *'morning*), and the remaining utterances *intermediate utterances* (such as *Good morning*).

The context of two speakers of MSC who meet on a sunny day

in Peking and start a conversation may elicit a great number of opening utterances. One of these may be the question *jīntiān tiānqi hěn hǎo, shì búshì* 'The weather is [very] nice today, isn't it?'. If this is the case, the question then becomes part of the context for what follows. Again, this somewhat more precise context may provide conditions for a wide variety of subsequent events: for instance, the question may be followed by further speech from the speaker who raised it, or it may be followed by silence, or by a response from the other speaker. The last possibility is perhaps the most probable, and the present example is based on it. Among the various responses of the other speaker several utterances might occur which could be grouped together in the way suggested above. If, for example, one of these utterances were the sentence *jīntiān tiānqi hěn hǎo* 'The weather is [very] nice today', if this sentence were not contained in any of the other possible responses, and if several other sentences contained in this sentence were among the other possible responses, a group of sentences could be established within which *jīntiān tiānqi hěn hǎo* would be the maximal utterance. The group limited by this maximal utterance would not be very large and it would consist of a definite number of members, that is the following six sentences: *jīntiān hěn hǎo* 'Today [it] is [very] nice', *jīntiān hǎo* 'Today [it] is nice', *tiānqi hěn hǎo* 'The weather is [very] nice', *tiānqi hǎo* 'The weather is nice', *hěn hǎo* '[It] is [very] nice', and *hǎo* '[It] is nice'. Of these six sentences *hǎo* is obviously the minimal utterance of the group, and the remaining five are the respective intermediate utterances.

At this point of the discussion the most relevant conclusion which can be drawn from this example is the limited and definite number of sentences within a maximal utterance group. Or, in other words, the fact that the group contains only the seven sentences (including the maximal utterance) listed above and not others, such as *tiān hěn hǎo* 'The heaven is [very] good', and *qì hěn hǎo* 'The air is [very] nice', both of which would be acceptable or *grammatical* sentences in other contexts, or such generally unacceptable or *ungrammatical* sentences as **qì hěn* 'The air very' or **jīn hǎo* 'Present is good'. One of the reasons why the number of sentences within the group is limited to the six sentences above is that the number of the smallest segments which they share or miss is definite and specific: all the sentences share the unit *hǎo* '[it] is good', and the units *jīntiān* 'today', *tiānqi* 'weather', and *hěn* 'very' are the only features which differentiate member sentences of pairs like *jīntiān hěn hǎo* 'Today [it] is [very] nice'—*hěn hǎo* '[It] is [very] nice', *tiānqi hǎo* 'The weather is nice'—*hǎo* '[It] is nice', and *hěn hǎo* '[It] is [very] nice'—*hǎo* '[It] is nice'. These four segments represent the smallest units which the speaker of MSC consciously operates with in the eventual process of his particular response in the respective context. If we decide to call such units *words*, we can say that an MSC word is the smallest unit which may function as an immediate constituent of MSC segmental sentences.

The purpose of the preceding example is to show that it is possible to establish units in MSC comparable with what we are accustomed to call words in European languages, but more than that, to demonstrate the need for doing so: the structure of an MSC sentence like *jīntiān tiānqi hěn hǎo* could not be fully explained in terms of other units (such as phonemes, syllables, or morphemes), since such an explanation would not distinguish between segments which represent immediate constituents of sentences and those which do not. This does not mean that data on the phonemic and morphological structure are irrelevant as far as MSC syntax is concerned; it simply means that beside these data a further concept of operational units is needed for a full explanation of the way large segments of MSC speech are organized. This concept makes it possible to draw a line between the grammatical disciplines of morphology and syntax, the former dealing with the inner structure of words, and the latter with their general behaviour in speech.

On the other hand, it has to be realized that words in MSC can be established only on the basis of actual structural features of MSC utterances, and that it is next to impossible to set up MSC words, or rather to find words in MSC by using the gauge of the set of features popularly associated with words in European languages. The essential part of this supposedly universal set of features (beside such irrelevant properties as the orthographic devices used for indicating the borderlines of words in alphabetic writing systems) is the feature of meaning, since it is the only feature in a sense common to presumably equivalent units in different languages. Thus, one expects to find a word in MSC which would mean the same as the English word *today*, the French word *aujourd'hui*, and the Latin word *hodie*. In the case of *jīntiān* 'today' and a certain proportion of other MSC units this approach seems to work. This, however, is more coincidence than proof that universals of this kind are valid, as could be shown on countless examples: the unit *jīn*, for instance, is not a word in MSC, although it means the same as the English word *present* or *now*.

The point is not that features of meaning have nothing to do with the status of MSC words, but that meaning is only a partial aspect of the total behaviour of the smallest operational units called words, and as such it is not a property sufficient for establishing these units.

Although it is not only possible but also necessary for the analysis of MSC to establish the smallest operational units (or words) without referring to the frame of popular universals, it is not always easy or unambiguous: not all MSC sentences can be as neatly analysed as *jīntiān tiānqi hěn hǎo*. Moreover, the results of the respective analysis of this sentence to its smallest structural constituents cannot be generalized for the whole of MSC as easily as the results of the phonemic and morphological analysis of a sample segment of an MSC utterance. The definition of MSC words as units which *may* function as immediate constituents of segmental sentences in the sense outlined above, marks words as units of a different kind than units of, so to speak, lower levels, such as morphemes. Morphemes, for example, were defined as the smallest units which *are* meaningful. The difference is reflected by the expression *may* as opposed to *are* in the two definitions: what is a morpheme in one MSC environment is a morpheme wherever else it occurs in MSC, but what is a word in one MSC context is not necessarily a word in another context. In the sentence *jīntiān tiānqi hěn hǎo* the segment *tiān* which is a morpheme meaning 'heaven, sky, day' is not a word; the same morpheme occurring in the sentence *tiān hēile* 'The sky became dark' is a word, since this sentence has the corresponding minimal utterance *hēile* '[It] became dark'. This dependence of word status on the environment in which the given segment occurs is not a feature specific to MSC. Examples of similar, although less common phenomena in European languages can easily be given. For instance, the status of the segment *black* varies considerably in English, as can be observed from sentences like *I have a black suit*, *Look at that black-bird*, *He's a blacksmith*, and *He's blackened my reputation*. However, the situation in MSC is somewhat more complicated and the problem of MSC words cannot be fully appreciated without a brief discussion of the factors which make the concept of their status more variable and also more difficult to apply in practical terms than we are accustomed to in the descriptions of European languages.

First of all, the structure of MSC sentences is a very complex affair; it will be shown later that MSC sentences, as well as sentences in other languages, cannot be described as linear chains of words, but rather as constructions containing hierarchies of relationships of different degrees between words and their arrangements. It is often not easy to extricate words from these relationships, or distinguish morphological from syntactic constructions within the intricate framework of sentence relationships. This presumably universal predicament of the smallest syntactic units in all languages is accentuated in MSC by the lack of an overall formal apparatus of indicators of word boundaries, such as the systems of affixes in some European languages, the distribution of juncture (cf. the difference between *night rate* and *nitrate* in English), or the patterning of word stress (cf. the regular stress on the penultimate syllable of a word in Polish). To give a simple example, it is difficult to evaluate the word status of all the morphemes occurring in the sentence *sān ge rén láile* '[Those] three people have arrived'. It is possible to imagine a context in which this sentence would have one corresponding intermediate utterance *rén láile* '[Those] people have arrived', and one minimal utterance *láile* '[They] have arrived'; according to this, the segment *sān ge* 'three [units of]' could be considered a single word, and yet the analogy between the construction *sān ge rén* 'three people' and constructions like *sān jīn chá* 'three pounds of tea' (*jīn* 'pound', *chá* 'tea') and *sān wèi rén* 'three people [of social importance]' makes this solution somewhat unconvincing. It is a little like questioning the word status of the segment *is* in *he is good* on the basis of a similar argument. Whatever the solution, the problem of the MSC sentence is slightly more tedious, since the segment *sān ge* does not give any formal indication as to its word status (compare with the indication conveyed by the English pattern *he -s*). The task of extricating MSC words from their environment is further made difficult by a feature shared probably by all languages with little paradigmatic morphology: it seems that these languages, unlike languages with complex systems of devices for modifying the formal shape of words (such as most European languages with the possible exception of English), depend comparatively heavily on rote repetition of utterances or their large segments, rather than on free manipulation with the smallest syntactic units. Consequently, the number of closely-knit phrases, idiomatic expressions, and other similar lexicalized items, is very high in normal MSC speech, and they often overlap in size with whole sentences. It is very difficult to evaluate the word status of their components without referring to questionable analogies, because such lexicalized expressions are not normally reducible to intermediate or minimal utterances. Thus, a sentence like *tā xīnyǎnr hěn duō* 'He takes no chances', or 'He takes nothing for granted' (literally, if one is allowed to use the expression, this sentence means 'He [has] a lot of holes in [his] heart', which is a phrase based on the traditional superstition concerning 'holes in the heart' as places where the elements of one's intelligence or foresight are stored), is a minimal utterance which cannot normally be reduced any further. The only way to analyse the word status of the components of this sentence is by analogy with sentences like *tā qián hěn duō* 'He [has] a lot of money' (which can be reduced further to such sentences as *tā hěn duō* 'He [has] a lot', *tā qián duō* 'He [has relatively] much money', etc. in some contexts), and *tā yǒu xīnyǎnr* 'He is smart' (or 'He has holes in [his] heart'). Such analogies are, however, a little like circumstantial evidence in court: on their own they cannot be sufficiently convincing.

Indistinct borderlines between the smallest syntactic units and their components are not only a reflection of the complexity of MSC syntactic relations in the synchronic sense, that is the complexity of the system of syntax as a generalization abstracted from the common speech behaviour of MSC speakers at the present time. This system itself is the result of a historical development, or rather a stage in a continuous historical process. It could be shown, however hypothetical the suggestion might be, that even the two examples given above could be interpreted in historical terms: a unit like *ge* (in *sān ge rén* 'three people') could be said to have reached a higher degree of grammatical formalization than the similar units *jīn* (in *sān jīn chá* 'three pounds of tea') and *wèi* (in *sān wèi rén* 'three people [of social importance]'), reflected beside other features by its atonicity, and idiomatic expressions like *tā xīnyǎnr hěn duō* 'He takes no chances' could perhaps be traced to a time when they had not yet become idiomatic. There are areas in MSC grammar where the historical aspects of indistinct borderline phenomena are even more apparent. One of such areas is that of the so-called *verb-noun* or *verb-object constructions*. Most of these are recurrent dimorphemic constructions functioning as single words in some contexts and as constructions of two words in others, for example *zǒulù* 'to walk' ~ *zǒu lù* 'to travel on foot' which may occur in such contexts as *zhè háiz huì zuòqilai, hái búhuì zǒulù* 'This child can sit up, [but he] cannot walk as yet', and *tā zǒule jǐ lǐ lù* 'He travelled several miles on foot'. There are a relatively great number of such constructions in MSC, and many of them are extremely frequent. They do not all behave in a uniform way: many of them are, so to speak, more morphological than others, and some occur solely as single words. In the last case, it is sometimes possible to find historical evidence for their syntactic origin: the word *zhīdao* 'to know', for instance, functioned originally as a syntactic construction of two words *zhī* 'to know' and *dào* 'the way, the principle' (which developed into the philosophical and religious term *Dào*, or as it is better known, the Tao of taoism), later as a kind of single intransitive verb *zhīdao* 'to know' (as in *nǐ zhīdao ma* 'Do you know?'), and at present it often functions also as a transitive verb *zhīdao* 'to know [something or someone]' (as in *nǐ zhīdao lù ma* 'Do you know the way?'). It could be shown that these constructions as a whole represent a subsystem in the process of transition from syntax to morphology, and that it is virtually impossible to draw a firm dividing line between syntactic and morphological constructions in this subsystem while the process is in progress.

The point of this discussion is that the concept of the smallest syntactic unit in MSC called word is very indistinct not because of our approach to it, but because the system of MSC of which the unit is a part is too complex for the imposition of clear-cut borderlines between its morphology and syntax. Such factors as the synchronic diversity of relationships between constituents of utterances, or the historical process of transition, are not the only ones which contribute to the complexity. Another important factor is the diversity of variants of speech behaviour within MSC: at the borderlines of what is called MSC it is possible to feel the influence of non-MSC dialectal behaviour which brings in minor features of different division between morphology and syntax than that normally accepted by most speakers of MSC. And yet, in spite of this seemingly monstrous complexity, there is in this respect very little in MSC that could not be associated with similar phenomena in any European language where the borderlines are ostensibly more clearly cut. It would be possible to find examples from English, for instance, for each of the cases mentioned above. The difference between MSC and English in this respect is not in the systems of the two languages, but in the degree to which either of the systems has been interpreted for practical purposes. When the smallest MSC syntactic units are discussed, the complexity becomes immediately apparent, because direct reference is made to the largely uninterpreted language material itself; in the case of English words, it is possible to refer to the accepted interpretation of the material in the form of the norm of Modern Standard English. It is, in fact, not only possible, but very difficult not to do so, since the norm, besides functioning as a kind of official set of rules for the game called language, very deeply influences our concept of English and our awareness of the status of its units. What we call English words are units partly set up in terms of the interpreting norm with all its delicacies, including the rules of English orthography. Since there is no correspondingly strong MSC norm in existence as yet, there is no practical interpretation available which would disguise the natural complexity of MSC language material. Most speakers of MSC are not accustomed to use the concept of the smallest syntactic units called words mainly because the writing system at present in use, the most concrete expression of language norm, does not indicate word boundaries. Even the awareness with which the units are operated varies between groups of speakers, differentiated mainly by the degree of education they have received: education means acquaintance with the traditional Chinese writing system which supports awareness of the morphological rather than the syntactic structure of the language. Thus, the question of MSC words will not be solved in detail (that is, solved for practical purposes; as was shown above, there is nothing to be solved in the theoretical sense) by improved linguistic techniques, but by the way MSC norm itself develops. Since the development of a language norm is a process which includes arbitrary decisions, it is impossible to do more than anticipate the general direction of the process. In the following sections of this chapter such anticipation, wrong or right, will have to be used tacitly in cases where the borderlines are not clear.

2. SYNTACTIC CONSTRUCTIONS

The indistinct borderline between MSC morphology and syntax is, apart from its importance for the concept of the smallest syntactic unit—the word, an indirect expression of the main features of the behaviour of small recurrent elements in MSC speech. It shows that the way in which these small recurrent elements are operated within the process of speech cannot be described as a kind of linear juxtaposing of clear-cut units governed simply by certain rules of what is usually called 'word order', since the relationships between the elements vary in their degree of closeness. If a fully close relationship such as that between the morphemes *zǒu* and *-le* within

the morphological construction *zǒule* 'to have gone' were used as
the starting point for evaluating the degree of closeness, it would
be possible to arrive finally at a fully open syntactic relationship
such as that between the words *māma* 'mother' and *zǒule* 'to have
gone' in the sentence *māma zǒule* 'mother has gone'; the indistinct
borderline between morphology and syntax discussed in the preceding section indicates that these two extremes delimit the range
of many relationships neither fully open nor fully close. A statement on MSC syntax has to reflect this feature of the arrangements of recurrent elements within MSC speech, if it is to be
complete.

The sentence *jīntiān tiānqi hěn hǎo* 'The weather is [very] nice
today' which was used in the preceding section for demonstrating
how the unit of the word can be established in MSC, reflects, as well
as any other sentence in MSC, different degrees of relationships
between words. First of all, this sentence contains four words
whose individual value for the sentence as such is not altogether
the same. As was pointed out earlier, this sentence has in the given
context a single corresponding minimal utterance *hǎo* '[It] is nice';
this word also occurs in all the intermediate utterances, and it can
thus be considered a kind of core of the sentence. The term *nucleus*
will be used for words which fulfil this function in MSC sentences,
and the relationships within sentences will be evaluated by observing how closely nuclei are related with other words on the one
hand, and what degree of closeness there is between the words
which are not the nuclei of sentences on the other hand. As follows
from the example on p. 93, any of the three words *jīntiān* 'today',
tiānqi 'weather', and *hěn* 'very' may constitute a sentence with the
nucleus *hǎo*, and their relationship with the nucleus is in that sense
equally close. There are, however, other features which can be
observed: two of the words, *jīntiān* 'today', and *tiānqi* 'weather'
either immediately precede the nucleus *hǎo* (in *jīntiān hǎo* 'Today
[it] is nice' and *tiānqi hǎo* 'The weather is nice'), or the word *hěn*
'very' occurs between them and the nucleus *hǎo* (in *jīntiān hěn hǎo*
'Today [it] is [very] nice' and *tiānqi hěn hǎo* 'The weather is [very]
nice'); the word *hěn* 'very' occurs only immediately preceding *hǎo*.
Moreover, the word *tiānqi* 'weather' occurs either immediately
preceding *hǎo* or preceding the words *hěn hǎo*, but it does not
occur in a position farther away from *hǎo*, as does *jīntiān* 'today'
in the maximal utterance *jīntiān tiānqi hěn hǎo*. On the basis of this
observation, it can be hypothetically concluded that each of the
three words is in a different degree of closeness with the nucleus

hǎo : *hěn* 'very' being most closely related with *hǎo*, and *jīntiān* 'today' being related with it most loosely. This can be indicated graphically in the following way:

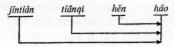

Fig. 21   Structure of the sentence *jīntiān tiānqi hěn hǎo*

The diagram suggests the other part of the hypothetical conclusion, which is that there is no difference in closeness in the mutual relationship between the words *jīntiān* 'today', *tiānqi* 'weather', and *hěn* 'very' themselves: these three words are not directly related with each other.

This conclusion is, of course, only hypothetical and not necessarily of any potential general value. It is necessary to test a conclusion of this kind on further material to show whether it is correct or not, and if it can be generalized in the form of one of the rules of syntactic arrangements of words in MSC sentences. First of all, the conclusion can be substantiated or refuted by negative evidence. As far as the example given above is concerned, it can be observed that the 'sentences' **hěn tiānqi hǎo* '[Very] weather is nice' and **hěn jīntiān hǎo* ['Very] today [it] is nice' are both ungrammatical, and that the sentence *tiānqi jīntiān hǎo* 'The weather today is nice', although grammatical, does not occur in the given context. This shows that the evaluation of the actual arrangement of the words in *jīntiān tiānqi hěn hǎo*, whether significant for the relationship between them or not, was correct. Further, the conclusion can be tested on the positive evidence of other similar sentences occurring in the same context or in other contexts. For the example above, it is possible to bring in the following relevant evidence of the positive kind. A sentence like *tiānqi tèbié hǎo* 'The weather is particularly nice' in the context of a preceding question *tiānqi zěnmeyàng* 'How is the weather' would in normal speech situations have the corresponding minimal utterance *tèbié hǎo* '[It] is particularly nice', but not just *hǎo* '[It] is nice'; this shows the occurrence of contexts which bring out the point that the degree of closeness is, in fact, greater between words like *hěn* 'very' or *tèbié* 'particularly', and *hǎo* 'to be nice', than between words like *tiānqi* 'weather' and *hǎo* 'to be nice', in sentences of this kind. Or, in other words, the last example shows that there are situations when a word like *tiānqi* 'weather' may occur in a sentence only when words like *tèbié* 'particularly' and *hǎo* 'to be nice' occur in the sentence. It can also be shown that the occurrence of a word like *jīntiān* 'today' in a sentence may be similarly conditioned by the occurrence of words like *tiānqi hěn hǎo* 'the weather is [very] nice' in the sentence: this can happen if the sentence *jīntiān tiānqi hěn hǎo* is a response to an MSC statement equivalent to 'You've been smiling all day long today, I wonder why you are so cheerful'. In this context, the corresponding minimal utterance is *tiānqi hěn hǎo* 'The weather is [very] nice', not just *hǎo* '[It] is nice'.

Even these few examples show that the hypothetical conclusion about the structure of the sentence *jīntiān tiānqi hěn hǎo* 'The weather is [very] nice today' reflects its inner relationships rather accurately, or at least better than a mere statement in terms of a linear juxtaposition of the words within the sentence, since the latter could not easily account for the kind of conditioned occurrence of words which takes place in certain contexts. The present conclusion also shows the need for establishing structural levels between the extreme levels of words and sentences, that is levels which reflect different degrees of closeness between words and their small arrangements within sentences. If we raise the concept of *syntactic constructions* opposed to the concept of words, as arrangements of two or more words on different structural levels of a sentence, including the final level of the whole sentence, it will be necessary for the description of MSC syntax to decide how many levels of syntactic constructions it is profitable to establish, and what are the relationships within them and between them. Before an attempt is made to do this (it can hardly be more than an attempt: apart from such problems as the indistinct borderline between morphology and syntax which make the task rather complicated, MSC linguistics has not yet reached the stage of analytical experience which would make more authoritative statements possible), it will perhaps be useful to give two further examples of MSC sentences which contain constructions of a different and more varied nature than those in *jīntiān tiānqi hěn hǎo* 'The weather is [very] nice today'.

The structure of the sentence *nǐ qián búgòu méiyǒu duō dà guānxi* '[It] doesn't matter too much [that] you haven't enough money' occurring in the context of a preceding statement by another speaker equivalent to 'I haven't enough money', is indicated by the diagram

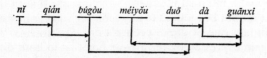

Fig. 22 Structure of the sentence *nǐ qián*
búgòu méiyǒu duō dà guānxi

The corresponding minimal utterance of this sentence is *méiyǒu guānxi* '[It] doesn't matter' (the fact that this is the minimal utterance rather than just *méiyǒu* '[It] doesn't' is indicated in the diagram by arrows pointing in both directions, and by connecting the centre of the link between *méiyǒu* and *duō dà guānxi* with the rest of the sentence), and there are ten intermediate utterances: *méiyǒu dà guānxi* '[It] doesn't matter much', *méiyǒu duō dà guānxi* '[It] doesn't matter too much', *búgòu méiyǒu guānxi* '[It] doesn't matter [that you] haven't enough', *búgòu méiyǒu dà guānxi* '[It] doesn't matter much [that you] haven't enough', *búgòu méiyǒu duō dà guānxi* '[It] doesn't matter too much [that you] haven't enough', *qián búgòu méiyǒu guānxi* '[It] doesn't matter [that you] haven't enough money', *qián búgòu méiyǒu dà guānxi* '[It] doesn't matter much [that you] haven't enough money', *qián búgòu méiyǒu duō dà guānxi* '[It] doesn't matter too much [that you] haven't enough money', *nǐ qián búgòu méiyǒu guānxi* '[It] doesn't matter [that] you haven't enough money', and *nǐ qián búgòu méiyǒu dà guānxi* '[It] doesn't matter much [that] you haven't enough money'. As the diagram shows, the occurrence of several words in the sentence is conditioned by the occurrence of others: *nǐ* 'you' does not occur if *qián* 'money' does not, *qián* 'money' does not occur if *búgòu* 'not to be enough' does not, *duō* 'too' does not occur if *dà* 'much' does not, etc.

The structure of the sentence *tāmen shì xuésheng* 'They [are] students' occurring in the context of a preceding question equivalent to 'What do your two brothers do' is indicated by the diagram

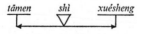

Fig. 23 Structure of the sentence *tāmen shì xuésheng*

The specific feature of this sentence is that it is simultaneously a

maximal and a minimal utterance, which means that in the given
context it cannot be reduced to any sentence smaller in size, which
would contain one of the respective word constituents. This feature is again expressed by the arrows pointing in both directions.
Moreover, this sentence contains the element *shì* beside the two
words *tāmen* 'they' and *xuésheng* 'student, students'; the function
of this element, indicated by the triangle pointing downwards, is
different from that of words as syntactic constituents in the sense
described earlier. It is not a unit which enters into relationships
with other units, but it rather indicates the kind of relationship
which other units enter into. As such, it is part of the general
pattern of the structural relationships within the given sentence.
Elements like *shì* will be called *markers*, and they will be discussed
in greater detail later.

The three examples above show that syntactic constructions
vary in size, in kind, and in structural complexity. The structure
of some sentences, such as *tāmen shì xuésheng* 'They [are] students'
is relatively simple, and it can be expressed in linear terms: the
relationship between the words within them is realized on a single
level. The relationship between the words in the sentence *nǐ qián
búgòu méiyǒu duō dà guānxi* '[It] doesn't matter too much [that]
you haven't enough money' is realized on at least four different
levels, and examples of structurally even more complex sentences
could be easily given. For our present purposes, it will be profitable
to establish three different kinds of levels, and three corresponding sorts of constructions. The first kind is represented by the level
nearest to the level of individual words: this is the level of very
close syntactic constructions of usually, but not always, two words,
indicated in the diagrams by the horizontal lines immediately below the underlined words. Constructions occurring on this level
will be called *syntagms*; they are the smallest arrangement of words
speakers of MSC operate with. The three examples above contain
four syntagms: *hěn hǎo* 'to be [very] nice' in *jīntiān tiānqi hěn hǎo*
'The weather is [very] nice today', *nǐ qián* 'you[r] money, and *duō
dà* 'too much' in *nǐ qián búgòu méiyǒu duō dà guānxi* '[It] doesn't
matter too much [that] you haven't enough money'; the whole
sentence *tāmen shì xuésheng* 'They [are] students' is also a syntagm.
The second kind is the final level which is indicated in the diagrams by the horizontal line farthest below the words. Sentences
are the respective constructions occurring on this level. Between
the level of syntagms and the level of sentences there may occur
one or more intermediate levels. This kind of levels is indicated by

all horizontal lines between the top and the bottom ones in the diagrams. All constructions occurring on these levels will be called *phrases*. The three preceding examples contain four phrases: *tiānqi hěn hǎo* 'the weather is [very] nice' in *jīntiān tiānqi hěn hǎo* 'The weather is [very] nice today', *nǐ qián búgòu* 'you haven't enough money', *duō dà guānxi* 'too much [consequence]', and *méiyǒu duō dà guānxi* '[It] doesn't matter too much'. It is not necessary to distinguish between different kinds of phrases at the moment, but more delicate distinctions will be made in their case later. It follows from this concept of structural levels that MSC syntax is understood as a system of hierarchies where units of one level, such as words, construct units of a higher level, such as syntagms. The level of phrases does not necessarily occur in all MSC sentences, and the level of syntagms may coincide with the level of sentences. There are also cases of sentences without the level of syntagms, such as sentences coinciding with single words (for example, *qù* 'Go!'). As the preceding examples show, the structural complexity of an MSC sentence, that is the number of syntagms and phrases it contains, depends to a certain degree on the number of words occurring in it. This is, however, a rather loose kind of dependence: there are cases of sentences containing the same number of words and differing slightly in complexity.

There are basically two kinds of syntactic constructions in MSC, speaking from the viewpoint of the character of the relationship between their constituents. These two kinds of constructions are indicated in the diagrams by arrows pointing in a single direction in some cases, and in both directions in others. In a somewhat oversimplified way of speaking, one of the two kinds (indicated by the single arrow) is represented by constructions which can be reduced to one of their constituents, and the other kind (indicated by the double arrow) is represented by constructions which cannot be reduced in this manner. The former are known as *endocentric*, and the latter as *exocentric* constructions. These two kinds of syntactic constructions occur in probably all known languages, but languages differ considerably in their mutual proportion. One of the most important general features of MSC syntax is the overall predominance of endocentric constructions on all structural levels: the occurrence of exocentric constructions in MSC is relatively rare, and there are very few syntactic constructions which are exocentric whenever they occur. This means that MSC constructions which are exocentric in some sentences or contexts are not necessarily exocentric in others. For example, the construction *méiyŏu guānxi* '[it] doesn't matter' (which was exocentric in one of the examples above) may occur as a maximal utterance in the context of the preceding question *yŏu guānxi méiyŏu* 'Does it matter or not?', and in this context it is endocentric

Fig. 24   Structure of the sentence *méiyŏu guānxi*

because it has a corresponding minimal utterance *méiyŏu* '[It] doesn't'. Notice that the similar English construction 'it doesn't' which is exocentric in the equivalent context, remains exocentric whenever it occurs in Modern Standard English.

The final distinction between different kinds of MSC syntactic constructions has to be made from the point of view of formal marking. There are syntactic constructions the inner relationship of which is indicated by markers (such as *shì* in *tāmen shì xuésheng* 'They [are] students'), while no such formal relationship indicators occur in others. The former constructions will be called *marked*, and the latter *unmarked*; both kinds, as well as marking in MSC in general, will be discussed in a further section of this chapter.

3. WORD CLASSES

The problem of MSC word classes, or 'parts of speech' in traditional linguistic terminology, is in many respects similar to that of the words themselves. The popular concept of distinct groups of words which share features of formal shape and general behaviour in sentences is again part of the presumably universal and obligatory characteristics associated with language: a language without 'parts of speech' is as nonsensical as a language without words. And, the same as in the case of words, a language is not only expected to have any kind of 'parts of speech', but groups of words characterized by rather precisely conceived features of morphological structure, syntactic behaviour, and above all meaning. For example, a language like MSC is commonly presumed to have among its 'parts of speech' a set of words which 'express actions or states', use some formalized means 'to express tenses', and function as 'predicates' in sentences, that is the sort of words we are accustomed to call verbs. The difficulty of finding sets of words in MSC conceived in this manner becomes obvious even after the briefest encounter with the language; again, the quest for word classes in MSC has resulted either in largely unsuccessful attempts to fit MSC into the pattern of more or less Latin-like 'parts of speech', or in the rejection of the concept of word classes for MSC altogether.

Yet the presumption about 'parts of speech', as well as that of words in MSC, is not completely unfounded. MSC words are not operated with in speech in a uniform and equal way, and it is possible to find a number of formal features (such as features of morphological structure) which are characteristic for some groups of MSC words, but not for others. Moreover, many groups of MSC words which are distinguished by common features of behaviour and form resemble, in the very general sense, the major 'parts of speech' of traditional European grammars. Thus, for example, the two MSC words occurring in the sentence *māma zŏule* 'Mother has gone' belong to two different groups which resemble English nouns and verbs respectively. The resemblance has several aspects: similarity in syntactic function (*māma* 'mother' can be said to function as the 'subject' of the MSC sentence, and *zŏule* 'to have gone' as its 'predicate'), in the features of morphological structure (the suffix *-le* in *zŏule* 'to have gone' can be said to serve the similar purpose of 'tense' as the respective form of the English verb 'to go') and in meaning.

This kind of superficial resemblance does not, however, go very far. If there is any common ground for MSC and a language like English in the respect of word classes, it lies much deeper than the level where similarities of the sort described above can be observed. This common ground is perhaps in the degree of complexity the two languages have reached in the development of their structural organization. This degree of complexity is simply reflected by the fact that either of the two languages contains groups of recurrent elements which are operated with in a distinctive way, and that these groups contain further smaller groups characterized by more delicate distinctive operational features. For example, the English expressions *my mother*, *he*, *I*, and *he bought a car and* are operated with in a distinctive way in some conditions, as can be seen from a sentence pattern like *X left*, where *X* may represent either of them; thus, they all belong to one distinct group of expressions. The first three are not, however, always operated with in the same way as the fourth, as can be observed from the sentence pattern *X can hardly believe that*, and thus they belong to a smaller more delicate distinct group. Further smaller groups can be established on the basis of such sentence patterns as *X does not understand*, *She is X*, etc. All such distinct operational groups are known as *form classes* (the term *form* denoting a meaningful arrangement of sounds of any size), and as follows from the example above, they may vary greatly in, beside other aspects, the number of their members in English. Strictly speaking, the most delicate form classes in English (as well as in any other language) are represented by single forms, since probably every English form may occur in at least one environment in which no other form normally occurs: for example, *apple* in relation to the pattern *He is the X of her eye*. What are called 'parts of speech' or word classes in English are, in fact, form classes of a special kind: they are form classes from which all non-word forms were excluded, and which were set up by using a certain degree of delicacy more or less arbitrarily agreed upon. The agreement was not reached with such arbitrariness as is usually applied in matters like norms of orthography, it is rather based on a number of considerations among which common sense and tradition presumably played an equal role. Common sense directed the hand when, for example, such words as *apple*, *tree*, and *mother* were placed within a single class, since their common distinctive features (such as their occurrence with the plural suffix -*s* and their similar functioning in sentences in conjunction with other words) make it more practical and sensible to treat them as a group, rather than as three separate classes which their specific distinctive features would call for. On the other hand, tradition modified (and sometimes contradicted) common sense by partly enforcing upon English an agreement reached earlier for a different, although not altogether unrelated language, namely Latin. The agreement about English word classes is thus the result of a specific approach to the distinctive features of English words combined with the influence of a specific kind of cultural tradition. It is not, and this is perhaps the most important point in this discussion, a direct reflection of an objective fact, neither a fact of English, nor a fact of language in general.

English and MSC share the common ground of the possibility of word grouping: MSC words can be classified in a way generally very similar to the kind of bringing together of English words of the same distinctive features on different levels of delicacy shown above. The corresponding agreement on MSC word classes has not, however, been fully reached as yet.[1] This does not mean that MSC has words which cannot be classified with the kind of common sense applied in the case of English; it merely stresses the important subjective element in the endeavour of word grouping: agreement is not easy to reach mainly because there is practically no 'parts of speech' tradition in the Chinese cultural area to guide the common sense, and because the imported tradition of Latin is based on so considerably different a frame of language reference that it confuses common sense rather than helps it.

The relatively short history of the 'parts of speech' problem in China is perhaps a clear demonstration of this predicament. Modern Chinese linguistics has been attempting for over seventy years[2] without considerable success to establish distinctive groups of MSC words on the basis of features commonly associated with word classes in European languages, that is features which are linked so closely with 'parts of speech' in the West that they have gained the status of universals in the mind of most educated Westerners. These are, very roughly speaking, features of three kinds. First of all, they are features of the formal shape of words, particularly the recurrent patterned features of their morphological structure, which can be interpreted as formalized expressions of such abstract grammatical categories as tense, gender, person, etc. Thus, the word *worked* in English is classified as a verb partly because of the suffix -*ed* which occurs in it and which places it among words occurring with this and several other suffixes (such as -*s* and -*ing*). Secondly, they are features of syntactic function, that is the way in which the given word is operated with in conjunction with other words, and which is generalized by such abstract concepts as subject, predicate, etc. Thus, the word *worked* is classified as a verb partly because of its behaviour in sentences such as *Mother worked hard*. Thirdly, they are common features of meaning, that is the element of meaning shared by the

---

[1] Before the impact of Western culture in China about a century ago, traditional Chinese linguists had, in fact, reached a kind of agreement in this respect: they distinguished words from markers, and treated every word as a separate form class, that is applying the highest possible degree of delicacy in evaluating the distinctive features of words. However, this approach, the most typical expression of which were commentaries to classical texts, has never been systematically applied to speech, and it has gradually disappeared since Chinese linguists began to acquaint themselves with the Western kind of linguistics.

[2] The first attempt to present a systematic description of 'parts of speech' of the European kind in Chinese was made by Mǎ Jiànzhōng in 1898. Although he himself applied the approach to classical written Chinese, his description served as a model for later analyses of MSC word classes.

given words. Thus, the word *worked* is classified as a verb partly because it is one of the words denoting actions in English. When this gauge of word class features is applied to MSC words, its limited usefulness does not become immediately obvious. For example, the MSC word *zŏule* 'to have gone' can be classified as a verb according to the gauge, because it occurs with the suffix *-le* which is in a way comparable with the English suffix *-ed*, because of its behaviour in sentences like *māma zŏule* 'Mother has gone', and because it denotes an action. The gauge does not, however, work with all MSC words, and it does not always work with every occurrence of a given word.

Features of MSC morphological structure are difficult to use as overall word class indicators, since the majority of MSC words do not contain any recurrent formal elements. Moreover, the occurrence of the relatively few elements of this kind in MSC words is generally governed by principles quite unlike those typical for European languages. The occurrence of affixes in English words, for instance, has a kind of binary significance, the absence of the affix being as significant as its presence. Thus, if an English noun may occur with a plural suffix, such as *students*, it denotes plural whenever it occurs with the suffix, and singular whenever it occurs without it (excepting such debatable cases as *many a student of Chinese*). The majority of comparable morphological elements in MSC have no such binary significance. The plural suffix *-men*, for example, indicates plural when it occurs in a word like *tóngzhìmen* 'comrades', its absence, however, is not significant: the word *tóngzhì* means either 'comrade' or 'comrades' (cf. *yí wèi tóngzhì* 'one comrade', and *sān wèi tóngzhì* 'three comrades'). Morphological devices of this kind are utilized in a much closer pattern with other grammatical devices in MSC than in European languages, and the indication conveyed by one device does not normally allow for the sort of redundancy contained in an English expression like *many comrades* (where the plural is indicated both by the word *many* as such, and the plural suffix *-s*). With the exception of word-formative affixes, most MSC formal morphological elements are governed by such principles of non-redundant distribution, and this naturally diminishes their usefulness as word class indicators: at best they can be fully utilized as such only in conjunction with other relevant features of words.

Features of syntactic function are the key features for establishing MSC word classes. This is mainly because considerations of syntactic functioning are directly related to the concept of form classes which, as was pointed out earlier, are the basic objective frame of reference for establishing the partly subjective groups called word classes. However, if the gauge of traditional European categories of syntactic function, such as 'subject' and 'predicate', is applied to MSC words, it immediately becomes obvious that an agreement on MSC word classes based on the syntactic features of words understood in terms of this gauge would first have to be preceded by an agreement on how the respective categories are represented in MSC. That this is not at all simple, is shown by the endless discussions of Chinese linguists, as old as discussions of word classes themselves, of problems like "what is the subject in the sentence *táishang zuòzhe zhǔxítuán* 'The presidium are sitting on the platform'?" (*táishang* '[on] the platform', *zuòzhe* 'to be sitting', *zhǔxítuán* 'the presidium').

Similarly, common features of meaning have proved to be of little practical use for establishing word classes in MSC. The problem with common meaning features of language forms in general is that they cannot be described with any degree of precision unless other features of the forms, features of syntactic function in particular, are taken into account. Generalizations such as 'a word denoting an action is a verb' used on their own may be helpful in some situations, but not in others, since they depend on largely subjective interpretations, such as what is meant by 'action'. It would hardly be profitable to discuss at this point the question of the nature of meaning in this general sense which has become one of the crucial questions of modern linguistics; since the problem of word classes in MSC is largely a problem of agreement on features of MSC words which will not only be considered more important than others, but which are also more reliable in the practical sense, it will perhaps be sufficient to say that common features of meaning are not suitable as one of the primary criteria for establishing MSC word classes simply because they are not reliable in practice on their own. For example, if the traditional European concepts of the common meaning features of nouns ('words designating or naming a person, living being, object, thing, etc.'[1]), substantives ('nouns, as well as any other words or groups of words used as nouns or instead of nouns', i.e. 'as or instead of words designating or naming...'), verbs ('words which express an action, a process, state or condition or mode of being'), adjectives ('words used to describe, qualify or modify a substantive'),

[1] The formulations of the respective concepts given here are taken from Mario A. Pei and Frank Gaynor, *A Dictionary of Linguistics*, New York 1954.

and adverbs ('words which modify a verb or adjective or another adverb') are applied to an MSC sentence like *bàba xiĕ de hăo* 'Father writes well; What father writes is good', at least the following two rather different conclusions can be reached:

(1) *bàba* 'father' is a noun, *xiĕ* 'to write' is a verb, and *hăo* 'well' is an adverb (the marker *de* denoting the relationship between the verb and the adverb);

(2) *bàba xiĕ* 'father writes' is a substantive (the marker *de* denoting that the group of words is used instead of a noun), and *hăo* 'to be good' is an adjective.

This example shows not only the unreliability of meaning criteria, but also their close dependence on features of syntactic function. Moreover it also shows to what degree the supposedly universal features of meaning are linked with individual languages. In MSC itself, the sentence *bàba xiĕ de hăo* does not mean either 'Father writes well' or 'What father writes is good', it means both at the same time: the difference is only between the two English equivalents of the sentence.

It is perhaps apparent from the preceding that the presumably universal features of words commonly associated with their word class membership are, in fact, typical concrete features of words in European languages classified by an agreement which was reached and developed in the European cultural area. The corresponding necessary agreement for MSC can perhaps roughly follow the European example, but since the features of MSC words are considerably more different from those of any European language than are the features of words of any two European languages, a new tradition of agreement on word classes in MSC is the only possible solution. This new tradition has actually been developing throughout the short history of MSC linguistics by a process of trial and error. Early attempts to fit MSC into the pattern of Latin, English, or other European systems of word classes were clearly unsatisfactory, and they were gradually modified by taking concrete features of MSC words into account. The agreement has not yet been fully reached, but it is possible to give at least the main points of the new tradition. The brief account which follows is, of course, only a tentative attempt to summarize the diverse experience of Western and Chinese scholars in this respect, and it does not intend to be in any way authoritative or exhaustive. The terms used here are basically those of Latin grammar modified in a way typical for the current English and American writings on MSC grammar; again, it should be emphasized that the actual terms, unlike the categories, are not very important.

MSC words as defined in the preceding section of this chapter (that is the smallest syntactic units, excluding markers) fall roughly into two large groups of the so-called *verbal* and *nominal expressions.* Each are characterized mainly by their syntactic function: verbal expressions are words which may function as the nuclei of sentences (see p. 100), and also words which occur only in syntagms or close phrases with nuclei; nominal expressions are words fulfilling other functions in sentences. Of the words occurring in the sentence *jīntiān tiānqi hěn hǎo* 'The weather is [very] nice today' discussed earlier, *hǎo* 'to be nice' and *hěn* 'very' are verbal expressions, *jīntiān* 'today' and *tiānqi* 'weather' are nominal expressions. Another feature distinguishing these two large groups of words is their occurrence with a negative prefix: all verbal expressions may occur with negative prefixes (with the exception of the word *yǒu* 'to have; there is' which occurs only with the negative prefix *méi-*, all other verbal expressions may occur with the prefix *bù-~bú-*, such as *bùhǎo* 'not to be nice' and *bùhěn* 'not very'), while no nominal expressions do (forms like **bùtiānqi* 'not weather' and **bùjīntiān* 'not today' are ungrammatical).

The two main word classes among verbal expressions are known as *functive verbs* (or only *verbs*) and *stative verbs* (or *adjectives*). Words of these two classes may function as nuclei of sentences, although they may, of course, also fulfil other syntactic functions. The borderline between the two classes is not very distinct, particularly since most words belonging to them share the ability to occur with the same set of formal morphological elements previously described as *verbal suffixes.* Their main formal distinction is their occurrence with other verbal expressions in syntagms: unlike functive verbs, stative verbs may occur in syntagms with a specific set of words among which *hěn* 'very' is the most common. Thus, *hǎo* 'to be nice' which occurs in *jīntiān tiānqi hěn hǎo* 'The weather is [very] nice today' is a stative verb, while *zǒule* 'to have gone', as in *māma zǒule* 'Mother has gone', is a functive verb (the form **hěn zǒule* 'very have gone' being ungrammatical). Several subclasses can be set up among stative verbs and particularly functive verbs. The two main subclasses among the latter are the so-called *resultative verbs* and *auxiliary verbs.* Resultative verbs are characterized most conspicuously by their distinctive ability to contain infixes (although they can also be defined by the distinctive features of their syntactic functioning). For example, the words *zuòwán* 'to finish [doing something]' and *chībǎo* 'to eat [one's] fill' belong to this subclass, since they both occur with the infixes *-de-* and *-bu-*: *zuòdewán* 'to be able to finish', *zuòbuwán* 'to be unable to finish', *chīdebǎo* 'to be able to eat [one's] fill', and *chībubǎo* 'to be unable to eat [one's] fill'. Auxiliary verbs, beside certain morphological features (most do not, for example, occur with all verbal suffixes), are mainly characterized by their occurrence in syntagms with other functive verbs. The words *yào* 'to want' and *huì* 'to know how; can' are auxiliary verbs, for instance, which occur in sentences such as *wǒ yào qù* 'I want to go' (*qù* 'to go [away]') and *tā huì yóuyǒng* 'He can swim' (*yóuyǒng* 'to swim'). The third major word class among verbal expressions are *adverbs*, words which occur only in syntagms with other verbal expressions, but do not normally function as nuclei themselves. The word *hěn* 'very' mentioned several times earlier (cf. *jīntiān tiānqi hěn hǎo* 'The weather is [very] nice today') is an adverb, and so are, for example, *mànmànr* 'slowly' (as in *mànmànr zǒu* 'to go slowly') and *jíle* 'extremely' (as in *hǎo jíle* 'to be extremely good').

Nominal expressions comprise several classes of words which all fulfil non-nuclear functions in sentences: they do not normally occur as nuclei, and they do not necessarily constitute syntagms with nuclei. Apart from other features, what distinguishes the individual classes is the way the respective words are arranged in patterns such as *tā nà liǎng ge péngyou* 'those two friends of his': the head of endocentric constructions of this kind is usually a *noun* (*péngyou* 'friend, friends') which may be preceded by a *number* (*liǎng* 'two [of]', as in *liǎng ge péngyou* 'two friends'), a *specifier* (*nà* 'that, those' as in *nà ge péngyou* 'that friend'), or both in the order specifier-number (as in *nà liǎng ge péngyou* 'those two friends'). *Measures* (such as *ge* '[unit of]') are words which occur between the head and the remaining part of such constructions; since they partly indicate the relationship between other words, they are on the borderline between words and markers, as will be pointed out later. Further members of such constructions may be *pronouns*, such as *tā*, 'he, his' in *tā nà liǎng ge péngyou* 'those two friends of his'. Each of these word classes can, of course, be characterized by many other features of syntactic function and also morphological structure. Perhaps the most important overall feature which distinguishes numbers, specifiers, pronouns, and to a certain degree also measures, from nouns (as well as all verbal expressions), is that the former group are word classes of restricted membership: each contains a limited and relatively small number of members (this is true in the practical sense even of numbers, although in their case there is the theoretical possibility of an unlimited group; the morphological constituents of numbers are, in any case, a limited group). It is thus possible to define each of these classes by enumerating its members. Subclasses can be set up in the case of each word class belonging to the group of nominal expressions. The two most important subclasses of nouns are *placewords* and *timewords*. Unlike other nouns, words belonging to these subclasses do not normally occur in endocentric constructions such as those described above; they either occur in syntagms with nuclei (such as the timeword *míngtiān* 'tomorrow' in *míngtiān qù* '[Let's] go tomorrow', or the placeword *zhèr* 'here' in *zhèr rènao* '[It] is noisy here', with the stative verb *rènao* 'to be noisy'), or they occur in constructions with nuclear phrases (such as *jīntiān* 'today' in *jīntiān tiānqi hěn hǎo* 'The weather is [very] nice today'). Placewords and timewords are also distinguished by various features of morphological structure and by occurrence in specific marked syntagms: many placewords, for example, contain the so-called positional suffixes (such as *-shang* 'on top of' in *zhuōzshang* 'on top of the table'), and they occur in such typical marked syntagms as *dào Běijīng qù* 'to go to Peking' (the marker *dào* 'towards' indicating the relationship between the verb *qù* 'to go [away]' and the placeword *Běijīng* 'Peking').

Even this very rough outline shows that the new tradition of MSC word classification has considerably modified the classical European 'parts of speech' model according to MSC word features whose relative importance has been agreed upon in a way similar to that which is in the background of the European model itself. Among the most important modifications is the strict binary distinction between nominal and verbal expressions, and the classification of words in certain ways comparable to adjectives in European languages (i.e. stative verbs) among verbal rather than nominal expressions. Both of these modifications are based mainly on the overall characteristic of MSC syntax which has been mentioned earlier, that is the prevalence of endocentric over exocentric constructions. This overall feature makes it possible to establish word classes partly according to the typical way in which the respective groups of words behave in endocentric constructions: verbal expressions including stative verbs occur mainly in the nucleus (or very close to it) of the closed pattern of endocentric layers called the sentence, while nominal expressions constitute mainly the non-nuclear outside layers of the pattern.

4. MARKERS

The units previously called markers are residual segmental features of MSC syntactic constructions: they are what would in some cases remain of the segmental structure of syntactic constructions if all words were removed from them. In that sense, markers are part of the framework of the syntactic constructions in which they occur, that is part of the set pattern of relationships into which words enter. Generally speaking, all markers share two distinctive features: they are not morphological constituents of words (it would, perhaps, be possible to say that they are bound forms related to syntactic constructions in a similar way as affixes are related to words), and they are units which have reached some degree of grammatical formalization. The former feature distinguishes them from other bound forms, and the latter from free forms. The latter feature of markers is an expression of their function: since they indicate relationships between words, they are, so to speak, part of the rules of language, and as such they are limited in number and each of them is associated with one of the rules; since they indicate relationships, their meaning is of a different kind than the meaning of words (it is called *grammatical meaning*, as opposed to *lexical meaning*), often possible to describe only in terms of the constructions they mark (such as *de* 'marker of subordinate relationships', or 'marker of endocentric constructions').

Although their distinctive features differentiate markers from bound constituents of words on the one hand, and from words on the other hand, the dividing lines are not always very clear on either side. MSC markers are not a very homogeneous group of units. They comprise forms which differ very little from such bound constituents of words as suffixes both in shape and meaning (for example, *de* which is atonic and has no lexical meaning similarly as a suffix like *-z*), as well as forms which are difficult to differentiate from words (such as *hěn* 'very' which may function as a marker). Individual markers differ considerably in their degree of *functional burdening*: some always fulfil the sole function of indicating relationships between words, while others fulfil this function only partly and not always. The marker *de* is of the former kind. The other end of the scale is represented by forms like *gěi* 'to give; marker indicating the relationship between certain nouns and verbs' which occurs both as a word (*wǒ gěi nǐ* 'I give [it to] you') or as a marker (*gěi tā jiè qián* 'Lend him [some] money': here it indicates the relationship between *tā* 'he' and *jiè qián* 'to lend money; to borrow money'), and even when it occurs as a marker, it retains a certain amount of word-like quality which is reflected in its not purely grammatical meaning (cf. *gěi tā jiè qián* 'Lend him [some] money' and *gēn tā jiè qián* 'Borrow [some] money from him'; although the grammatical relationship in these two sentences is very similar, their meaning is different, the difference being carried by the partly lexical meaning of the markers *gěi* and *gēn*).

It was mentioned earlier that classification of words is not part of traditional Chinese linguistics, that is classification of words into classes or 'parts of speech'. The distinction between words and markers, however, belongs to this tradition: the old Chinese terms *shízì* 'full words' and *xūzì* 'empty words' (the latter is used for markers; in more recent terminology the similar terms *shící* and *xūcí* are used instead) express the concept of different proportions of lexical meaning used by Chinese linguists to distinguish between what are called words and markers here. That the concept of lexical meaning as the distinctive feature of words as opposed to markers is not the most fruitful in this as well as other cases, is perhaps rather well demonstrated by the diversity of various traditional and modern Chinese opinions on where the dividing line between words and markers lies: traditional Chinese linguists considered practically all minimal forms beside what would be called nouns as 'empty words', while contemporary Chinese linguists, although they lay the dividing line roughly where it is put in this book, disagree on points such as on which side of the line several classes like pronouns and adverbs should be placed.

It will not be attempted here to establish the dividing line between bound constituents of words, markers, and words with greater clarity than is usually done in the existing descriptions of MSC. It will, however, be possible to point out that there are other criteria beside that of the degree of lexical meaning which can be applied to this purpose. For example, the kind of formal analysis used for establishing words which was demonstrated earlier (see p. 91 ff.) can also be used for distinguishing words from markers. From the point of view of this analysis, markers are forms which usually cannot be eliminated on their own in the process of the maximal-to-minimal-utterance reduction in any of its individual stages. Thus, the sentence *gěi tā jiè qián* 'Lend him [some] money' can be reduced to *jiè qián* 'Lend [some] money' in some contexts, but not to *tā jiè qián* 'He borrows money; He lends money' in any context: the marker *gěi* can be eliminated only together with *tā* 'he', that is when the construction it marks is eliminated from the sentence. This feature differentiates markers from words which can be eliminated on their own during the process of reduction; it does not, however, differentiate them from bound constituents of words, as the latter can also be eliminated only together with other forms. For instance, the sentence *tāmen zǒule* 'They have gone' can be reduced to *zǒule* '[They] have gone', but not to *tā zǒule* 'He has gone', eliminating only the suffix *-men*. To distinguish between markers and bound constituents of words, the structure and size of the forms they occur with has to be taken into account. While bound constituents of words occur only with forms which can at best be interpreted as single words (that is, if their status of word constituents is disregarded, such as *tā* 'he' in *tāmen* 'they'), all markers may occur with constructions of words (such as in *gěi wǒ mǔqin jiè qián* 'Lend my mother [some] money', where the marker *gěi* indicates the relationship between *jiè qián* 'to lend money; to borrow money' and the construction of two words *wǒ mǔqin* 'my mother', in the immediate vicinity of which it occurs).

There are, nevertheless, some situations when markers can be eliminated from sentences on their own. For example, a sentence like *wǒ de mǔqin zǒule* 'My mother has gone' can be reduced to *wǒ mǔqin zǒule* 'My mother has gone' in most contexts. In such situations, however, the elimination of the marker does not represent the same kind of step typical for the individual stages of the maximal-to-minimal-utterance reduction. Where this elimination is possible, the difference between the structure and meaning of the two sentences (the one with the marker and the one without it) is minimal, and in normal speech the two sentences (such as *wǒ de mǔqin zǒule ~ wǒ mǔqin zǒule* 'My mother has gone') are free variants in the given context, rather than two different steps in the process of reduction. It is possible to speak of a free choice between a marker or zero in situations of this kind. This choice is never free in all contexts: the sentence *wǒ de mǔqin zǒule* 'My mother has gone' has no variant without the marker in a context such as that of the preceding question *nǐ de mǔqin zǒule, háishi tā de mǔqin zǒule* 'Has your mother gone or has his mother gone?'. The occurrence of some markers is thus sometimes partly redundant, but never fully redundant.

Beside free choice between a marker or zero in some situations, there are also cases of conditioned choice between one marker or another. When there is the sole possibility of the latter, the situation is invariably of the kind when the given marker cannot be eliminated from the sentence on its own. For example, an introductory statement in a conversation (when the preceding context is purely situational) *tā xiězì tèbié hǎo* 'He writes characters particularly well' cannot be reduced to *tā xiězì hǎo* 'He writes characters well' in this context: the latter would not be considered a 'full sentence'; it would be like saying *He writes better* in English in the same situational context, which would puzzle the listener and lead to questions like *Better than who?*. However, sentences such as *tā xiězì fēicháng hǎo* 'He writes characters exceptionally well' or *tā xiězì hěn hǎo* 'He writes characters [very] well', etc., might equally well occur in this context. The forms *tèbié* 'particularly', *fēicháng* 'exceptionally', *hěn* 'very', etc., serve a double purpose in such cases: they are, on the one hand, markers, because they cannot be eliminated from the sentences on their own, and, on the other hand, they are operated with as typical words, since they can be substituted in terms of word class membership (similarly as *tā* 'he' in *tā xiězì tèbié hǎo* 'He writes characters particularly well' can be substituted by *wǒ* 'I' to form a different sentence). This kind of choice between one marker or another, which was called conditioned because the given sentences are not members of the same maximal-to-minimal-utterance reduction group, is a reflection of the indistinct dividing line between words and markers: there are forms which are both markers and words. The whole word class of measures mentioned in the preceding section, for example, consists of forms of this kind. In historical terms, this phenomenon could be explained as a feature of the gradual formalization of linguistic units. In these terms it would be possible to follow the development of certain forms from words to markers and perhaps further to bound constituents of words, with some of these forms being in transition from one stage to another in MSC. However clarifying this historical concept of the problem may be, the synchronic description of MSC can hardly account for this phenomenon without introducing the borderline category of *semi-markers*. Again, this is another situation where the lack of a norm leaves the problem open and exposes language as a fluid system to which rigid categories cannot be easily applied.

Markers occur on all levels of MSC syntactic constructions, and the occurrence of individual markers is governed not only by the type of constructions, but also by the level the given constructions represent in sentence structure. There are consequently two ways in which markers can be classified from the viewpoint of their function in syntactic constructions. On the one hand, markers can be divided into *endocentric* and *exocentric* according to the type of constructions they mark. A typical endocentric marker is the form *de* mentioned several times earlier; such markers as *shì* (as in *tā shì xuésheng* 'He [is] a student'), *yě* 'also' (as in *tā huì hējiǔ yě huì chōuyān* 'He [can] drink and [also] smoke'; *hējiǔ* 'to drink [alcoholic beverages]', *chōuyān* 'to smoke [cigarettes]'), and *dōu* 'all' (as in *Zhāng xiānsheng, Wáng xiānsheng, Liú xiānsheng dōu shì hǎo rén* 'Mr Zhāng, Mr Wáng, [and] Mr Liú are [all] nice people') are typical exocentric markers. On the other hand, it is possible to classify markers according to the level of syntactic constructions on which they occur. Since markers which occur on the level of syntagms may also occur on the level of phrases (this is given by the features of markers as opposed to bound constituents of words: members of marked constructions may be either single words or constructions of words), three main groups of markers can be set up:

(1) *Phrase markers*, that is markers occurring on syntagm up to phrase level. The most common markers belonging to this group, such as *de*, are highly formalized, but there are also some semi-markers in it, such as all measures, and also forms like *gěi* and *gēn* (cf. the sentences *gěi tā jiè qián* 'Lend him [some] money' and *gēn tā jiè qián* 'Borrow [some] money from him').

(2) *Simple sentence markers* which are markers occurring on all levels up to the level of sentences containing single nuclei. Some of these markers are highly formalized, such as *shì* (as in *tā shì xuésheng* 'He [is] a student'), but most are semi-markers, such as various adverbs occurring in syntagms with nuclear stative verbs (*fēicháng* 'exceptionally' and *tèbié* 'particularly' in the introductory statements *tā xiězì fēicháng hǎo* 'He writes characters exceptionally well' and *tā xiězì tèbié hǎo* 'He writes characters particularly well', for example). Among semi-markers belonging to this group *hěn* 'very' is more formalized than others; in many sentences it has almost no lexical meaning at all (as in *tā xiězì hěn hǎo* 'He writes characters [very] well').

(3) *Complex sentence markers* which normally occur only on the level of sentences containing two or more nuclei. Most, perhaps all of these are semi-markers, and their typical feature (although not wholly restricted to this group) is that they commonly occur in pairs. For example, the sentence *tā suǒyǐ hěn pàng, yīnwei tā*

chīfàn chī de tài duō '[The reason why] he is [very] fat [is] because he eats too much' contains such a pair of markers: *suǒyǐ . . . yīnwei* '[the reason why] . . . [is] because'.

5. SENTENCES

In the section dealing with MSC syntactic constructions, sentences were described as constructions occurring on the lowest level, or the level most distant from the level of words, of the respective pattern of relationship hierarchies. This statement calls for a more detailed discussion, since as it stands it could lead to a somewhat circular concept of MSC syntactic structure, sentences being defined as ultimate syntactic constructions, and syntactic constructions as expressions of relationships within sentences.

The difficulty with defining sentences, not only in MSC but in any other language as well, is the variety and complexity of forms which are to be covered by the definition. The concept of a maximal closed unit of structure and meaning usually associated with the category of sentence, is notoriously difficult to interpret in terms of concrete features. The sentence has consequently always been a unit posited and tacitly accepted by linguists rather than precisely defined. As far as MSC is concerned, it is hardly possible to attempt at a more suitable definition of the sentence for both these general reasons, and also reasons specific for a language which is relatively little explored and the general features of which are not as clearly pronounced as those of languages with a firmer norm. Nevertheless, the concept of the unit can perhaps be supported by a closer observation of relevant speech phenomena other than those discussed in the preceding sections of this chapter, that is features of MSC utterances other than words, markers, and their arrangements. The relation of these features to words, markers, and their arrangements, is similar in the broad sense with the relation between suprasegmental and segmental features on the phonemic level (such as within a syllable). It is possible to speak of the segmental and suprasegmental features of utterances, the former represented by arrangements of words and markers, and the latter primarily by *rhythm* and *intonation*.

Rhythm is a feature of continuous speech resulting from the distribution of stressed and unstressed syllables. In MSC, two stressed syllables do not normally occur in close sequence uninterrupted by one or more unstressed syllables or a pause (see also p. 82), and utterances thus appear as regular arrangements of stressed syllables alternating with unstressed syllables and occasional pauses. Since sequences of two or more unstressed syllables, unlike sequences of stressed syllables, are common in MSC, the actual arrangement of stressed and unstressed syllables in an utterance may take many shapes. This arrangement is not, however, free: beside the necessity to break sequences of stressed syllables, it is governed by several important factors. The most prominent among these factors is given by what may be called *fixed points of stress* in MSC speech. Fixed points of stress are of two kinds: they are either the established patterns of stressed and unstressed syllables of some polysyllabic words (for example, the first syllable in [ˈjǐts₁] *yǐz* 'chair' is stressed, and so are the first and the third syllable in [ˈt'úṣū̠ˈkuǎn] *túshūguǎn* 'library', the remaining syllables being always unstressed in both words; this kind of established stress patterning is a morphophonemic feature, see p. 83, and it is known as *word stress*), or they are the unstressed atonic syllables which represent certain markers, such as *de*. Within the fixed points of stress, stressed syllables may occasionally become unstressed, but the permanently unstressed syllables, of which at least one is contained in a fixed point, never become stressed. Fixed points of stress thus represent elements sufficiently rigid not to yield to other rhythmical tendencies of utterances. On the contrary, the rhythm of an utterance modifies itself in accordance with the fixed points of stress it contains. In utterances which do not contain any fixed points of stress (usually sentences containing only monosyllabic words), the natural tendency towards *regular alternation* of one stressed syllable and one unstressed syllable takes over: this tendency itself is another important factor in the rhythmical shaping of utterances. A fixed point of stress in an utterance does not necessarily have to be represented by the occurrence of word stress or of an atonic syllable representing a marker. It can also be given by *ad hoc* emphasis: in the sentence *tā qù* 'He will go' which is normally stressed [t'āˈtɕʻỳ] in the context of a preceding question such as *tā qù búqù* 'Will he go [or not]?', the stress pattern may become [ˈt'ātɕʻỳ] in the context of a question like *wǒ qù háishi tā qù* 'Shall I go or will he go?': a fixed point of stress is created here by the emphasis on *tā* 'he'. This kind of stressing, which may be called *emphatic*, is another factor in the rhythmical shaping of utterances. The final important factor is the *overall tempo* of speech. This factor does not considerably influence the basic pattern of the distribution of stressed and unstressed syllables in an utterance,

but it contributes to its final shape: in slow careful speech, the
number of stressed syllables and pauses tends to be relatively
high, while in rapid speech most pauses disappear, and there
remain very few stressed syllables interrupted by rather long
sequences of unstressed syllables. The following account of an
experiment with a speaker of MSC will perhaps show how the final
rhythmical shape of an utterance results from the combining of
the individual factors.

The speaker was asked to say 'He walks slowly' in MSC. His
reply was tā zǒulù hěn màn (tā 'he', zǒulù 'to walk', hěn 'very',
màn 'slowly'), stressed ['t'ātsǒu'lùxǒn'màn]. This is a case of a
sentence with no fixed point of stress: the constituents are all
monosyllabic words (with the possible exception of zǒulù 'to walk'
which is a unit on the borderline between a single word and a
construction of two words, see p. 97; whatever it is here, it is not
a unit with an established stress pattern), there is no atonic syllable
representing a marker among them, and since this is an unemphatic
sentence said in fairly slow tempo, the factor of the natural tendency towards regular alternation is here the only one in action.
The specific choice of whether the first syllable should be stressed
or not was influenced by what could be called *partly fixed points
of stress*: the construction zǒulù 'to walk', although its stress pattern is not established, is more commonly stressed [tsǒu'lù] rather
than ['tsǒulù], and the semi-marker hěn 'very' is usually unstressed;
thus, the stressing [t'ā'tsǒulù'xǒnmàn] would not normally be
acceptable, unless some other factor, such as emphatic stress on
hěn 'very', were present. The speaker was then asked to transform
this sentence into a somewhat more emphatic variant according
to the model tā shuōhuà hěn duō 'He talks [very] much' (tā 'he',
shuōhuà 'to talk', hěn 'very', duō 'much')→tā shuōhuà shuō de duō
'He talks a lot' (i.e. 'He [as far as] talking [is concerned] talks
much'). His immediate reply was tā zǒulù zǒu de màn stressed
['t'ātsǒu'lù‖'tsǒutə'màn] with a brief pause between lù and the
repeated zǒu. This kind of stressing is a combination of two processes: in the first part of the utterance the stress pattern is the
same as in ['t'ātsǒu'lùxǒn'màn] tā zǒulù hěn màn (beside the
partly fixed point of stress in zǒulù, the rhythmical impression of
tā zǒulù hěn màn uttered by the speaker shortly before probably
contributed to this), while the pattern of ['tsǒutə'màn] zǒu de màn
is given by the fixed point of stress of the atonic syllable representing the marker de. Within the segment zǒu de màn, the fixed point
of the atonic syllable enforces stressing on both sides, that is

both on *zŏu* and *màn*; this, however, leads to a sequence of two stressed syllables at the point where the two patterns meet (*[... ˈlùˈtsŏu ...]), and this unpermitted sequence is broken by a pause ([... ˈlù‖ˈtsŏu ...]). This phenomenon of pauses brought about by combining rhythmical patterns of speech segments is rather interesting from the viewpoint of how normal MSC speech is organized: it suggests that speakers of MSC (and perhaps not only of MSC), beside operating with such units as words, also operate with relatively short segments consisting of syntactic constructions, linking such segments together successively. By 'normal speech' we mean here the kind of immediate unpremeditated utterances of most situations in common language communication. That this so-called normal speech differs to a certain degree from the 'abnormal', that is premeditated speech (any kind of prepared or rehearsed language communication produces 'abnormal' speech: stage language, lecture style, and also what underlies any written communication; what is felt as the artificial nature of the material in even the best language textbooks is mainly the result of its being based on 'abnormal' speech), is demonstrated by the next step in the experiment. When the speaker was asked to repeat the utterance *tā zŏulù zŏu de màn*, he automatically modified its stressing to [tʻāˈtsŏulùˈtsŏutəˈmàn], adjusting the pattern of the first part to that of the second part, and thus eliminating the pause and bringing the factor of regular alternation into harmony with the factor of the fixed point of stress in the whole utterance. Later on, the speaker was asked to repeat the same utterance many times with increasing tempo. His first few responses were fairly quick [tʻāˈtsŏulùˈtsŏutəˈmàn] with the same rhythm as in the slower tempo, followed by several [tʻāˈtsŏulùtsŏutəˈmàn], again with basically the same rhythm, but with the repeated *zŏu* reduced to an unstressed syllable, and then by several [tʻātsŏuˈlùtsŏutəˈmàn]. The last series of repetitions represent a step back to an adjustment of the original pattern of 'normal' speech [ˈtʻātsŏuˈlù‖ˈtsŏutəˈmàn]: the elimination of stress on the repeated *zŏu* by the increased tempo permitted the partly established stress on *lù*, which in slow tempo yielded to the fixed point of stress of the atonic *de*, to come back into play. In the last few most rapid repetitions only the last syllable was stressed: [tʻātsŏulùtsŏutəˈmàn]. Finally, the speaker was asked to emphasize different parts of the utterance, and this resulted in the following patterns: [ˈˈtʻātsŏulùtsŏutəˈmàn] *tā zŏulù zŏu de màn* 'HE walks slowly [, not YOU]', [tʻāˈˈtsŏulùtsŏutəˈmàn] *tā zŏulù zŏu* *de màn* 'He WALKS slowly [but he can run quickly]' (where *zǒulù* 'to walk' was presumably opposed to *pǎo* 'to run', etc.), [t'ātsǒuᴵᴵlùtsǒutəᴵmàn] *tā zǒulù zǒu de màn* 'He WALKS slowly [but he can ride a horse quickly]' (where *zǒulù* 'to walk' was presumably opposed to *zǒumǎ* 'to ride a horse', etc.), and [t'ātsǒuᴵlù-tsǒutəᴵᴵmàn] *tā zǒulù zǒu de màn* 'He walks SLOWLY [, not quickly]'. The factor of emphatic stress modified in each case the rhythmical shape of the utterance in accordance with one of the two basic patterns (the 'normal' one characterized by stressed *lù*, and the 'abnormal' one characterized by stressed initial *zǒu*, with the respective stressing of their environment), with the effect of very strong stress on one syllable or another.

Rhythm is thus the result of a combination of factors, some of which prove to be stronger than others in the given situation. As was shown above, MSC speech can be divided into segments within the borderlines of which these factors operate in harmony. These segments are divided from each other by pauses, and it is then possible to say that MSC utterances consist of one or more segments of homogeneous rhythm delimited by pauses. Before the importance of this for the definition of MSC sentence is pointed out, it has to be noticed that not all pauses in MSC speech are obligatory: the pause in [ᴵt'ātsǒuᴵlù‖ᴵtsǒutəᴵmàn], for example, does not necessarily occur in rapid speech, not mentioning its lack in 'abnormal' speech. On the other hand, there are pauses in MSC speech which occur with all the repetitions of utterances regardless to changes in tempo or other factors. Pauses of this kind occurred before and after each repetition of the given utterance during the experiment described above; another example of such a pause is in the utterance [t'ātsǒuᴵlùtsǒutəᴵmàn‖ᴵtʂỳjiàŋt'āᴵkǎn-puʂàŋᴵɕiʌwǔtəxuǒᴵtʂʽɤ̌] *tā zǒulù zǒu de màn. zhèyàng tā gǎn-bushàng xiàwǔ de huǒchē* 'He walks [too] slowly. He will not catch the afternoon train this way.' Such obligatory pauses dividing different rhythm patterns from each other coincide rather accurately with the borderlines of sentences, that is units of 'closed structure and meaning'. The point of this whole discussion is, then, that MSC sentence can perhaps be partly defined, by taking into account the very concrete features of stress and pause patterning, as the maximal unit of rhythmical homogeneity. It is, however, difficult to say how far this suggestion will prove to be reliable, since very little is still known about the respective suprasegmental features of MSC utterances.

The general features of MSC intonation are very similar to those of rhythm. The same as rhythm, intonation materializes in the form of closed patterns coinciding with utterances or segments of utterances divided from each other by pauses. The patterns, again the same as stress patterns, are composed of successions of the relevant suprasegmental features of syllables modified to a certain degree within the patterns' limits into a homogeneous shape: in the case of intonation the relevant features being tones. In an earlier chapter of this book it was shown how an intonation pattern is formed (see pp. 39–40). MSC sentence can, in view of this, and on the basis of the same argument as that used for rhythm, perhaps be partly defined as the maximal unit of intonational homogeneity. However, although the concept of intonation patterns as features highly relevant to defining sentences has been commonly accepted in modern linguistics, not only is too little known about MSC intonation to apply the concept in practice, but it is also very difficult to design methods and techniques for finding out about it. The main problem is that intonation features are almost inextricably combined with the tonal and stress features of syllables in MSC speech, and it is not easy to state precisely where the one ends and the other begins. This is presumably a problem of other tonal languages beside MSC as well. It is thus possible to make only very rough and tentative statements on MSC intonation at the moment.

What mainly differentiates MSC intonation from the intonation of a language like English is, on the one hand, the general lack of established overall contours (cf. the typical intonation contours distinguishing segmentally identical English sentences), and, on the other hand, the occurrence in MSC of segmental elements which are constituents of intonation patterns. The latter in particular can perhaps be considered a device which sets apart intonation from tonal features in a tonal language; it does, however, complicate the matter even further, since it makes MSC intonation a partly segmental feature. It will be shown further what these segmental constituents of intonation patterns are and how they are operated with; the only remotely comparable phenomenon in a language like English are interjections: for example, the interjection *Oh* in *Oh, he didn't come* can be said to contribute to the function fulfilled by the respective intonation contour of *he didn't come*, thus in a sense being part of the given intonation pattern.

There are basically two types of intonation contours in MSC: the contour of unemphatic statements (regardless whether these are declarative, interrogative, etc.), and the contour of emphatic statements (such as urgent questions, strict orders, exclamations, etc.). The former is characterized by the generally level pitch contour mildly falling towards the end, as described on pp. 39–40. The latter cannot be described in general terms: it materializes as an exaggeration of the respective tonal features of either all or more commonly only some syllables within the given statement (the quality of the exaggeration being of a similar kind as that which takes place in stressed syllables, see p. 40 ff.). Although other minor types and subtypes could perhaps be established, the main distinctions between intonation patterns more delicate than the distinction indicated by the unemphatic and emphatic contours, are given by the occurrence and choice between a number of segmental elements. These elements, called *particles* (in sinological literature this term is, however, often used in a much broader sense: it commonly also refers to other units, such as bound constituents of words and markers), are invariably atonic syllables of the V or CV type of structure which occur at the beginning, but most commonly at the end of segments delimited by obligatory pauses (hence *initial* and *final sentence particles*), and also at the end of segments followed by non-obligatory pauses. Initial sentence particles, usually divided from the rest of the utterance by a pause, resemble English interjections, and they serve mainly to distinguish different types of emphatic statements (thus usually combining with the emphatic intonation contour): for example, *a, zhè kě guài* 'Oh, isn't this strange!', *ai, nǐ lái bùlái* 'Well, are you coming or not?', *e, tā zǒule* 'What, has he gone?', *aiya, nǐ zhēn chéng* 'Hey, you are terrific!', *yo, nǐ yòu láile* 'Oh dear, you've come again!', etc. Particles occurring at the end of segments delimited by non-obligatory pauses are similar to final sentence particles (most of them occur in both positions) in form, and, the same as initial particles and some final sentence particles, they occur in various subtypes of emphatic statements, accompanied by emphatic intonation contour. The part of the utterance preceding them contains the most emphasized segment; for example, *nǐ a, zhēn bùhǎo* 'You, oh well, [you] are no good', *tā ne, shì wǒ de qīnqī* 'He, oh, [he] is a relative of mine', etc.

Two kinds of final sentence particles can be distinguished according to the type of intonation contour of the statements in which they occur. One kind occur in statements with emphatic intonation contour, such as *jīntiān tiānqi hǎo a* 'The weather is [really] nice today!', *nà tài piányi la* 'That's too cheap, [indeed]!', and *nà zěnme bàn ne* 'What [on earth] can be done about that?'.

The other kind (although some particles may occur with both types of intonation contour) are combined with unemphatic intonation contour, and they distinguish unemphatic statements of different kinds. These different kinds of unemphatic statements are often segmentally identical otherwise, for example *qù* '[I'll] go', *qù me* '[Will you] go?', and *qù ba* '[Let's] go'. Final sentence particles of this kind may, however, complement other devices distinguishing such kinds of statements as interrogative and declarative, for example in *nǐ xiāngxìn bùxiāngxìn ne* 'Do you believe [it] or not?' where the question is primarily indicated by the positive-negative verbal construction *xiāngxìn bùxiāngxìn* '[do you] believe or not'.

Final sentence particles and particles occurring before non-obligatory pauses have the same pitch features as other atonic syllables, which means that their position within the natural range of voice pitch is governed by the tone of the preceding syllable (see pp. 43–44). Their pitch features thus provide a kind of coda to the given intonation contour. Initial sentence particles are also atonic, that is they cannot be said to have the distinctive features of one of the four tones. They do, however, vary in their pitch contours, the variations representing the respective openings of different intonation contours. Thus, for example, the falling or rising pitch contour of the initial particle *e* contributes to the two intonation contours of *e* [falling], *tā zǒule* 'Oh, he has gone' (unemphatic statement), and *e* [rising], *tā zǒule* 'What, has he gone?' (emphatic statement).

Despite problems which arise when the little known and often somewhat undiscernible suprasegmental features of MSC utterances are applied to establishing the unit of sentence in practice, the concept of the MSC sentence as a construction of segmental units with a closed homogeneous pattern of rhythm and intonation is on the whole more illuminating than the more traditional definition of the sentence as a closed unit of structure (i.e. segmental structure) and meaning. Beside other advantages, this concept makes it possible to account for what traditional grammars consider as 'incomplete sentences', that is sentences which are not closed units of structure and meaning, and which, in fact, represent a large proportion of normal speech segments. Before this aspect of the concept is exploited in some detail, it will be useful to take a closer look at the segmental structure of MSC sentences conceived in this way, and in terms of units discussed in the preceding sections of this chapter. In the following rough out-

line, the segmental structure of 'complete sentences' will be used
as the basis for the discussion. The reason for this is purely practical, since it is easier to discuss the segmental structure of 'incomplete sentences' in terms of 'complete sentences' than the
other way round. It is rather difficult to make a general statement
on what precisely is a 'complete sentence' and what is not, since
the distinction between the two is largely an artificial device. For
the purpose of the following outline MSC 'complete sentences' will
be roughly understood as the most common sentences occurring
outside any directly relevant speech or situation context. The most
typical condition in which such sentences occur in normal language communication is the beginning of a speech act, such as the
opening of a dialogue or a monologue not referring to the environmental situation in which it takes place. For example, the first
sentence of a narrated story is invariably complete in this sense.

An MSC sentence may be either *simple* or *complex*. Complex sentences consist of two or more *clauses*; a clause is a subtype of
phrase which resembles a simple sentence (see further) in segmental structure, but which represents only a part of a closed
suprasegmental pattern. The construction of clauses within a
complex sentence may be either endocentric or exocentric, and
their relationship may be marked or unmarked. *Yáng xiānsheng
shì Shànghǎirén, Yáng tàitai shì Tiānjīnrén* 'Mr Yang is from
Shanghai, Mrs Yang is from Tientsin' is a typical unmarked exocentric complex sentence, *Yáng xiānsheng shì Shànghǎirén, Yáng
tàitai yě shì Shànghǎirén* 'Mr Yang is from Shanghai, Mrs Yang
is also from Shanghai' is a marked exocentric complex sentence
(the marker being *yě* 'also'). Endocentric complex sentences are
represented by constructions of clauses denoting a rich variety of
relationships; most of these sentences are marked and the number
of markers which may occur in them is much higher than that of
exocentric complex sentence markers. An example of an unmarked
endocentric complex sentence is *qìchē bùhuílaile, wǒmen zǒu ba*
'[Since] the car is not coming back, let's go'; *yīnwei tā bùxǐhuan
wǒ, suǒyǐ wǒ búyào dào tā nàr qù* 'Because he doesn't like me,
[therefore] I don't want to go to his place' is an endocentric complex sentence marked by *yīnwei . . . suǒyǐ* 'Because . . .[therefore]'.

A simple MSC sentence consists of a single clause which itself
may occur as a phrase or even a syntagm. A minimal simple sentence (and thus also a minimal clause) may be represented by
either of several types of syntagms, the most frequent of which are
the following two: an unmarked endocentric syntagm of a verbal

9—C.L.T.

expression (a functive or a stative verb) and a nominal expression
(a noun or a pronoun), or an exocentric syntagm of two nominal
expressions (nouns or pronouns) marked by one of a few markers,
among which *shì* is the most common. The first type is a construction of a *verbal nucleus* and a *nominal referent*, and it can be
further divided into two subtypes according to whether the nucleus
is a functive or a stative verb: the former subtype constitutes
functive sentences (such as *māma zǒule* 'Mother has gone'), the
latter *stative sentences* (such as *māma cōngming* 'Mother is clever').
Complete stative sentences consisting of a syntagm-clause are
relatively rare, they are normally phrases containing an endocentric syntagm of an adverb and a stative verb, and a nominal
referent, such as *māma hěn cōngming* 'Mother is [very] clever'.
The head of the respective endocentric syntagm is the stative verb,
the adverb is its expanding element (or *attribute*), in this case
called *adverbial modifier*. The second most common type of syntagms constituting minimal simple sentences (exocentric syntagms
of two nominal expressions) are marked constructions of two
nominal nuclei called *equational sentences* (such as *tā shì xuésheng*
'He [is] a student'). The overwhelming majority of all MSC simple
sentences are either sentences of these two types or their *expansions*. Expansions of the minimal types are represented by simple
sentences in which either the nuclear component or the nominal
referent, or both, are endocentric or exocentric syntagms or
phrases, rather than single words. So, for example, the nucleus of
a functive sentence may be a marked or unmarked endocentric
construction of a functive verb and one or more nominal expressions fulfilling the function of further nominal referents (e.g. *wǒ
gēn tā jiè qián* 'I borrow money from him' which is an expansion
of *wǒ jiè* 'I borrow; I lend', and in which *tā* 'he' and *qián* 'money'
are such additional nominal referents in construction with the
verbal nucleus *jiè* 'to borrow; to lend'; the relationship between
tā and *jiè* is marked by *gēn*, the relationship between *jiè* and *qián*
is unmarked), or a marked or unmarked endocentric construction
of a functive verb and an adverb or another word in the function
of an adverbial modifier (as in *māma mànmànr zǒuzhe* 'Mother is
walking slowly', or in *māma míngtiān zǒu* 'Mother will go tomorrow', where the adverb *mànmànr* 'slowly' and the timeword
míngtiān 'tomorrow' function as adverbial modifiers), or an exocentric construction of two or more functive verbs, each functioning as a nucleus (as in *tā yě kànzhe yě tīngzhe* 'He is [also] looking
and [also] listening', where *kànzhe* 'to be looking' and *tīngzhe* 'to

be listening' constitute an exocentric syntagm marked by *yě . . . yě* '[also] . . . and [also]'), to give just a few examples of the most typical cases. Similarly, a nominal referent (as well as a nominal nucleus) may be an endocentric construction of a nominal head and one or more attributes (as in *wǒ de māma zǒule* 'My mother has gone', where *wǒ* 'I' functions as the pronominal attribute of the nominal head *māma* 'mother' in the construction marked by *de*, in *cōngming de rén bùduō* '[There] are not many clever people', where the nominal head *rén* 'people' is preceded by the stative verbal attribute *cōngming* 'to be clever' and the marker *de*, or in *láile sān ge chuān dàyī de rén* '[Some] three people in overcoats came', where the nominal head *rén* 'people' forms a phrase with two attributes: the number *sān* 'three' and the semi-marker *ge* '[unit of]', and the syntagm of a verb and a nominal referent *chuān dàyī* 'to wear an overcoat' whose relationship to the nominal head is marked by *de*), or an exocentric construction (as in *māma bàba dōu láile* 'Both mother [and] father came', where *māma bàba* 'mother [and] father' is an exocentric construction marked by *dōu* 'all, both'), or even a clause-like phrase (as in *wǒ bùxǐhuan tā chōuyān* 'I do not like [that] he smokes [cigarettes]', where the additional nominal referent of the verbal nucleus *bùxǐhuan* 'not to like' is represented by *tā chōuyān* 'he smokes [cigarettes]'), etc.

It is important to add a few words at this point on the controversial question of 'word order', or, in the broader sense, of the order of the arrangements of words and syntactic constructions in MSC sentences, primarily within endocentric constructions. As was suggested earlier, the concept of 'word order' is not sufficient for the description of MSC syntax which can be better and more accurately discussed in terms of structural hierarchies. Nevertheless, the specific sequence of words and constructions is obviously an important feature of MSC sentence structure. It is often maintained by traditional linguists that one of the characteristic features of Chinese syntactic constructions (i.e. endocentric syntactic constructions) is the sequence expanding part-core (that is, attribute-head, modifier-nucleus, etc.). Although this is certainly not true as a general rule for MSC, it is true of the majority of unmarked endocentric constructions. Examples given in this chapter are, however, sufficient proof that this sequence is not typical for marked endocentric constructions, and that there are also unmarked endocentric constructions in which the order is reversed (such as in *hǎo jíle* 'to be extremely good'). Since there is no generally valid rule of order in MSC syntax, its full description must, therefore, contain statements on the order within individual kinds of constructions, marked or unmarked, on all levels.

As far as complete sentences are concerned, the description of MSC sentence structure (which cannot, of course, be attempted in a book of this size) would be an account of the features of words and constructions fulfilling the functions outlined above, and of their order of arrangement. This, however, would not be a full description of MSC syntax on sentence level, since it would not cover what for the lack of a better term were called incomplete sentences. It was mentioned earlier that the structure of MSC incomplete sentences can be described in terms of complete sentences. However, an exact way of doing that has not yet been discovered. Traditional grammar usually applies the concept of ellipsis to solve this problem: the structure of a sentence like *qù* '[I] shall go' (a sentence, that is 'a construction of a segmental unit with a closed homogeneous pattern of rhythm and intonation', which may occur as an answer to *nǐ qù búqù* 'Will you go or not') is then explained by presuming the omission of the respective nominal referent (or 'subject' in the traditional terminology) *wǒ* 'I'. Although this approach involves somewhat uncomfortable subjective presumptions, it can, in a way, account for the structure of some incomplete sentences, provided that the conditions of omissions are fully described.

There are, however, many incomplete sentences the structure of which cannot be described by ellipsis. When, for example, a speaker at a political rally in Peking addresses his audience by the opening sentence *tóngzhìmen* 'Comrades!', it is obviously impossible to suggest what precisely was omitted from this sentence. Similarly, the sentence *a* [falling] 'Oh!' can hardly be described in terms of ellipsis, since according to the concept of MSC sentence structure used here, it is a sentence with zero segmental unit constituent (*a* being the segmental constituent of the intonation pattern); even if *a* in this case were described as an 'interjection', it would be equally impossible to state exactly what complete sentence it 'stands for'. Moreover, a common property of many incomplete sentences in MSC is not only the presumed omission of one or more words, but also the fact that the word or words which occur in them lack their characteristic grammatical features. A typical example of this is given by C. F. Hockett in *A Course in Modern Linguistics* (New York 1960, pp. 248–249). In his example, the sentence *wǒ kāi* 'I shall drive' is said by one of two people who have just walked up to a motorcar. The functive verb *kāi* 'to open;

to drive; to run (as of a shop)' happens to belong to a group of functive transitive verbs in MSC which in complete sentences occur only with two or more nominal referents (as in *wǒ kāi chē* 'I shall drive a car', *wǒ kāi chuānghu* 'I shall open a window', etc.). The occurrence of the respective nominal referents in a sentence containing a functive verb like *kāi* is not only essential for the grammatical completeness of the sentence, but also for what may be called the grammatical completeness of the functive verb itself (this is reflected in meaning: cf. the different meaning of *kāi* in the sentences *wǒ kāi chē* 'I shall drive a car' and *wǒ kāi chuānghu* 'I shall open a window'). This so-called grammatical completeness of words in complete sentences is achieved by devices of many kinds: a word may reach it by either morphological or syntactic means. The word *hǎo* 'to be good; to be well; to be nice' is, for example, grammatically incomplete in the incomplete sentence *tā hǎo* 'He is good' (that is, if this incomplete sentence occurs in the kind of context typical for complete sentences), but it is grammatically complete in such complete sentences as *tā bǐ wǒ hǎo* 'He is better than I am', *tā hěn hǎo* 'He is [very] good', and *tā hǎole* 'He got better'. The point with the sentence *wǒ kāi* 'I shall drive' in Hockett's example is that it is an incomplete sentence, and yet the functive verb *kāi* in this sentence *in the given context* is grammatically complete. A complete sentence such as *wǒ kāi chē* 'I shall drive a car' would, in fact, be unacceptable in the given context: the context makes the verb *kāi* grammatically complete similarly as the various syntactic and morphological devices make the word *hǎo* grammatically complete in the three complete sentences above.

This example which shows the importance of the feature called grammatical completeness in MSC, also suggests a possible solution to the problem of the full description of MSC syntax on sentence level including incomplete sentences. This solution is in conceiving the unit of sentence as the constituent of a larger unit containing a further constituent of what is denoted by the rather imprecise term context. The solution is perhaps more promising than what the crude and subjective devices of traditional linguistics such as ellipsis could be hoped to yield; and yet, its implications are too staggering to permit any further elaboration here. What the solution implies is that the structure of the sentence in a language such as MSC, and this may perhaps be true of any language, cannot be fully described and understood without an organized classification of phenomena partly outside the borders of the sentence, and partly even outside the system of the language, and without a realization of the relations between sentence structure and these phenomena. This means more than a grammar of language units larger than the sentence, which in itself is a formidable thought. It also means that the place of a given language in its non-language environment must be clarified for the purpose of a full description of the language. Although such categories of traditional linguistics as meaning are obviously insufficient for the clarification, modern linguistics has not yet, however, discovered better ones. It is thus only possible to observe that certain aspects of MSC syntax remain unclear not only because we know too little about MSC itself, but also because we still know very little about the systems called languages in general, and about the relation between languages and non-language phenomena.

CHAPTER V

THE NORM

I. TRENDS IN MSC VOCABULARY
AND GRAMMAR

MSC as the contemporary standard form of oral communication
in China is a very recent phenomenon with almost no direct tradition reaching farther back than the beginning of this century. Its
immediate predecessor known as *guānhuà* or Mandarin which had
been the common language of Chinese officialdom through several
centuries was a standard considerably different from MSC, and
also any language standard of the modern West, both in its general
character and range of use: it was not, in fact, a specific form of
Chinese different from any of the 'natural' dialects but a specific
application of the educated variant of Peking dialect to the sole
purpose of oral communication among imperial officials who
represented a minute fraction of the Chinese population. The birth
of MSC, the norm of which is still relatively weak partly because of
its very short history, coincides with the birth of modern China,
and it is an integral part of the process of the vast social, political,
and cultural changes which have been taking place in China since
her first massive contacts and conflicts with the modern Western
world. It is important to realize that MSC, as well as any other
modern standard language, is necessarily a partly artificial system:
beside embodying trends typical for the natural process of language development, it also permits the influence of largely subjective and deliberate acts aimed at the achievement of not wholly
linguistic goals. Moreover, it is a system in the formation of which

the educated minority plays the most important creative role, and the tools of their trade tend to leave a distinct mark on the product. As a result of this, the major trends in the development of MSC show the strong influence of various forms of writing: MSC, like other standard languages, is thus a form of oral communication bearing the traces of the back-feeding influence of what had originally been recorded language. In this sense, perhaps the strongest concrete factor in the gradual development of the oral standard was the new written style which appeared after the rejection of the classical *wényán* by the May 4th Movement of 1919, the beginning of the modern Chinese cultural revolution. The concept of the oral standard grew stronger and more precise in the wake of the emerging new writing, and the spread of MSC in speech followed the penetration of the written standard in the non-intellectual strata of Chinese society in the process of school education and movements for popular enlightenment, as well as in the struggle of political ideas and the upheavals of war. The influence of writing on the development of the oral standard has become particularly strong during the last two decades characterized by the overall impact of the endless stream of political messages delivered by the mass media, as well as modern theatre and films.

The various trends contributing to the formation of both the new written style and subsequently the oral standard reflect the complexity of modern China in the mixture of new and old, native and foreign, local and national, and in the fluctuating role of personal individuality in a growingly regimented society. The classical *wényán* was rejected as a means of written communication as a whole, but some of its features have still been utilized in writing, and through writing they have also penetrated into the oral standard. The telegraphic terseness of *wényán* units and their constructions was found suitable for purposes similar to those for which the style of newspaper headlines and advertisements was developed in the West. The most typical area in MSC speech where the influence of *wényán* is clearly felt is that of the so-called political slogan, that is the part of MSC which has become surprisingly similar to the Newspeak of Orwell's *Nineteen eighty-four*. As far as lexical items are concerned, the majority of newly coined terms for various categories of political life have been formed by making use of the inventory of basic *wényán* units and arranging them according to the rules of *wényán* syntactic patterning. All the so-called stump compounds (see p. 79) are constructed in this way, and also larger lexical items, such as the brief slogans summarizing the contents of this or that political movement, which belong among what were called inorganic elements in MSC earlier (see pp. 81–82). A recent example of the former is the new name chosen in August 1966 for the street in Peking where the Russian embassy is located, and which has been translated in the British press as 'The Street of Struggle Against Revisionism'. The name is *Fǎnxiūlù*; both its first two morphemes (the last morpheme *lù* 'road, avenue' is a common final constituent in the names of large streets in Peking and elsewhere) *fǎn* and *xiū* occur as free morphemes in MSC: *fǎn* is a functive verb not followed by unmarked nominal referents, meaning 'to rebel', as in *jūnduì fǎnle* 'The army rebelled', 'to turn over', as in *bǎ zhǐ fǎnguolai* 'to turn the [sheet of] paper over', or 'to make noise', as in *nǐ dào wàibianr qù fǎn* '[You] go and make noise outside', while *xiū* is a functive verb commonly followed by such referents, meaning 'to build', as in *xiū fángz* 'to build houses', 'to repair', as in *xiū biǎo* 'to repair watches', or 'to trim', as in *xiū zhǐjiar* 'to trim [one's] nails'. In *Fǎnxiūlù* they are both used with the typical meaning and grammatical function they have in *wényán*: *fǎn* 'to oppose' which can be followed by unmarked nominal referents (in MSC, this meaning is preserved in such words as *fǎnduì* 'to oppose' and *fǎnkàng* 'to resist', and also in words where it occurs as a kind of equivalent of the prefix 'anti-', such as *fǎn-dǎng jítuán* 'anti-Party clique'), and *xiū* 'to improve, to correct, to revise, correction, revision', that is a word functioning either as a functive verb or a noun in *wényán* (as preserved in MSC words like *zìxiū* 'to improve oneself, self-improvement', *xiūgǎi* 'to alter, to revise', or *xiūzhèngzhǔyì* 'revisionism'). The name *Fǎnxiūlù* could, in fact, be explained as an abbreviation of *Fǎnduì-xiūzhèngzhǔyì-lù* 'The Avenue of Opposing Revisionism', and there is little doubt that this is precisely how it was conceived; nevertheless, the inspiration from *wényán* is obvious, and the fact that the respective abbreviation was chosen without hesitation instead of the unabbreviated variant shows the power of the tendency to the usage of *wényán*-like patterns in this and similar cases. Many of such names and terms, and particularly larger items used as the summarizing slogans, are not only expressions newly contrived on the basis of *wényán* units but also items borrowed for the given purpose from *wényán* as a whole. So, for example, the slogan *bǎihuā qífàng, bǎijiā zhēngmíng* '[Let] a hundred flowers blossom [and] a hundred schools of thought contend' raised during the brief period of what appeared to be a political and cultural thaw in 1956–1957, is composed of two old *wényán* expressions, the latter originally referring to the diverse schools of philosophy in the pre-imperial era. Most of such expressions straightforwardly taken over from *wényán* have acquired a different meaning and function in the revived modern usage. For example, the classical expression *yīng xióng* 'to be brave and of superior virtues', originally referring to the qualities of outstanding noblemen, was deliberately chosen to designate the popular heroes of war and labour in Mainland China, and it is now used in MSC as a single word *yīngxióng*, either a stative verb 'to be brave', or more frequently a noun 'hero'. The influence of *wényán* in this sphere is not limited to small lexical items or larger inorganic expressions. Very often the syntactic patterning of *wényán* including the usage of *wényán* markers is productively applied to arranging MSC units in slogans and various political phrases. The result is a rather strange mixture of colloquial and literary elements with a somewhat pompous effect. A typical example of this is the now very commonly used *wényán* pattern of a nominal expression followed by a verbal expression whose relationship is marked by *wèi* and *ér*: *wèi* N *ér* V 'to do V for the sake of N', as in *wǒmen yīnggāi wèi hépíng ér fèndòu* 'We must struggle for peace'. One of the very rare (and severely suppressed) cases of Mainland Chinese political verbal humour of the 'fifties reflected by the phrase *wèi rénmínbì ér fèndòu* 'to struggle for People's Currency', a kind of equivalent of 'to keep up with the Joneses', shows that the ornate artificiality of these heterogeneous phrases is still felt, and that it can be deliberately utilized to mock the slogan style.

The amount of *wényán*-like catchwords and phrases referring to the everyday affairs of social and political life has grown so large in MSC speech since their first appearance in the early days of the Republic some fifty years ago that the first impression a Chinese-speaking foreign visitor gets in present-day Peking is of being surrounded by people who use hardly understandable phrases sounding like pieces of an ancient code imbedded into an otherwise modern language pattern. This is in a way a paradoxical turn in the development of MSC, since the classical written style which was the primary target of the attack of the cultural revolution in 1919 has, at least in the limited sphere of the political slogan, gained a status in speech which it had probably never had in the days when *wényán* was the sole means of written communication. At the same time, again as a result of the corresponding trends in writing, MSC has by now admitted, particularly into its vocabulary, items which not only in the times of Mandarin but also in the period immediately following the beginning of the cultural revolution of 1919 were considered substandard or even vulgar. So, for example, the formerly substandard colloquial expression *bāofu* '[cloth] bundle, wrapper' is now used in MSC with the derived meaning '[ideological] burden', that is the kind of obstacle in thought carried over to the new society from the old times. The word *àiren* which used to mean 'lover' and which was almost tabooed in polite conversation before 1949 (it still makes most Chinese intellectuals living abroad blush), has now acquired a perfectly respectable meaning of 'the beloved one' in MSC, and it is also used in the meaning of 'wife' or 'husband' as a substitute in some contexts for such old terms as *tàitai* 'madam, married lady', now despised in Mainland China.

In comparison with elements of Chinese tradition such as *wényán* and the formerly substandard styles, what generally contributed much more to the way both the new written style and MSC, in that order, have grown into their present form, was the impact of the West. In the very broad sense, it can be said that hardly any aspect of modern Chinese life remained untouched by Western influence since the Opium Wars in the middle of the nineteenth century. In the cities in particular, relics of purely Chinese formal traditions of any kind, reaching from clothing to political thought (perhaps with the sole exception of food), have now become as scarce and isolated as museum pieces, and they are gradually vanishing even from the bastion of tradition, the village countryside. What this meant for the development of the standard language hardly needs a lengthy explanation. In the first place, the vocabulary reflecting practically all spheres of life went through a radical process of change in which a vast number of words and expressions were invented or taken over from foreign languages, and others were forgotten or adapted to suit the needs of the new reality. The number of lexical items which have appeared since the beginning of massive Western influence is actually so great that it now represents a substantial part of current MSC vocabulary. In an earlier chapter of this book (see pp. 65–67), examples were given of two structural types of newly coined words, namely sound borrowings from European languages and borrowings from Japanese. Borrowings of this kind are not, however, the most typical among the new lexical items in MSC. The great part of the new vocabulary are words constructed by arranging existing

Chinese morphological units in accordance with the rules of Chinese morphological patterning. Most technical and semi-technical terms, for example, including such common words as *qìchē* 'motorcar' (a subordinate compound of *qì* 'steam, vapour', a bound morpheme, and *chē* 'vehicle', a free morpheme), and *fēijī* 'aircraft' (a subordinate compound of *fēi* 'to fly', a free morpheme, and *jī* 'machine', a bound morpheme) were coined in this way. Because of the weakness of the norm in the early years of the cultural revolution of 1919, Western influences resulted in a kind of lexical chaos in many parts of the new vocabulary. Two or several terms for individual entities came into use simultaneously and have in many cases coexisted for a long period of time. One of the most common phenomena of this kind are coexisting pairs of technical terms, one member of each pair being a sound borrowing, and the other a word constructed from Chinese morphemes in terms of MSC morphology, such as the two currently used terms for 'microphone' *màikèfēng* (a sound borrowing from English), and *chuányīnqì* (*chuán* 'to pass on', *yīn* 'sound', and *qì* 'implement', all three bound morphemes). Although there is now a strong tendency towards standardizing the relevant parts of MSC vocabulary by selecting one of such groups of synonymous terms as normative (in the case of pairs of terms like *màikèfēng* and *chuányīnqì*, the sound borrowing is invariably rejected), the situation is at present still rather unstable. The rapid process of Western-influenced changes in MSC vocabulary has not, however, resulted only in a somewhat chaotic state which the emerging norm will have to clear up in the long run. Perhaps its more important consequence is the present high overall feeling of flexibility about the lexical system among speakers of MSC, for which there is no equivalent phenomenon in any Western language community. The norm simply stabilizes the rules within the limits of which very little, beside the core of a relatively small number of items, is considered impermissible to alter, and which have regulated but not slowed down the process of changes in MSC vocabulary.

Contrary to the popular belief, Western influence on new Chinese writing and MSC is not limited solely to the sphere of vocabulary. One of the major sources of inspiration for the early pioneers of the new written style was Western literature: not only its content and structure became models to modern Chinese writers but also its purely formal features, including the specific linguistic aspects reflected by its written media. Chinese purists of the 'twenties used to complain about the 'translationese' of contemporary writers, that is the kind of style characterized by involved long sentences peculiarly structured and generally resembling bad translations from some foreign language. The tendency towards letting foreign grammatical and stylistic features exert influence on the new writing has not, however, diminished with the progress of time, although it has gradually become less crude. On the contrary, quite obviously under the growing influence of a similar and even more powerful invasion of Western political writing, much of what was originally felt as alien 'translationese' has become an accepted part of the structure of the new written style, and it has furthermore found a firm foothold in the oral standard as well.

In morphology, foreign influence is mainly responsible for the great increase in the number of polymorphemic words. With the exception of sound borrowings, all newly coined MSC words are polymorphemic, and the general trend from monomorphemic to polymorphemic units has begun to be reflected even in the older parts of MSC morphological system. Generally speaking, wherever there is the possibility of choice between a monomorphemic and a polymorphemic construction, the latter tends to win; polymorphemic members of pairs or groups of synonyms seem to be gaining the status of more respectable expressions, while the corresponding monomorphemic units are acquiring the connotation of an often undesirable and substandard colloquiality. This is happening irrespective of the original stylistic features of the given expressions. For example, the most common word for 'to be beautiful' used to be *měi* in MSC until relatively recently (as in *fēngjǐng hěn měi* 'The scenery is [very] beautiful') and this word had an elegant equivalent *měilì* which was used exclusively in writing; at present, the air of elegance and sophistication associated with *měilì* has practically disappeared, and it is used in MSC as well, gradually pushing out the monomorphemic *měi*: sentences like *fēngjǐng hěn měilì* 'The scenery is [very] beautiful' are now very common in MSC. Another example is the growing use of the form *shǐyòng* 'to use, to make use of' which until not long ago had been considered suitable only in written technical or documentary style; this form is gradually substituting not only the somewhat archaic *shǐ* which had been used solely in writing, but also the corresponding monomorphemic word *yòng* in MSC. Even more striking than the growing number of such polymorphemic words as these, that is words containing two or more root morphemes, is the rapid increase in word-formative and grammatical affixation in MSC. The appearance of new words with word-formative affixes is apparently part of the process triggered off by the impact of the new polymorphemic vocabulary: there are hundreds of such words, and their number steadily grows with every new '-ism', '-ist', and '-ity', e.g. *xiūzhèngzhǔyìzhě* 'revisionist' with the suffix *-zhǔyìzhě* equivalent to '-ist' (the suffix *-zhǔyì* meaning '-ism'), and *fàngshèxìng* 'radioactivity, to be radioactive' with the suffix *-xìng* equivalent to '-ity'. The increasing use of grammatical affixes cannot, however, be explained only in terms of the respective process of vocabulary development. It was pointed out in the preceding chapter on MSC syntax that grammatical affixes on the whole belong to the system of devices which make a sentence complete. It was also suggested that there is a certain balance in MSC between these devices and what was called context: if a sentence is made complete by its specific context, the non-contextual devices, including many grammatical affixes of the word constituents, may become redundant and not occur. The problem is that although this is still generally true in MSC, the present trends in its grammar seem to indicate that the balance has begun to shift in favour of a much greater redundancy in the occurrence of the non-contextual devices. It is rather difficult to say what has brought this shift about, and the most likely suggestion that this is the result of the influence of European languages with their highly developed (and also highly redundant) systems of paradigmatic morphology is merely one of many possible hypotheses in this respect. Nevertheless, one feels that the distinct tendency, mainly in the written style but penetrating with amazing rapidity into MSC as well, to have the key verbs in the sentence always neatly equipped with one or more suffixes (the occurrence of the suffix *-zhe* has greatly increased in MSC perhaps because of this tendency: functive verbs with this suffix tend to be used as nuclei in sentences where their simpler variants without the suffix would have normally occurred in earlier MSC, such as the formerly rare form *yǒuzhe* 'there is, there has been' instead of *yǒu* in sentences like *Zhōngguó yǒuzhe liǎng zhǒng jīběn máodùn* 'There have been two kinds of basic contradictions in China'), and to set apart words belonging to different classes by largely redundant features (the form *-d*, for example, now tends to be used as a kind of general adverbial suffix, and it often occurs in adverbs which had not normally contained it, such as *tóngshíd* 'simultaneously' instead of the formerly only permissible variant *tóngshí*), can hardly have originated elsewhere than from the practical experience with *verbum finitum* and the typical formal characteristics of word classes in European languages. One is also reminded of such facts as that the people who now set the tone in writing and indirectly also in speech in Mainland China were partly brought up on the hasty and truly bad translations of Marxist writings mainly from Russian which had been mass-produced and exported from Moscow from the 'twenties onwards.

The trend towards greater redundancy in the use of formal grammatical devices is also reflected by the steady increase in the formal marking of syntactic constructions. In some cases, the occurrence of redundant markers may have been brought about by the direct influence of European prepositional phrases. For example, the now very fashionable functive verb *fúhé* 'to correspond [to], to be in harmony [with]' which may be followed by unmarked nominal referents, as in *fúhé shìshí* 'to correspond [to] facts, to be justified by the facts', now very often occurs before nominal referents marked by the redundant *yú* (originally a highly literary form now appearing both in writing and MSC as a kind of all-purpose marker of certain nominal referents), such as in *fúhé yú rénmín de lìyì* 'to be in harmony with the interests of the people'. In other cases, redundant marking accompanies the Western-influenced shift towards the increased use of formerly rare or unfavoured types of syntactic constructions. A typical example of this is the growing usage of the marker *bèi*. This marker used to occur almost exclusively in constructions containing a functive verb and two nominal referents, the unmarked one denoting the performer of the given action, and the marked one the receiver of its effects, as in *wǒ bèi tā dǎle yí dùn* 'I was beaten up by him' (*wǒ* 'I', *tā* 'he', *dǎle yí dùn* 'to have beaten up, to have been beaten up'); it is now also commonly used in formerly rare constructions containing a single nominal referent, such as *wǒ bèi dǎle yí dùn* 'I was beaten up'. Its occurrence in the latter type of constructions is redundant, since a single nominal referent in them denotes the receiver of the given action (unless there is something in the context which specifically marks it as denoting the performer): *wǒ dǎle yí dùn* also means 'I was beaten up'. What had originally been a marker is thus gradually becoming a kind of verbal prefix, and MSC seems to be developing, under the influence of European languages, the category of verbal passive which had not existed in its grammatical system. Although purists still object to such phrases as *xìn bèi xiěle* 'The letter was written' (instead of *xìn xiěle*), the norm of MSC has in general yielded to this trend.

Another case of Western influence in the respect of shift towards
originally unfavoured syntactic constructions is the arrangement
of certain functive verbs and marked adverbial modifiers denoting
place. For example, the verb *zhù* 'to live [at], to be staying [at]'
used to occur almost always preceded by such adverbial modifiers,
as in *wǒ zài fàndiànli zhù* 'I am staying in a hotel'; its occurrence
before these adverbial modifiers was very rare and it was not
considered strictly correct. By now it is used before adverbial
modifiers of this kind very commonly, as in *wǒ zhù zài fàndiànli*
'I am staying in a hotel'. The same goes for verbs like *shēnghuó*
'to live, to lead a life': constructions such as *shēnghuó zài èrshí
shìjì* 'to live in the twentieth century' are now far more common
than their formerly favoured variants like *zài èrshí shìjì shēnghuó*.
The influence of equivalent patterns in Western languages, mainly
English and Russian, resulting in these cases in the shift of preference towards previously unfavoured syntactic arrangements had
here a secondary stylistic consequence: the originally more common patterns are now considered somewhat old-world and
affected.

The wide scope of Western influence on MSC grammar can
finally be exemplified by changes in the functional versatility of
some syntactic units. This phenomenon which usually takes the
form of a word originally belonging to one class beginning to be
used as a member of another class, is not new from the viewpoint
of the historical development of Chinese (cf. the example of
zhīdao 'to know' on p. 98 the changing functioning of which
suggests a similar phenomenon taking place in the pre-MSC
period); however, it is much more common at present, and the
changes are now much more rapid and abrupt. In MSC, this
phenomenon is part of the Western-influenced process of growth
and change whose other aspects are the development of the new
vocabulary and the general increase in the flexibility of both
vocabulary and grammar. An example of this is the relatively
recent change in the word-class status of *kēxué* 'science', originally
a noun, which is now commonly used also as a stative verb, as in
zhè zhǒng xiǎngfa bùkēxué 'This way of thinking is unscientific'.
Similarly, the word *kuāndà* 'to be broad, to be broad-minded',
originally a stative verb, now also occurs as a functive verb with
unmarked nominal referents following it, as in *kuāndà péngyou*
'to treat friends leniently'.

Another strong formative factor in the development of both
the new written style and MSC has been the constantly increasing

communication between speakers from different dialectal areas. The breakdown of largely isolated tight social units of the imperial era and the unprecedented movement of large parts of the population during the turbulent years of the civil war and the Sino-Japanese conflict played an important role in this respect as well as the later growth of the power of the centralized government reaching into the farthest corners of the country by the means of modern communication devices. Again, this has led to a highly flexible attitude towards what would have been felt as impermissible local dialectal expressions at the break of the century. It is perhaps mainly in the respect of a certain degree of permissiveness towards the most common features of individual Chinese dialects that MSC differs from its most immediate formal basis of Peking dialect. MSC now not only permits the usage of such words as *gǎo* 'to be, to do, to engage in' (as in *gǎo hóngwèibīng* 'to be a Red Guard', *nǐ zài zhèr gǎo shénme* 'What are you doing here', and *gǎo guānxi* 'to engage in a [sexual] relationship'), which used to belong to the vocabulary of some non-Mandarin dialects, mainly Xiāng (see p. 16), and which was unknown in Peking until rather recently, but it has also grown very tolerant towards such features as the from the point of view of Peking dialect wrong usage of markers, for example *bǎ* in *bǎ kuàiz chīfàn* 'to eat with chopsticks' (which happens to mean 'to eat chopsticks' in Peking dialect, as opposed to *yòng kuàiz chīfàn* 'to eat with chopsticks'). Similarly as in other aspects, the social events of the last two decades increased the tendency of MSC to embody diverse dialectal features. For one thing, the earlier linguistic snobbery of the speakers of 'pure Peking dialect' became politically somewhat tedious after 1949: the majority of the present core of Communist Chinese political leaders are not speakers of Peking dialect, and they have developed a kind of dialect somewhat jokingly labelled as *gànbùhuà* 'cadre language' which, beside a solid proportion of political phrases, bears the traces of the several dialects through the areas of which the Communist revolution moved towards Peking. Although MSC remained largely unaffected by the fashion still popular among many petty Party cadres 'to speak like the leaders' (which means speaking MSC with a trace of non-Mandarin accent, such as saying *si* instead of *shi*, getting one's tones a bit mixed up, etc.), the pre-1949 aversion of MSC speakers towards non-Mandarin dialectal expressions has considerably softened up at the present time.

   Among the factors in the development of MSC which have all in general contributed to its growing flexibility in the historical, social, and geographical sense, the influence of the individual is naturally the least tangible. Perhaps the only sphere where it can be concretely pointed out as one of the major formative factors is the literary style of the 'twenties and the 'thirties. Of the authors who have considerably influenced the direction in which the new written style, and to a certain degree also the oral standard have developed, Lu Hsün (the pen-name of Zhōu Shùrén, 1881–1936) is perhaps the most important. His main part and that of others was not so much in enriching the new written style by personal innovations, for which the lack of a norm provided a wide ground, as in their active contribution towards establishing a proportion between the various existing tendencies in the formative process of the development of the written style, and towards speeding up the process.

It is necessary to stress that trends in present-day MSC which may seem to reflect solely the specific social, political and cultural situation in contemporary China, are, in fact, a mere culmination of a development started several decades earlier, a stage in a process in its very general features not dissimilar from that which had led to the formation of standards in European languages. Roughly speaking, the main similarity is in basing the standard on the educated variant of the area traditionally considered central in the political and cultural sense, and at the same time opening it to the influence of a wide range of factors with the aim of reaching a sophisticated and flexible tool of communication acceptable to as large a section of the population as possible. In a way, establishing a standard language means setting a normative proportion between sophistication, flexibility and chaos: only the future development of MSC, which is still much farther away from its normative stage than any of the major Western standard languages, will show to what degree the search for an optimum proportion will prove successful.

2. THE WRITING SYSTEM

Since this book deals mainly with oral communication, the Chinese writing system falls, strictly speaking, outside the frame of its main topics. Moreover, the subject of Chinese script is so vast that even a brief description of the system would hardly be possible here. Nevertheless, the main features of the script must be pointed out in the context of this chapter for the simple reason that writing is not as irrelevant to language in general as linguists sometimes believe, and that it is, in fact, a highly important element in the formative process of the special kind of language a standard such as MSC is. The point is that a standard language is almost always linked with writing in many ways. It was, for example, shown in the preceding section that MSC has been developing in close relationship with the new written style. Perhaps the most important feature in this respect is that the people who contribute most actively to the development of the standard are the literate and educated minority whose language awareness and behaviour are not only strongly influenced by the general features of the written style they use, but also, in a very subtle sense, by its technical means, that is the script in question. It will perhaps become clearer further on just how this delicate influence of the writing system on language behaviour materializes in the case of MSC speakers. For the moment, it will be useful to remember how deeply our own notions and feelings about the structure of our language are conditioned by the writing system we use: such categories as phonemes and words are easily acceptable and 'natural' to an educated speaker of a European language because the script he uses reflects them more or less systematically, while other categories, such as morphemes and intonation patterns which are not or not always indicated in the writing system, remain limited to the sphere of specialized linguistic disciplines. It is also possible to imagine, on the basis of our own experience, that given an opportunity to contribute creatively to the development of a standard language, people would in general employ only the categories they are aware of, an important part of which they realize because of the specific features of the script they use.

To be precise, there are two kinds of script now in use by speakers of MSC: the traditional character writing system, and one or another transcription aspiring to become the future Chinese script. For all practical purposes, however, the former is still the only one functioning as an accepted common device of written communication in China, and the only system exerting the kind of influence on the language behaviour of MSC speakers suggested above. The latter will be discussed in the final section of this chapter; at this point, the discussion will be restricted to the specific features of the character script which is now the only existing Chinese writing system in the proper sense.

Since Westerners first met this writing system, they have called it many names. The two most common terms which are still used at present reflect attempts to describe the nature of this script as opposed to that of an alphabet: *pictographic*, which is meant to indicate that the basic units of the script (*pictograms*) are pictures of objects and acts both by origin and in their present shape (furthermore, the term suggests that the script works as a kind of system of visual symbols for the things one talks about, thus pointing to meaning rather than sound), and *ideographic*, which implies that the writing system uses units (*ideograms*) symbolizing 'ideas' or abstract concepts of objects, acts, and qualities. The basic summarizing judgment on the Chinese writing system expressed by both these terms is that it is a script which, unlike an alphabet, does not record sounds but in one way or another indicates meaning. Whether this judgment is true or not is of great importance for any discussion on the role of the script as a formative element in the development of MSC, and in order to test its validity, it will be useful to point out some of the main features in the development of the Chinese script as opposed to that of an alphabet, and also the way in which the two kinds of script function in relation to the respective languages.

The early history of the major writing systems used today is not, as could be expected, very well known. The only conspicuous feature which unites the scripts relevant to this discussion is that there were pictures somewhere in their beginnings. This is undoubtedly true of such diverse writing systems as the Latin alphabet and the Chinese script, but it is equally uncertain if pictures were the only elements in writing at the very beginning, and if they were, precisely how they were used. The earliest specimens of the Chinese script dating from about 2000 B.C. are too scanty and too mysterious to serve as a clue in this respect, while the first large set of examples preserved mainly on oracle bones and shells comes from a period (about 1400–1200 B.C.) when the writing system had basically reached its final stage of development. The traditional Chinese division of characters (that is, units of an already developed writing system) into six different classes (this division was first made around 1100 B.C. in the book of classics known as *Zhōu lǐ* 'The Rites of [the state] Chou'), does, however, indicate some kind of historical process, since it is based on the concept that some classes of characters developed from others, the primary classes being represented by pictures. There are, in fact, four such primary classes in this traditional division: straightforward pictures of objects (such as ⌡ denoting 'a man' which gradually developed into its present form 人), pictures meant to indicate various abstract concepts as acts or events (such as 大 denoting 'big', that is 'a man looking big or trying to look big', now written 大), combinations of existing pictures indicating more complex concepts (such as 林 denoting 'a forest', a reduplication of the form 木 denoting 'a tree', that is a picture of a tree with the branches on the top and roots below, which developed into the present 林), and modifications of existing pictures indicating subclasses of objects or acts (such as 尸 denoting 'a corpse', that is a twisted form of the 'man' picture, which became the present 尸).

Unless it were somewhat unrealistically presumed that a clever man once sat down and invented the whole set of symbols belonging to these four groups in a day or two when he had nothing more urgent to do, the possibility of a process from a simple picture to a more complex one suggests itself rather clearly. This goes even more for the step towards the last two classes which, as will be seen later, contain forms based on pictures but formed according to other principles than those of visual symbolization. Whatever the case, the way the presumably original set of simple pictures later enriched by more complex ones was used as a script is not known. There is, however, some strongly suggestive evidence from other old cultural areas where similar scripts were used, including those which had been the cradle of the ancestors of the Latin alphabet such as ancient Egypt, and also from several civilizations which have used similar writing systems until very recently, such as that of North American Indians. All these scripts seem to have shared the common feature of being communication systems not directly related to any particular language: the arrangements of picture units communicated messages which could be linguistically interpreted in different ways, both in a single language or in different languages. Readers of early Westerns will recollect that the prominent white figure in the message painted on a strip of hide might be read as anything from 'Big White Chief' to 'the President of the United States' in English or in several Indian languages, and that no specific expression or sound in any of the respective languages was explicitly indicated by the whole figure or any of its parts. The relationship between what can be called *source* (that is, the actual object, situation, or whatever else is commented upon), the script, and the language, can be indicated in the case of the picture writing system by a triangle, where the two full lines denote direct symbolization, and the broken line indirect symbolization:

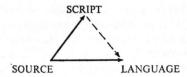

Fig. 25   Relationship between source, language, and non-linguistic script

The usage of a picture script thus means the existence of two largely independent communication systems in the given language community: the script and the language. Although there is undoubtedly some relationship between the two systems (since language is historically always the prior system, identification of source features and their coding into pictures is necessarily influenced by the specific way the given language symbolizes the source), the relationship is not direct, or, in other words, it is not a one-to-one relationship: items in language cannot be systematically and unambiguously associated with items in script and vice versa. For the purposes of this discussion, scripts of this kind will be called *non-linguistic*. Although it is not certain if any community ever used a fully non-linguistic script, all the early picture writing systems seem to have belonged basically to this type, and it may be suggested that the ancient Chinese script represented by the four classes of characters mentioned above was one of them, as well as the ancestors of the Latin alphabet.

The part of the judgment on the nature of the Chinese writing system which refers to its being a pictographic script is thus true as far as its origins and perhaps also its early stages of development are concerned. However, it is also true in the same sense for a script such as the Latin alphabet, and this part of the judgment is consequently not very helpful. The still common opinion popular even among many linguists is that while such scripts as the Latin alphabet developed from their pictographic beginnings into writing systems substantially different, the Chinese script never really got past its pictographic stage. That this is an erroneous concept is demonstrated by the last two classes of Chinese characters representing forms which have presumably developed later than those of the first four classes. An example of a typical member of the fifth class of characters (known as *phonetic loans*) will perhaps clearly show that the Chinese script, or at least a part of it, reached relatively early a point far beyond the picture stage: the form 米, originally a picture denoting 'a kind of wheat' (cf. the picture denoting 'a tree' on p. 149), began to be used for 'to come', and it is still used that way today (the present form being 來). Just when this happened is not known, as the form occurs in both meanings in the earliest available texts (later a different form developed for 'a kind of wheat', and the previously ambiguous character retained the sole meaning 'to come'), but the principle is obvious: instead of inventing a new written symbol for 'to come', an existing symbol denoting something completely different was borrowed for the purpose. It has been proved by historical linguists that the basis for such borrowing was the fact that the respective language symbols, that is the expressions for 'a kind of wheat' and 'to come' were identical or similar in sound. The same principle was in a more sophisticated way eliminating ambiguity applied in the case of the sixth class of characters presumably representing the final stage in the development of Chinese script. These characters called *phonetic compounds* consist basically of two parts: one (called *a phonetic*) is usually a picture borrowed to denote something else in the same way as in the case of the fifth class, and the other (called *a radical*) is an added element, also a picture, indicating the fact and the nature of the borrowing. For example, the character whose present form is 扣 and which indicated 'to strike' was constructed from what is now 口 (originally a picture of the open mouth 日) indicating 'mouth', and 扌, a graphic variant of 手 (originally a picture of an open hand 手) indicating 'hand', both of which existed and still exist as separate symbols in the system. The former was the borrowed phonetic (even in MSC, 口 and 扣 represent units very similar in their phonemic structure: *kǒu* and *kòu*), and the latter the radical added as an indication that the whole form was borrowed and denoting something connected with manual action.

The last two classes of characters not only show that the Chinese writing system was not fully a picture script at the time when the earliest massive evidence existing today originated, but they also point to the important fact that at some stage in the development of the Chinese script a revolutionary change took place which made it a system different from what were called non-linguistic writing systems here. The case of the fifth class of characters means that at some point written symbols began to be closely associated with specific arrangements of language sounds rather than with features of the so-called source: if there were no such association, the usage of a single symbol for two completely different source items such as 'a kind of wheat' and 'to come' would have been impossible. Characters of the sixth class (which, incidentally, represent the overwhelming majority of script units today, while the remaining ones have been reinterpreted in terms of the sixth class: characters of the first class are, for example, understood as radicals with zero phonetics, etc.) indicate that the association which began to take place was not made only between script units and specific arrangements of language sounds, since language units identical or similar in sound and different in meaning were associated with different written symbols, such as 口 'mouth' and 扣 'to strike' originally representing two fully or almost fully homophonous expressions. The presumption of a change is, of course, equally conjectural as the proposition of the kind of development suggested above (which, if it actually took place, was probably much more complicated in any case); nevertheless, the picture elements in the Chinese writing system indicate that the script had once been fully or partly non-linguistic, and the presumption of a change is further made fairly plausible by taking into account evidence of similar situations elsewhere than in China. On the whole, it seems that communities which used or use a basically non-linguistic script are more primitive than those using writing systems of a different kind, and it is possible to come to the hypothetical conclusion that certain developments in the social life of a community using a non-linguistic script invariably bring about the revision of this writing system which is obviously rather inefficient by its nature. Theoretically, there are two possible ways for carrying out such a revision: either by improving the non-linguistic script and developing it into a more complex system of direct source-script symbolization, or by discarding the non-linguistic writing system and substituting it by something more suitable. Since the former possibility has never successfully materialized anywhere in the world (no non-linguistic writing system exists today which could satisfy the needs of modern communication), it seems obvious that the latter possibility was generally the more acceptable one. The practical solution was equally obvious: disregarding the cases of communities which rejected their own non-linguistic writing systems and adopted alien scripts of more advanced communities, what happened in one way or another everywhere else was that instead of designing some totally new system of symbolization and thus prolonging the coexistence of two independent systems of communication, people have adapted the hitherto non-linguistic script to match the already existing complex system of communication, that is the given language. The script thus became a system of symbols of symbols, and units of the writing system were assigned to some language units or others in a one-to-one proportion. The resulting change in the relationship between source, language, and script can be indicated in the respective triangle as

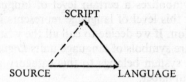

Fig. 26   Relationship between source, language, and linguistic script

The important point is that this happened both in the case of the Latin alphabet (or rather its predecessors, that is the Phoenician script, and even in the last stages of the development of the Egyptian writing system), and the Chinese writing system. The difference between the two systems is not that each developed in a substantially different way or that each now represents a different stage of the same process. They have both gone through a similar process and they have both reached an equivalent stage of development; what makes them different is the concrete solution of assigning the script units to language units. While in the case of the Latin alphabet the language units which script units were ultimately assigned to were more or less phonemes, the units of the Chinese writing system were assigned to language units of, so to speak, a higher level. The two systems thus differ in nothing less and nothing more than the *level of representation* of language units by script units. In view of this, the statement on the Chinese writing system reflected by the terms pictographic and ideographic is, at least as far as the present features of the system are concerned, partly wrong and partly incomplete: Chinese script is pictographic by its origin, but it is not pictographic in its present function, since characters are not used as pictures of objects and acts but as 'pictures' of certain language units, and it is not ideographic, since characters are not direct symbols of ideas or abstract concepts but symbols of certain language units (which in their turn may perhaps be considered as symbols of ideas or abstract concepts but this is not a directly relevant consideration). The summarizing judgment on Chinese script as a system indicating meaning rather than sound is, in a way, true but it is also rather incomplete and imprecise. It would be more correct to say that the units of the Chinese writing system represent certain language units which are partly characterized by specific features of meaning: again, the main point is that the Chinese writing system represents or symbolizes a certain level of language in the first place, and what this level of language represents is only a secondary consideration. If we decide to call all the writing systems the units of which are symbols of language units *linguistic scripts*, the Chinese writing system belongs to this category as obviously as does the Latin alphabet.

The problem which remains to be discussed, before the way in which Chinese script exerts influence on the language awareness and behaviour of MSC speakers can be suggested, is exactly what language units do the units of the Chinese writing system represent. Although the following statements in this respect may be valid for Chinese script in its whole post-picture period, they are meant to refer primarily to the state of its contemporary system which coincides with the birth and subsequent development of MSC.

Since no systematic relationship between the script units called characters or any of their parts, and phonemes or arrangements of phonemes smaller than the syllable can be established, the only units which can be associated with characters on the phonemic level are syllables: when an MSC sentence is written down in characters (such as 今天天氣很好 *jīntiān tiānqi hěn hǎo* 'The weather is [very] nice today'), there are invariably as many characters as there are syllables. There are very few cases where this is not true, the most common of these being instances of the way the so-called erisation (see pp. 71–73 and 86) is reflected in writing: any of the word-formative suffixes sharing the shape -*r* is, phonemically speaking, a subsyllabic element which clusters together with the syllable it follows (such as *huà* + *r*→*huàr* 'picture'), but it is written by a separate character 兒; thus, wherever it occurs, a single syllable is represented by two units of the script such as 畫兒 *huàr* 'picture'. Such inconsistencies are, however, of little importance, since they are limited to a very small number of cases. What is much more important is the fact that the association between MSC syllables and characters does not represent a one-to-one relationship. Although the number of syllables and the number of characters in corresponding segments of speech and written text largely coincide, and although one character almost always represents only one syllable (again, there are minor exceptions to this), the same syllable is not necessarily always represented by the same character. For example, the character 今 always represents the syllable *jīn* but this syllable may be represented by at least ten other characters: 巾,斤,筋,津,矜,金,禁,衿,襟, and 浸. What obviously matters here are the different meaningful units which the individual occurrences of the same syllable represent: *jīn* is represented by 今 only when it means 'present, now' (as in 今天 *jīntiān* 'today') but not when it means 'towel, kerchief, scarf' (when it is written 巾, as in 毛巾 *máojīn* 'towel'), 'a catty [unit of weight almost equivalent to the English pound]' (when it is written 斤, as in 公斤 *gōngjīn* 'kilogram'), 'muscle' (when it is written 筋, as in 筋肉 *jīnròu* 'muscle'), etc. The relationship between characters and MSC linguistic units is thus not a relationship on the phonemic level, since phonemic units are not meaningful.

Although many words can be associated with single characters, characters cannot always be associated with words or their arrangements. The Chinese writing system in no way indicates borderlines between basic syntactic units as the various systems using the Latin alphabet do, that is by larger spaces between individual letters. The potential one-to-one relationship between script units and meaningful MSC linguistic units which then obviously suggests itself is that between characters and morphemes. On close examination, this is an almost fully one-to-one relationship, as can be seen from the example of *jīn* given above: the individual characters represent the different morphemes sharing the respective phonemic shape. The close association between syllables and characters on the one hand, and between many words and characters on the other hand, is, in fact, an indirect expression of this relationship, since the overwhelming majority of MSC morphemes are represented by single syllables on the phonemic level, and many words are represented by single morphemes. All the minor inconsistencies in the one-character-per-syllable pattern can be explained in the terms of the relationship between characters and morphemes: for example, the monosyllabic form *huàr* 'picture', which is written by two characters, represents two morphemes (*huà* 'to draw, picture' and the word-formative suffix

-r). On the other hand, the overall one-to-one relationship between MSC morphemes and characters has its own exceptions.
First of all, only segmental morphemes are represented in the
writing system, which means that the script does not reflect morphologically distinctive suprasegmental features (such as the UU
stress pattern, see p. 87). As far as segmental morphemes are
concerned, the one-to-one relationship is broken in two major
kinds of cases: all polysyllabic morphemes are represented by
groups of two or more characters, and there are also instances of
groups of morphemes represented by single characters. In the
former case, the disproportion can be explained by the peculiar
way in which foreign expressions are borrowed in Chinese: as was
pointed out earlier, presumably all polysyllabic morphemes in
MSC are of foreign origin (see p. 65 ff.), and the process of borrowing includes the segmentation of the foreign expression into MSC-
like syllables. The fact that these syllables acquire a quasi-
morphemic value because of, or partly because of, the need to write
them down, shows the force of the overall pattern of the syllable-
morpheme-character relationship, while the fact that the respective
polysyllabic units ultimately remain monomorphemic reflects their
foreign origin. Cases of single characters representing groups of
morphemes are examples of inherent inconsistencies typical for a
writing system as such. To be of any practical value, a writing system must have a certain proportion of stability and permanence;
once established, its principles and rules based on the features of
the respective language (in the case of linguistic scripts) tend to
remain unaltered despite the subsequent development in the language which may lose these features and acquire new ones. Many
of the well-known inconsistencies of Western orthographies are of
this kind. In most of these orthographies which are all based on the
one-to-one relationship between phonemes and individual letters
of one alphabet or another, there are cases of single letters representing more than one phoneme and vice versa. In the English
writing system, for example, the letter *c* represents at least two
different phonemes (as in *cut, cylinder*, etc.), while the inconsistent
representation of single phonemes in different ways is reflected
in G. B. Shaw's suggestion to spell the word *fish* as *ghoti*: *gh* as in
enough, *o* as in *women*, and *ti* as in *cautious*. In MSC, the inherent
discrepancy between script and language is mainly exemplified by
groups of two or more morphemes which are represented by single
characters; in most of these groups (some of which were mentioned in Chapter III, see pp. 87–88): *hǎo* 'to be good' and *hào*

'to be fond of', for example, are written with the same character
好), the respective morphemes show similarities which suggest a
common point of origin. Despite all these and other discrepancies
in the one-to-one relationship (some of them may be due to the
simple fact that the Chinese script, as well as any other writing
system, has not been faultless to begin with; it is, after all, a
human product), the fact that the linguistic unit on which the
whole system of Chinese script is built is the morpheme is beyond
doubt. If the need is felt to use a special term for such a script, a
morphemic writing system is perhaps the most suitable one.

A morphemic script, such as the Chinese writing system, is a
subtype of linguistic scripts. Among the existing linguistic scripts
it is a very uncommon subtype; the most wide-spread are the so-
called *phonemic* scripts some of which, such as the writing systems
using the Latin alphabet, are largely based on the association of
the basic script units with phonemes (and also of groups of script
units with words as a secondary association), while others, called
syllabic scripts, such as the present Amharic script or the Korean
writing system (the basic units of the latter can, however, be
reduced to elements of phoneme representation; the non-Chinese
part of the Japanese script called *kana* is perhaps a better example
of a syllabic writing system used in the Far Eastern area), associate
basic script units with syllables.

The main features of the Chinese writing system can be pointed
out in comparison with the kind of phonemic script such as that
used by speakers of English. Since the number of morphemes is
incomparably greater in any language than the number of its
phonemes, the most conspicuous feature of all morphemic scripts
including the Chinese writing system is the multitude of their basic
units: compared with the twenty-six letters of the English alphabet,
the Chinese writing system operates with literally thousands of
characters. It is difficult to say just how many characters actually
exist today (it is like trying to give the number of existing English
morphemes: considerations of frequency, historical coverage, the
degree of inclusion of proper names, etc., are relevant factors in
this respect): one of the largest Chinese dictionaries known as
Kāng-xī zìdiǎn 'K'ang Hsi Dictionary' (K'ang Hsi being the style
of the second emperor of the Ch'ing dynasty who reigned in the
years 1662–1723) which was completed in the eighteenth century,
lists about fifty thousand characters, while between two to three
thousand characters are usually said to be used actively by literate
speakers of MSC for purposes of everyday written communication.

Moreover, since it is necessary to preserve distinctions between the individual members of such a large set of symbols, characters are, on the whole, graphically much more complex than the letters of an alphabet. The graphic complexity of characters is tradition- ally measured by the number of 'strokes', that is uninterrupted lines counted according to the rules of correct writing by hand; the number of strokes in characters of the traditional system, that is before the introduction of simplified characters (see the final section of this chapter), varied between one (such as ➝ repre- senting the morpheme *yì~yí~yī* 'one') and over thirty (such as

齉 representing the morpheme *nàng* 'to be thick [of voice]' which

contains thirty-six strokes), while most characters fell within the range of seven to seventeen strokes. The practical disadvantages of such a script when compared with an alphabet are obvious: for instance, the Chinese writing system poses an incomparably heavier burden on the mechanical memory of its users and it makes such matters as printing a very complex affair.

Beside such relative practical shortcomings, the Chinese mor- phemic script has various advantages over a phonemic writing system. First of all, it is a more stable system in the historical sense, since it reflects the morphological level of language which develops and changes much more slowly than the phonemic system. The amount of inconsistencies in contemporary Chinese script which are due to changes in the morphological system of the language is incomparably smaller than the typical inconsistencies of most European orthographies, although the Chinese writing system has been used more or less in its present form much longer than any of the modern European scripts. Moreover, it is a writing system the use of which is not limited to a small language community, such as all phonemic scripts are. Since dialects of one language, as well as languages in general, normally share more of morpho- logical than phonemic features, it is relatively easy for speakers of different dialects of one language or even of different languages to use the same morphemic script. This does not mean that, as one of the most common fallacies about the Chinese script posits, this is possible without any difficulties. To read and write in a mor- phemic script means to learn the basic features of the morpho- logical system of the dialect on which the script is based, which in the case of the Chinese script is more or less Northern Chinese (see p. 16). This, however, is much easier for a speaker of, say, one of the dialects of Cantonese than if he had to learn the features of a Northern Chinese dialect's phonemic system as well, in which case he would be in the same position as a German wanting to write in Dutch without knowing any Dutch. Beyond a certain point, the usage of the Chinese writing system by speakers of non-Northern Chinese dialects, and particularly of another language, becomes very tedious (this is probably the main reason why all non-Chinese communities which had once used the Chinese script either abandoned it altogether, such as the Vietnamese and the North Koreans, or supplemented it with their own additional subsystems, such as the Japanese), but the point is, on the whole, much farther from the original centre than in the case of a phonemic script. Finally, the Chinese morphemic writing system is particularly adaptable as far as the tendency towards compactness, common to all scripts, is concerned. Generally speaking, every linguistic script, for obvious practical reasons, attempts to convey as much as the respective language does with minimal effort, which means that linguistic writing systems tend to omit recording as many fully or partly predictable and redundant language elements as possible. Most linguistic scripts have no symbols for such suprasegmental features as stress and intonation, and some phonemic writing systems even omit symbols for certain segmental phonemes (such as the traditional Hebrew and Arabic scripts which do not always indicate vowels), since the occurrence of the respective features can be fully or partly presumed by speakers of the given languages reading written texts. In some specific conditions when otherwise distinctive features become irrelevant, such reductions may become particularly drastic, as for example in the style of English cablegrams. Morphemic scripts can, on the whole, afford much greater compactness than phonemic writing systems mainly because they often distinguish features which are distinguished solely by distribution in the respective language. For example, the syllable *yǒu* represents several MSC morphemes one of which is a bound morpheme meaning 'friend'; this morpheme occurs, among others, in the word *péngyou* 'friend'. To say 'friend', one always uses the whole word *péngyou*, but one can write it down merely by using the character representing the morpheme *yǒu* 'friend' which is 友. This is possible because in the script, unlike in the language, this unit can never be mistaken for the homophonous free morpheme *yǒu* 'to have, to exist' which is written 有. This feature became one of the main principles on which the classical written style called *wényán* was based. However, the possibility of achieving a great degree of compactness is an advantage of dubious value: in the long run it led, in the case of the Chinese script, to the development of a complex system of written communication almost unrelated to language and consequently partly deprived of the main positive feature of a linguistic writing system as opposed to a non-linguistic script: the simplicity given by a single principle of symbolization. As a result, the classical written style finally had to be rejected by obviously drastic and painful measures.

The way in which using a morphemic writing system may exert influence on the language behaviour of the literate speakers of the respective language is suggested by the typical features of such a script. To learn how to use a linguistic writing system means, in a sense, to accept a kind of analysis of the language one speaks; since every linguistic script reflects primarily one particular structural level of the given language, the people who use a linguistic script necessarily become conscious of the features of the level of their language which the script reflects and interprets. This phenomenon is, apart from other aspects, obviously the basis for the common kind of popular beliefs about individual languages and language in general. On the one hand, educated speakers of any language tend to think of their own language in terms of the writing system they use, that is in terms of the kind of analysis the given script reflects, and to apply the concepts of script categories to language features. On the other hand, literate speakers of one particular language tend to consider the kind of analysis their script represents as generally valid for all languages. All this results in the sort of popular distortions and misunderstandings which annoy linguists when they discuss language and languages with non-linguists at sherry parties; what is more important, however, is that it also results in a very acute awareness of some language features, and a surprising lack of sensitivity to others, among the majority of people who are in a position to influence the development of the language standard. In the case of literate speakers of Chinese, the awareness is focused on morphological features, or to be precise, on the way these features are interpreted by the morphemic script. Many of the trends in MSC mentioned earlier in this chapter can be traced down to the influence of this factor. The modern revival of *wényán* in the sphere of political slogans, for example, shows that the kind of delicate 'morpheme awareness' which is limited in the West to the few who are interested in such matters as etymology, is common to most people in China who can read and write, and that this awareness is a strong active factor in their language behaviour. Similarly, the way in which foreign borrowings are ascribed quasi-morphemic values before they are accepted, and the general tendency towards coining new expressions rather than accepting their foreign models, are not merely expressions of national pride, but also reflections of uneasiness about elements which lack the immediate clarity of morphological features 'proper' language units are expected to possess. The awareness may, however, have even deeper effects on the development of the language standard than in the sphere of lexical items. It would be possible to suggest that the process of grammatical formalization in the case of many units which are approximating the status of affixes or markers has never reached the ultimate stage partly because the awareness of the original morphemic value of the respective units is continually supported by the usage of the script. Whether this is true or not is, of course, difficult to prove; nevertheless, the unusually indistinct borderlines between grammar and lexis mentioned several times earlier in this book seem to indicate the influence of a factor conspicuously lacking in the languages of communities using a different kind of writing system.

The proof may perhaps materialize if and when the morphemic script is substituted by a phonemic writing system, that is if the cautious preliminary steps taken in that direction by the Communist government in Mainland China ever reach that stage. In this context, it is interesting to take notice of one aspect of the present situation in the respect of script reform. One of the points of resistance to the introduction of a phonemic script in China is apparently the fear of breaking away from the rich cultural tradition of the country, since the adoption of a different writing system would make anything written in characters inaccessible to the majority of the literate population. This argument appears in various forms in all the relevant discussions carried on the pages of articles and books dealing with the reform of the Chinese writing system published in China (and particularly elsewhere), and its basic line of reasoning never seems to be questioned. And yet there are probably as many Chinese who daily read their Mencius as there are Englishmen who regularly sit down to Plato's Dialogues in Greek, and the average literate Chinese understands the original text of Mencius perhaps just a little better than an Englishman qualified only by his ability to read and write comprehends Beowulf. The fear of losing continuity is perhaps substantiated by unspoken considerations of a different kind. It may be the expression of unwillingness to part with the kind of tradition projected into the intrinsic features of the morphemic script, the influence of which still functions as an integral part of the conscious language behaviour of the literate speakers.

3. THE RULES

The development of any standard language is basically given by the social, political and cultural needs of a given community at a given period. The needs themselves are not always clear, however, and they are not necessarily shared by all members of the community with sufficient lack of ambiguity to result automatically in straightforward practical steps. A great many things about the standard language have to be agreed upon, and within the process of agreement decisions, often arbitrary, have to be taken. So, for example, an existing dialect has to be chosen as the basis for the standard, delicate points of its grammatical system have to be exposed to subjective rulings on their propriety and correctness, the vocabulary has to be firmly established by selecting some lexical items and rejecting others, and, as the part of the general standardization which, as was shown in the preceding section of this chapter, is not wholly irrelevant to the standard language, and which in practice usually assumes primary importance, rules concerning the writing system and the written style have to be set up. It is precisely the factor of arbitrary decisions which makes the standard language a linguistic body of a special kind: the final result is neither a, so to speak, natural language system, nor is it a system completely reorganized by deliberate acts, but it has elements of both. This character of standard languages makes them relatively difficult to describe in purely linguistic terms. It has been very common among linguists to neglect the complex nature of standard languages on the one hand, and to treat them as natural language systems; on the other hand, the specific features of standard languages have been considered as features of languages in general, including natural language systems. The man in the street goes even further: to him, language is often solely the set of arbitrarily decided rules. It will perhaps be useful to attempt to summarize briefly at this point the main events connected with decision making which have taken place in the process of the development of MSC, in order to separate the arbitrary factor from features of a natural language system.

The concept of MSC as a whole has itself been partly deliberately developed to its present form through several stages. At its beginnings, after the foundation of the Republic in 1911, there was the desire to establish in China a standard language equivalent in all respects to the standards of Western languages. The desire was not very concrete; in practice, it meant little more than taking over the tradition of using the educated variant of Peking dialect, which had been the standard form of oral communication among imperial officials since 15th century called *guānhuà* (i.e. Mandarin: this semi-standard was also utilized in a limited degree by pre-Republican reformers at the end of the nineteenth century as an instrument for spreading education in the country), as the oral norm, and giving it a new name *guóyǔ* 'National Language'. The name itself was borrowed from Japan where, around 1900, the successful standard language movement had impressed the numerous students from China who later became an important element in Chinese cultural and political life. The first steps towards making the desire less vague took place by setting up such organizations as the National Language Research Committee (in 1916), the purpose of which was to suggest decisions aimed at the unification of the National Language. The work of the Committee was, however, directed more towards the script than the language in the most immediate practical respects; its language projects, such as the survey of Chinese dialects and the compilation of a normative dictionary, bore fruit much later than the crucial period of the 'twenties. In the beginning, the concept of the language standard consequently grew more precise by trial and error rather than by an organized effort. Perhaps the most influential factor in this respect during the initial period was the outburst of writing in the new style which followed the rejection of *wényán*. This style called *the new báihuà*, or only *báihuà* (usually translated as 'vernacular'; the etymology of the Chinese term which means something like 'plain language' is not quite certain), grew partly out of the tradition of popular old *báihuà* writing mainly represented by the great medieval novels such as *Hóng lóu mèng* 'The Dream of the Red Chamber', which had not been considered proper literature by pre-Republican *literati*, and partly under the influence of Western literary styles as the written counterpart of *guóyǔ*. Within several years after the May 4th Movement in 1919 which represents the main point of break with the old written culture, certain distinct trends in writing emerged mainly as far as the proportion of such formative components as the features of old *báihuà*, dialects other than the educated variant spoken in Peking as reflected in writing, foreign borrowings, personal innovations, and remnants of *wén-yán* were concerned, and these trends influenced the changing shape of the concept of the standard language itself. It was not until the early 'thirties when an awareness of where the trends were leading to and what the broader consequences of the development might be grew among the leaders of the various cultural and political movements. At that time questions of the language standard, written style, and script became to an unusually great degree part of the fierce ideological struggle on the Chinese political scene. The concept of *guóyǔ* which had gradually developed into a kind of sophisticated lingua franca primarily of the small educated minority, was attacked by left-wing intellectuals as a tool of the bourgeois conspiracy, and a scheme of the so-called *dàzhòngyǔ* 'Language of the Masses' inspired mainly by the experience of contemporary Soviet Russian attempts at a cultural revolution among the Chinese living on Russian territory, was put forward by them as the revolutionary alternative. The concept of *dàzhòngyǔ* was quite different from that of *guóyǔ*: its main points were much less sophistication and rejection of Peking dialect as the only basis of the standard (the advocates of *dàzhòngyǔ* were, in fact, proposing to establish five different language standards, one for each of what they considered as the main dialectal areas). Unlike the case of *guóyǔ*, the scheme of *dàzhòngyǔ* had not, however, been tested in practice, and it remained a theory before the beginning of the Sino-Japanese war in 1937, which interrupted the organized efforts of the standardization movement for two decades. Some of the ideas of the scheme were, however, embodied in the concept of language standard adopted by the Communist government after 1949. This concept of the so-called *pǔtōnghuà* 'Common Language' is largely based on the latter stage of *guóyǔ* (the two terms *guóyǔ* and *pǔtōnghuà* are now almost synonymous, *guóyǔ* being used by most Chinese living outside Mainland China), but in some of its aspects, particularly in its stressing of non-sophistication and non-exclusiveness, traces of the *dàzhòngyǔ* principles can be felt. Since 1949, activities related to language standardization have become much more organized than they had ever been before, and they have been centrally coordinated with the movement for script reform and with linguistic research in such organizations as the *Zhōngguó wénzì gǎigé wěiyuánhuì* 'Committee for the Chinese Script Reform', bodies sponsored by the government and having a considerable amount of decisive power. Nevertheless, the concept of the standard language, although it became relatively much more precise, is still not comparable in clarity with any Western norm, and its slow development shows the limits to which the element of subjective decisions can influence the course of events in the process of standard language formation.

Since its very beginning, the modern movement for language standardization has been closely connected with linguistic research. This is, of course, not surprising, as any practical normative decisions could be made only on the basis of data provided by a detailed description of the language situation. However, the slow and tentative progress of the movement in its initial stages was partly due to the fact that there had been very little tradition in China of the kind of linguistics which could be applied to the purpose of standardization, until the beginning of this century. In old China, scholars interested in language problems had been devoting their attention almost exclusively to texts, that is texts written in the *wényán* style, and dealing with actual language problems only as secondary when textual interpretation required reference to the underlying language phenomena. Before the modern impact of Western scholarship, there had been no descriptive linguistics in China to speak of, and when it was born (the first Chinese descriptive grammar of a kind was written by Mǎ Jiànzhōng in 1898), it imitated its Western models so closely that the first results were more or less mere attempts to apply the specific categories of the grammar of one Western language or another to a selected set of Chinese data. Mǎ Jiànzhōng's description was based on the model of Latin grammar, while most of the books on Chinese grammar published in China until the late 'thirties imitated such standard works on modern European languages as Henry Sweet's *New English Grammar*. The more sophisticated and independent descriptions written during the Sino-Japanese war by Lǚ Shúxiāng, Wáng Lì, Gāo Míngkǎi and others had little influence on the process of standardization mainly because the movement itself stagnated during this period, and the influence of Russian linguistics (which had an earlier tradition among the followers of *dàzhòngyǔ*), mainly after the publication of the anti-Marr article on language and linguistics under Stalin's name in 1950, meant a step back towards another, although less crude application of alien models. The most important feature of the post-1949 period is that the state sponsored standardization movement has harnessed linguistics to its services; this, on the one hand, resulted among others in the final appearance of the first draft of a normative grammar of MSC meant mainly for educational purposes (published in 1956), but, on the other hand, regimented linguistic research to such a degree that matters not directly related to standardization are now publicly ignored by linguists in Mainland China.

Although the systematic description of MSC as a whole by Chinese linguists has not yet broken the bonds of blind application of questionable universals and reached a level from which standardization could considerably profit, modern linguistic research in China has been rather successful in several narrow disciplines, and in a few isolated areas it consequently contributed to the development of the MSC norm to a substantial degree. This applies to dialectal survey, lexicography, and the study of word-formative morphology in particular: in all three cases there had been some scholarly tradition in China to begin with, and some of the large scale projects of linguistic research launched in the 'twenties and the 'thirties, led by such prominent linguists as Zhào Yuánrèn (known in the West as Yuen Ren Chao), Luó Chángpéi, Lí Jǐnxī, and Lù Zhìwéi laid a modern foundation of a highly sophisticated quality which could substantiate some of the crucial decisions necessary in the process of standardization. The results of the dialectal survey, although still far from complete, contributed greatly to a more precise concept of the relationship between MSC and natural dialects, including the dialect of Peking. Research in lexicography enabled the compilation of the first large monolingual dictionary of MSC called *Guóyǔ cídiǎn* 'Dictionary of the National Language' (the first edition of this dictionary was completed in 1943; its revised and abbreviated edition known as *Hànyǔ cídiǎn* 'Dictionary of Chinese' has now become the most popular middle-range dictionary of MSC), which represents the first step towards a normative dictionary comparable in status with such works as the Oxford Dictionary in Great Britain. Work on a normative dictionary of this kind is, in fact, in progress at the Institute of Linguistics of the Academia Sinica in Peking. Analysis of MSC word-formative morphology, the results of which were presented in such works as Lù Zhìwéi's *Hànyǔ de gòucífǎ* 'Word-formation in Chinese' of 1957, has been of great importance for establishing the norm in many respects, the unification of technical terminology in particular.

In general, the modern Chinese movement for language standardization has always been associated with, and often subordinated to the movement for a reform of the writing system.

This in itself is not unusual, since problems of script norm are commonly found of greater immediate importance than questions of the standard language for purposes of nation-wide communication and education. The former are also more obvious and tangible, and to a certain degree easier to solve, as they involve almost exclusively the sole factor of arbitrary decisions. On the other hand, the fact that a movement for script reform could acquire such strength in a country with one of the longest uninterrupted traditions of writing in the world is somewhat surprising and calls for some explanation. The way a writing system may exert influence on the language behaviour of educated speakers was suggested in the preceding section of this chapter; since a substantial reform of script could be expected to have some effect on the development of at least some features of the standard language, it is also important from this viewpoint to take notice of what has actually been happening with the Chinese writing system during the period of formation of MSC.

In the preceding section of this chapter some of the general advantages of the Chinese morphemic script were mentioned. Moreover, it could be added that the adoption of a morphemic script is particularly suitable in a language community using a language like Chinese, that is a language the morphemes of which coincide with a homogeneous set of phonemic units and also with many basic syntactic units. Thus, in the theoretical sense, the morphemic writing system was and still is the almost ideal kind of script for speakers of Chinese, and this is perhaps the main reason why it has been used in China for at least three millennia without any substantial change. The practical shortcomings of the script, mainly the high number of its units and their complexity, are not objective disadvantages. A morphemic writing system takes a long time to learn and it has to be constantly practised but this does not really matter much until time becomes money. It is also a serious obstacle in popular enlightenment and general education on all levels: one has to learn how to read and write before one can start to learn things which can be learned from books, and if it takes several years to master the script, a hard-working peasant will never get past the initial stage, and even an intellectual will have relatively little time left for things not immediately connected with written culture. This, however, is of little importance in a society which has no need for literate peasants and the economic structure of which requires craftsmen rather than scientists. Chinese society had been precisely of this kind until it came into massive contact with the dynamic Western world, and it was not until the moment of this contact that the disadvantages of the morphemic script became apparent. On the contrary, they had been advantageous for the preservation of the basic social and economic structure of imperial China: the relative complexity of the script made it an ideal exclusive tool of communication between the ruling few throughout the country, a kind of sophisticated code which was particularly suitable as the mechanics for building up the tradition of an intricate written culture accessible only to the small leisure minority of the population. The fact that at a certain moment in Chinese history steps began to be taken towards reforming or even discarding the traditional morphemic script is thus not a proof of its intrinsic deficiencies, but an indirect reflexion of the breakdown of the social and economic structure of old China.

It is significant from this point of view that the first steps towards reforming the morphemic writing system were taken on a large scale in China only during the last decade of the nineteenth century, that is about fifty years after the First Opium War and the subsequent penetration of the Western element into China. They are represented by a number of schemes proposed by various Chinese scholars in the years 1892–1910, among which Wáng Zhào's system of 1900 was the most successful and the only one which gained some support of the authorities. All these schemes were proposing a phonemic script, and they differed only in practical solutions: in the number of symbols, their form (either letters of the Latin alphabet, symbols derived from simple characters, or purely arbitrary symbols), and in the choice of the dialect the script was to be based on. Their authors relied mainly on the tradition of Western transcriptions of Chinese which started with the missionary Matteo Ricci's early scheme of 1605, and by the end of the nineteenth century reached its peak with such systems as Thomas F. Wade's transcription of 1867 which is still used today in the English-speaking world in its modified 'Wade-Giles' version, as it first appeared in H. A. Giles' *Chinese–English Dictionary* of 1912, and which was, in another modified version, adopted in China for purposes of the telegraphic communication of proper names some time after 1880. The early Chinese schemes remained, however, more or less private attempts of individual enthusiasts, and it was not until the first years of the Republic that script reform became a state sponsored affair. The purpose of the first official Chinese phonemic transcription called *zhùyīn zìmǔ* 'Pronunciation

Alphabet' (also known as National Phonetic Alphabet, first published in 1918 and in 1920 introduced into schools) was to serve as
a stepping stone towards learning the characters, and also as a
tool for promulgating the National Language. Its other aim was
to prepare ground for further reforms ultimately leading to a
substitution of the morphemic script by a phonemic writing
system. The Pronunciation Alphabet scheme of a phonemic
transcription the symbols of which were adapted forms of simple
characters, was followed by the second official system called
guóyǔ luómǎzì 'National Romanization' (also known as Gwoyeu
Romatzyh or G. R., adopted by the government in 1928), which
used letters of the Latin alphabet for transcribing segmental
phonemes and also tones. Similarly as in the case of the National
Language, the National Romanization scheme about which there
was a vague hope of making it the substitute for characters in the
long run, was attacked by intellectuals of the extreme left who
started propagating the rival scheme of *lādīnghuà* 'Latinization'
(also known as Latinxua, first published by Qū Qiūbái in 1929),
inspired and partly outlined by several Russian sinologues such
as A. A. Dragunov who participated in the projects of cultural
reform among the Chinese population of the Russian Far East.
The struggle of the two schemes never ended in the victory of
either one. The Sino–Japanese war and the subsequent civil war
which resulted in the foundation of the Communist state in Mainland China interrupted the movement for a script reform, but
perhaps the main reason why neither of the two major schemes
could finally succeed before these events and establish itself as the
potential replacement for the morphemic script was the fact that
the main condition for introducing a phonemic writing system did
not exist at the time: a sufficiently precise and strong language
norm had not yet become a reality in China. It was pointed out
earlier that one of the disadvantages of a phonemic script in comparison with a morphemic writing system is the limitation of its
use to a linguistically closely-knit community. The only possible
basis on which a single phonemic script could be introduced in
China was to create such a closely-knit community artificially,
that is by developing a standard language. The degree to which
adopting a phonemic script depended on the development of language norm was perhaps fully realized only by the Communist
government: it was only after 1949 that the movement for script
reform became fully coordinated with organized efforts at language standardization, and that the previously somewhat Utopian

schemes of phonemic script were replaced by more realistic plans. As regards the script itself, the government renewed the movement for reform in two ways: the morphemic script was revised by simplifying the most commonly occurring characters so as to remove at least one of the disadvantages of the script during the time when it still would have to be used (this scheme was approved by the Communist National Assembly in 1956, and the revised simplified script is now used throughout Mainland China), and a new phonemic transcription called *pīnyīn zìmǔ* 'Phonetic Alphabet' was designed (the final version of this transcription known as Pinyin, based roughly on the Latinization scheme but also using elements of the National Romanization, was approved in 1958). Before 1967, when the movement for script reform suffered a presumably temporary setback through the upheavals of the so-called cultural revolution, the Pinyin transcription had been gradually introduced as a secondary writing system in schools, and also used in various public inscriptions. Although its ultimate purpose is to replace the morphemic script, no deadlines have been set, and the issue is not being forced. The Communist Chinese authorities are cautious, apparently realizing that the norm of the language must be firmly established before a phonemic script can be introduced as the sole writing system.

Since the Chinese morphemic script has not yet been substantially reformed in practice, it is difficult to estimate what will happen if and when it is replaced by another, presumably phonemic writing system. This will obviously take place, if it ever does, when the language norm is more firmly established, that is when the oral standard which the script would represent becomes a fact of life in China. If the phonemic script were once accepted, it could be expected to influence the language behaviour of future generations, and ultimately have an effect on the further development of the norm itself. At the moment, it is only possible to presume that such a development would undoubtedly influence the general awareness among literate speakers of the structure of the language, and that the now so typical sensitiveness of educated Chinese to the morphological features of MSC would partly disappear. Just how this would be reflected in their language behaviour remains to be seen if the present trends in the development of language norm and in script reform reach their final aims. As well as in many other respects, China is a fascinating living experiment in language and its function in modern society; the experience which may be gained by observing the development of MSC can be of considerable importance for our understanding of language in general.

LIST OF LINGUISTIC TERMS

The following alphabetically arranged list contains general linguistic terms briefly described as they are used in this book. Terms which are used only for MSC or which can be described only for individual languages are not listed: such terms are explained in the book itself.

acoustic analysis: Analysis of the physical features of sounds in general, speech sounds in particular.

adverbial modifier or *modifier:* A subtype of attributes; the function of what is defined as an adverb (or its expansion) in the given language, in endocentric constructions the heads of which are represented by what are defined as verbs in the given language.

affiliation or *linguistic affiliation:* The relationship between particular systems of sound communication given by their common historical origin and reflected in their common distinctive features.

affix: A bound morpheme characterized mainly by its grammatical meaning and stereotype distribution in words; affixes are further classified as *prefixes* (those which precede root morphemes), *suffixes* (those which follow root morphemes), and *infixes* (those which occur between root morphemes).

affricate: See *consonant.*

allomorph: A concrete representation of a morpheme.

allophone: A concrete representation of a phoneme.

alveolar: See *consonant.*

alveopalatal: See *consonant.*

aspirated: See *consonant.*

aspiration: The release of a brief puff of air through the oral cavity without vocal bands vibrating, most commonly after producing a consonant.

attribute: The member of an endocentric syntactic construction which does not belong to the same form class as the whole construction.

back: See *vowel.*
bilabial: See *consonant.*
borrowing: A lexical item borrowed by one language from another language.
bound form: A language form which represents a unit of a certain level and which never represents a unit of a higher level alone.
bound morpheme: Generally any morpheme which does not represent a word in a given case; a morpheme which never represents a word in particular.
breathed: See *onset.*

central: See *vowel.*
citation form: An isolated language form uttered by a speaker outside any normal speech situation, usually for purposes of linguistic analysis.
clustering: Merging of two or more units into a single unit.
compound: A word containing two or more root morphemes.
consonant: A speech sound produced by placing a considerable obstruction to the outflow of air through the oral cavity. Different types of consonants can be established from the following points of view:

(1) The place of the obstruction and the organs which participate in creating it (see Fig. 27) distinguish consonants such as *bilabial* (both lips in area *1*), *labiodental* (lower lip and upper teeth in area *2*), *dental* (tip of tongue and back part of upper teeth in area *3*), *alveolar* (tip or middle of tongue and alveolar ridge in area *4*), *alveopalatal* (tip or middle of tongue and the front section of the hard palate in area *5*), *palatal* (middle of tongue and the hard palate in area *6*), *velar* (root of tongue and velum in area *7*), and *glottal* (edges of the vocal bands in the space between vocal bands and the attached carti-lages which is known as the glottis).

(2) The kind and degree of obstruction distinguish consonants such as *stops* (complete closure suddenly released), *nasals* (complete closure accompanied by outflow of air through the nasal cavity, see Fig. 31), *fricatives* (partial closure restricting but not stopping the outflow of air), *laterals* (complete closure in the centre of oral cavity accompanied by restricted outflow of air on its sides), and *affricates* (complete closure released into partial closure).

(3) The state of vocal bands during the production; consonants produced while vocal bands are vibrating are *voiced*, consonants produced while vocal bands are not vibrating are *unvoiced*.

(4) What immediately follows the production of the sound; con-sonants which are immediately followed by a brief puff of air without

vocal bands vibrating are *aspirated*, consonants not followed by such a puff of air are *non-aspirated*.

(5) The general shape of the tongue during production (see Fig. 30); consonants produced while the tongue is more or less flat or with its middle arched upwards are *plain*, consonants produced while the tip of the tongue is sharply raised and the middle of the tongue pressed downwards are *retroflex*.

(6) The typical position within larger segments in a given language; for example, MSC consonants which occur only at the beginning of syllables are *initial*, those which occur at the end of syllables are *final*.

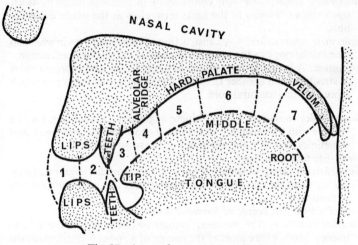

Fig. 27   Areas of consonant production

construction: The arrangement of two or more units of a given language and the relationship within this arrangement.

context: The general relevant situation in which a language form occurs in normal speech; consists of other language forms in its environment or of non-language phenomena or both.

continuous: Referring to constructions or other arrangements the components of which are in immediate succession.

coordinate: Referring to constructions each component of which participates in their structure in an equal manner.

degree of formalization: The amount of grammatical meaning a language form has acquired, usually reflected in the phonemic and phonetic shape of this form.

dental: See *consonant*.

dialect: A system of sound communication among some members of a particular language community; similarly as language itself, it is partly defined by its distinctive features, and partly established on the grounds of cultural and historical considerations.

diphthong: See *vowel.*

discontinuous: Referring to constructions or other arrangements the succession of whose components is interrupted by the occurrence of units or unit components not belonging to these constructions or arrangements.

duration: The relative dimension of a speech sound or speech sounds in time; the physical correlate of length.

endocentric construction: Any construction of language forms in which one member belongs to the same form class as the whole construction.

exocentric construction: Any construction of language forms in which no member belongs to the same form class as the whole construction.

expansion: A language form which is larger in size and more complex in structure than another language form which it contains and which represents its structural core.

final: (1) See *consonant*; (2) In Chinese linguistics the total features of a syllable with the exception of the initial consonant or semivowel, and sometimes also with the exception of the respective tone.

form: See *language form.*

form class: A group of language forms which share important features, among them the occurrence in grammatically identical environments in particular.

formalization: See *degree of formalization.*

formant structure: The number, mutual position, and shape of frequency bands where most of the energy of a vowel is distributed; the physical correlate of vowel quality.

free form: A language form which represents a unit of a certain level and which may also represent a unit of a higher level alone.

free morpheme: Generally any morpheme which represents a word in a given case; a morpheme which may represent a word in particular.

fricative: See *consonant.*

front: See *vowel.*

function: The role played by a language form or language form component in the grammatical system of a language.

functional burdening: The relative proportion of grammatical meaning as opposed to the proportion of lexical meaning of a language form.

fundamental frequency: The number of complete repetitions of a complex sound wave within a set period of time, measured in cycles per second; the physical correlate of pitch.

glottal: See *consonant.*

grammar: See *grammatical system.*

grammatical meaning: Meaning of a language form which can be understood and described only by referring to other language forms.

grammatical system or *grammar:* The total of all relevant general features of a given language; in a more limited sense, the morphology and syntax of a given language.

head: The member of an endocentric syntactic construction which belongs to the same form class as the whole construction.

high: See *vowel.*

homophone: A language form identical in phonemic shape with another language form but different in distribution and meaning.

IC: See *immediate constituent.*

idiolect: The speech behaviour of a single member of a language community.

immediate constituent or *IC:* The maximum structural component of a language form (or a language form component), i.e. a component which itself does not constitute a part of another larger structural component of the same language form (or language form component).

infix: See *affix.*

initial: (1) See *consonant*; (2) In Chinese linguistics the initial consonant or semivowel of a syllable.

intensity level: The total amount of energy present in a complete repetition of a sound wave, measured in ergs per cycle, but more commonly in terms of power in microwatts, and even more commonly in the relative units called decibels; the physical correlate of loudness.

intonation: A suprasegmental feature of a relatively large speech segment, mainly or partly characterized by a typical pitch contour.

juncture: The transitional feature of the link between successive syllables.

labiodental: See *consonant.*

language: In general, a system of communication by sound among human beings; a specific language is a particular system of sound communication partly defined by its distinctive features and partly established on the grounds of cultural and historical considerations, among members of a particular community.

language form or *form:* (1) Any meaningful sound or arrangement of sounds which occurs in a given language; (2) Any concrete variant of a given language, such as a dialect or a style.

language norm: The total set of rules concerning the standard language, established partly arbitrarily by members of a particular language community; usually closely connected with the respective norm of writing.

lateral: See *consonant.*

length: A relative feature of speech sounds which causes them to be recognized as longer or shorter than others; the perceptional correlate of duration.

level: See *structural level.*

lexical item: A member of the vocabulary of a given language.

lexical meaning: Meaning of a language form which can be understood and described without referring to other language forms.

linguistic affiliation: See *affiliation.*

loudness: A relative feature of speech sounds which causes them to be recognized as louder or less loud than others; the perceptional correlate of intensity level.

low: See *vowel.*

marker: A bound morpheme or any other bound form which does not occur as a word constituent; a bound constituent of syntactic constructions.

meaning: The non-formal feature of a language form common to all the situations in which the language form is used.

medial: See *vowel.*

mid: See *vowel.*

modifier: See *adverbial modifier.*

morph: A single instance of a minimal meaningful unit in speech.

morpheme: A minimal meaningful unit of a particular language.

morphological: Referring to morphology or one of its aspects.

morphology: The way in which morphemes participate in the structure of words in a given language, and the features and behaviour of morphemes in a given language in general; also the study of this.

morphophonemic feature: In general, any phonemic feature of a morpheme; a phonemic feature conditioned by morphological factors in particular.

morphophonemics: The total of morphophonemic features of a given language; also the study of these features.

nasal: See *consonant.*

nasalization: The participation of the outflow of air through the nasal cavity in the production of a speech sound (see Fig. 31).

nasalized: See *vowel.*

nominal referent or *referent:* The function of what is defined as a noun (or its expansion) in the given language, in endocentric, potentially exocentric constructions the heads of which are represented by what are defined as verbs in the given language.

non-aspirated: See *consonant.*

non-nasalized: See *vowel.*

norm of writing or *written norm:* The total set of rules concerning the orthography and the written style, established arbitrarily by members of a particular language community; usually based on the respective language norm.

nucleus: The head of the construction which is the head of all constructions in a sentence; a syntactic function in languages characterized by
the predominance of endocentric over exocentric constructions,
usually but not necessarily represented by what are defined as verbs
in the given language.

onset: The transition between silence and the production of a vowel;
breathed onset is a transition from silence through free outflow of air
without vocal band vibration to vowel production, without any closure or semiclosure at any point.

orthography: The conventionalized way of using a writing system by
members of a language community.

palatal: See *consonant.*

paradigmatic: Referring to *paradigmatic patterning.*

paradigmatic patterning: Any way in which the forms of a given
language can be grouped together to make the abstraction of a
common significant pattern possible; in particular the way in which
all or most words of a given language can be divided into groups
characterized by sets of affixes which occur in these words.

pause: A moment of silence of any dimension in time, in the speech of a
single speaker.

phoneme: A minimal unit of a particular language which may distinguish its language forms.

phoneme component: A speech sound which does not represent a
phoneme in a given language but only a part of a phoneme.

phonemic or *phonological:* Referring to phonemics or one of its aspects.

phonemic script: See *phonemic writing system.*

phonemic shape: The phonemic features of a language form.

phonemic solution: The way in which speech sounds occurring in a given
language are classified in terms of phonemes and phoneme components.

phonemic status: The position of a given speech sound in relation to the
phonemic system, i.e. its occurrence or non-occurrence as a minimal
unit distinguishing language forms.

phonemic writing system or *phonemic script:* A writing system the basic
units of which are symbols of phonemes.

phonemics or *phonology:* The way in which phonemes participate in the
structure of larger units in a given language, and the features and
behaviour of phonemes in a given language in general; also the study
of this.

phonetic: Referring to phonetics or one of its aspects.

phonetic shape: The phonetic features of a language form.

phonetics: The physical features, production, and behaviour of speech
sounds in general or of speech sounds of a particular language; also
the study of this.

12—C.L.T.

phonological: See *phonemic.*

phonology: See *phonemics.*

pitch: A relative feature of speech sounds which causes them to be recognized as higher or lower than others; the perceptional correlate of fundamental frequency.

plain: See *consonant* and *vowel.*

prefix: See *affix.*

referent: See *nominal referent.*

retroflex: See *consonant* and *vowel.*

rhythm: The distribution of stressed and unstressed syllables in relatively large segments of speech, and the characteristic features of this distribution in a given language.

root: See *root morpheme.*

root morpheme or *root:* A free morpheme, or a bound morpheme characterized mainly by its lexical meaning and largely unpredictable distribution in words.

rounded: See *vowel.*

sandhi: Mutual influence of language forms or their components reflected in their phonetic shape.

script: See *writing system.*

segmental: Referring to a segmental feature.

segmental feature: Any feature of language forms which can be described in terms of vowels and consonants.

semivowel: A speech sound sharing the features of vowels and consonants, i.e. a vowel-like sound characterized by its approximation towards a consonant-like obstruction.

sentence: A construction of a segmental unit with a closed homogeneous pattern of rhythm and intonation.

simple vowel: See *vowel.*

simple word: A word containing a single root morpheme.

standard language: A system of sound communication selected and developed by members of a particular language community as the proper and correct form of speech behaviour; usually but not necessarily the basis of the written style used by members of the given community.

stop: See *consonant.*

stress: In general a suprasegmental feature distinguishing segmentally and otherwise suprasegmentally identical language forms, which is mainly or partly characterized by a relatively high degree of loudness.

structural: Referring to structure or one of its aspects.

structural level or *level:* An artificial cut through the system of a language established by applying a single criterion in analysing the language.

structure: The general features of the way in which units of a given language are arranged.

style: A variant of a language or dialect characterized mainly by a specific selection of language forms.

subordinate: Referring to constructions whose individual components do not participate in their structure in an equal manner.

suffix: See *affix.*

suprasegmental: Referring to a suprasegmental feature.

suprasegmental feature: Any sound feature of language forms which can be described only in terms of modification of the segmental features of these forms.

syllable: A minimal phonemic unit which may contain a suprasegmental feature as one of its immediate constituents.

syntactic: Referring to syntax or one of its aspects.

syntax: The way in which words participate in the structure of larger units in a given language, and the structure of units larger than words in a given language in general; also the study of this.

tempo: The number of speech sounds produced in a set period of time.

tone: (1) In general a suprasegmental feature distinguishing segmentally identical language forms, which is mainly or partly characterized by a typical pitch contour; (2) A tone phoneme or toneme.

toneme: A tone which has the status of a phoneme in a given language.

transcription: A system of arbitrary graphic symbols for recording speech sounds or the phonemes of a given language (exceptionally other units), used for specialized purposes, such as linguistic description or language learning.

triphthong: See *vowel.*

unit: (1) An abstraction of language forms or their components which occur on a specific structural level of a given language and which share one or more distinctive features important from the point of view of the structure of the language; (2) An element of a writing system.

unrounded: See *vowel.*

unvoiced: See *consonant.*

utterance: Any segment of speech preceded and followed by a relatively long pause.

velar: See *consonant.*

verbal nucleus: A nucleus which is represented by what is defined as a verb in the given language.

vocabulary: The total of language forms, mainly words and constructions larger than words in a given language, each of which is characterized by a high degree of recurrence and a distinctive and largely unpredictable feature of meaning.

voiced: See *consonant.*

voicing: The participation of vocal band vibration in the production of a speech sound.

vowel: A speech sound produced by modifying the shape of the oral
  cavity but not considerably obstructing the outflow of air passing
  through it. In normal speech (i.e. with the exception of whispering),
  all vowels are produced while the vocal bands are vibrating. Different
  types of vowels can be established from the following points of view:

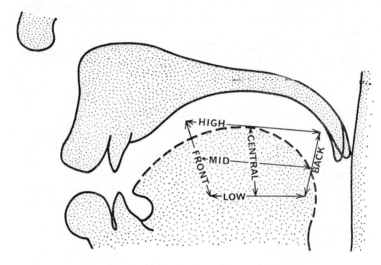

Fig. 28   Positions of tongue in vowel production

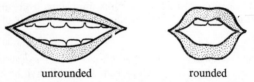

unrounded   rounded

Fig. 29   Shape of lips in vowel production

(1) The shape of the oral cavity during production which is mainly
given by the position of the bulk of the tongue (see Fig. 28); the position of the tongue along the vertical axis conditions the difference
between *high*, *mid*, and *low* vowels, while the raising of the respective
part of the tongue along the horizontal axis conditions the difference
between *front*, *central*, and *back* vowels.

(2) The shape of lips during production (see Fig. 29); vowels produced with the corners of lips contracted are *rounded*, vowels produced with spread lips are *unrounded*.

(3) The general shape of the tongue during production (see Fig. 30); vowels produced while the tongue is more or less flat or with its middle arched upwards are *plain*, vowels produced while the tip of the tongue is sharply raised and the middle of the tongue pressed downwards are *retroflex*.

(4) The retention of the shape of the oral cavity during production; vowels produced while the shape of the oral cavity remains more or less the same are *simple*, vowels produced while the oral cavity distinctly shifts through two or three characteristic shapes are *diphthongs* or *triphthongs*. The partial sounds of diphthongs and triphthongs are *vowel components*.

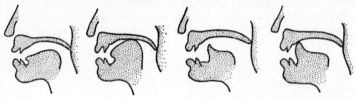

plain vowel   plain consonant   retroflex vowel   retroflex consonant

Fig. 30   Examples of differences in the general shape of the tongue during vowel and consonant production

(5) The degree to which air is permitted to flow through the nasal cavity during production (see Fig. 31); vowels produced while the nasal cavity is closed are *non-nasalized*, vowels produced while the nasal cavity is partly or fully open are *nasalized*.

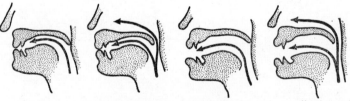

non-nasal consonant   nasal consonant   non-nasalized vowel   nasalized vowel

Fig. 31   Examples of the participation of the nasal cavity during consonant and vowel production

(6) The typical position within larger segments in a given language; for example, MSC vowels which occur in the middle of syllables are *medial*.

vowel component: See *vowel*.

vowel quality: The feature of individual vowels which causes them to be recognized from each other; the perceptional correlate of formant structure.

word: The smallest unit which the speakers of a given language consciously operate with, or the smallest unit which may function as an immediate constituent of segmental sentences.

word class: A form class all members of which are words.

word-formative morphology: The way in which root morphemes participate in the structure of words in a given language; also the study of this.

writing system or *script:* A system of arbitrary graphic symbols used for purposes of written communication by members of one or more language communities.

written norm: See *norm of writing*.

written style: In general, a system of written communication among human beings; a specific written style is a particular system of written communication used by members of one or more language communities.

SELECT BIBLIOGRAPHY

Only standard works published in English which are, in the author's opinion, of basic importance for Modern Chinese descriptive and applied linguistics are listed here. Most of the books and articles whose titles are given below contain further bibliographical data. For a detailed select bibliography of contemporary works on Modern Chinese see the section 'Langue' of the *Revue Bibliographique de Sinologie*, a yearly periodical published at the Hague by Mouton & Co. since 1957. The most complete publicly accessible bibliography of works on MSC is contained in *Report No. 5* of the Ohio State University Project on Linguistic Analysis, Columbus, Ohio, 1953. The brief introductory notes and comments on the individual titles listed below express the private opinion of the author of this book, and their only purpose is to serve as a rough guide to those who are completely unfamiliar with Modern Chinese linguistics.

TEXTBOOKS

John DeFrancis, *Beginning Chinese, Intermediate Chinese*, and *Advanced Chinese* (each with a separate character text). New Haven, Conn. and London: Yale University Press, 1963–1966.

Perhaps the most comprehensive and best organized course in MSC existing at the moment. It is accompanied by tapes, and it can be profitably used even for self-teaching purposes. Its only major shortcoming is that it reflects a stage in the development of the language which already belongs to the past, at least as far as Mainland China is concerned, primarily due to the fact that it was compiled with the help of MSC speakers who have not lived in Mainland China since the late 'forties. However, since this is reflected only in the more delicate aspects of vocabulary and the even more delicate features of grammar as they are presented in the textbook, it does not diminish the general value of the course to a considerable degree. The textbook is being supplemented by readers compiled by the same author.

M. G. Tewksbury, *Speak Chinese*. New Haven, Conn.: Yale University Press, 1948. (Revised first section published in 1955.)

An earlier, somewhat mechanical, course whose major advantage is that it is followed by a useful series of readers and other material published by the Institute of Far Eastern Languages of Yale University. It is even less up-to-date than DeFrancis' textbook by which it has now been superseded. Also accompanied by tapes.

Y. R. Chao, *Mandarin Primer* (with a separate character text). Cambridge, Mass.: Harvard University Press, 1948. (Also later printings.)

By now a rather out-of-date course which has, however, the advantage of being written by the Nestor of Modern Chinese linguistics. Its language, although slightly oldfashioned, is lively and fresh, and the book has the charm typical for all Yuen Ren Chao's writings. It has a very useful and interesting introductory part, and it is accompanied by a set of records.

Modern Chinese Reader (in two parts). Peking: 'Epoch' Publishing House, 1958.

A course by far inferior to the preceding three in method and presentation but more up-to-date in the language material it is based on. It is being followed by elementary readers also published in Peking.

DICTIONARIES

At the moment, there exists no large MSC–English dictionary which could be used as the sole basic source of information on MSC vocabulary and also for reading modern Chinese texts: large Chinese–English dictionaries which provide some information on MSC beside other historical and stylistic levels, mainly *Mathews' Chinese–English Dictionary*, are generally inferior in lexicographical standard, and their coverage of MSC is not sufficient. The three dictionaries listed below are mainly suitable for beginners or for a given specific purpose; for more detailed comprehensive data it is necessary to refer to large monolingual dictionaries of MSC, such as *Hànyǔ cídiǎn* 'Dictionary of Chinese', or one of the few good large dictionaries of MSC and a language other than English. Kuraishi Takeshirō's MSC–Japanese *Iwanami Chūgokugo Jiten* is an outstanding example of the latter: its arrangement and exemplification are so lucid and exhaustive that it can be profitably used even without any knowledge of Japanese. Apart from

the English–Chinese section of the *Dictionary of Spoken Chinese* listed
below, there is no reliable basic English–MSC dictionary available at
present. Dictionaries of this kind published in the West (such as J. C.
Quo's *Concise English–Chinese Dictionary, Romanized*) are invariably
too small and lacking in exemplification, while those published in China
are explanatory (Chinese items contained in them are often loose
descriptions rather than equivalents of the English lexical items), and
consequently almost useless for speakers of English.

W. Simon, *A Beginner's Chinese–English Dictionary of the National
Language* (*Gwoyeu*). London: Lund Humphries & Co., 1947. (Revised
edition 1957.)

A reliable middle-size dictionary containing useful information of
many kinds beside the basic word list. It is somewhat too complicated
for real beginners owing to the use of the Gwoyeu Romatzyh transcription. Suitable for language learning and for reading simple
modern texts. It does not include most of the common lexical items
which have appeared in MSC since 1949.

Dictionary of Spoken Chinese. New Haven, Conn. and London: Yale
University Press, 1966.

A dictionary based on the principle of maximum coverage and
exemplification of a minimal set of lexical items. It consists of a
Chinese–English and an English–Chinese section, and it contains a
brief description of MSC grammar. This dictionary is extremely good
for language learning but, since it lists only a small number of lexical
items, it is unsuitable for reading any but the most elementary texts.
It is, in fact, a revised edition of the War Department *Dictionary of
Spoken Chinese* published in 1945 as a U.S. Army manual; the original edition, although less up-to-date (the new edition includes many
post-1949 lexical items) was nevertheless superior to the new edition
in lexicographical standard and in the general linguistic standard of
the introductory description of MSC grammar.

Y. R. Chao and L. S. Yang, *Concise Dictionary of Spoken Chinese*.
Cambridge, Mass.: Harvard University Press, 1947. (Also later
printings.)

This is a classified list and description of MSC morphemes rather
than a dictionary in the broader sense. As such it is the most exhaustive
and accurate source of information and an indispensable manual.
However, since it does not list polymorphemic items systematically,
its practical use for language learning and text reading is limited.

GENERAL DESCRIPTIONS

Beside brief discussions such as that contained in the Introduction to
Yuen Ren Chao's *Mandarin Primer*, there is no single comprehensive

general source of information on MSC in English. The books listed below describe Chinese from the historical and comparative points of view; as such, they are mainly useful for establishing the place of MSC within the broader frame of reference of history and linguistic affiliation, but they do not provide many data on MSC itself.

B. Karlgren, *Sound and Symbol in Chinese*. London: Oxford University Press, 1923. (Revised edition published in Hong Kong and London: Hong Kong University Press and Oxford University Press, 1962.)

One of the popular books by the most prominent modern Western sinologue. It is rather out of date by now and it contains many half-truths and misconceptions. As a simple general introduction to the subject it has not, however, been surpassed as yet.

R. A. D. Forrest, *The Chinese Language*. London: Faber and Faber, 1948. (Revised edition 1965.)

A considerably more detailed and more recent essay concentrating mainly on the question of Chinese dialects; in general approach, it is not, however, much more advanced than Karlgren's book.

C. F. Voegelin and F. M. Voegelin, Ed., 'Languages of the World: Sino–Tibetan' (Fascicles 1–5). In *Anthropological Linguistics*, vol. 6 (1964), no. 3, and vol. 7 (1965), nos. 3–6.

A large comparative description of Sino–Tibetan languages containing an excellent brief discussion of MSC. The existing edition in *Anthropological Linguistics* is, however, full of misprints and other technical errors, and it can be referred to only with extreme caution.

PHONEMICS

C. F. Hockett, 'Peiping Phonology'. In *Journal of the American Oriental Society*, *67* (1947), pp. 253–267. Also in M. Joos, Ed. *Readings in Linguistics*. New York: American Council of Learned Societies, 1957 (also later editions), pp. 217–228.

C. F. Hockett, 'Peiping Morphophonemics'. In *Language*, *26* (1950), pp. 63–85. Also in M. Joos, Ed., *Readings in Linguistics*, pp. 315–328.

Two articles of key importance not only for MSC phonemics but also for modern phonemic theory in general.

GRAMMAR

For a brief description of MSC morphology and syntax see the Introduction to each of the two editions of the *Dictionary of Spoken Chinese*, and the Introduction to Yuen Ren Chao's *Mandarin Primer*. The

Concise Dictionary of Spoken Chinese also contains a relevant Introduction.

Y. R. Chao, *A Grammar of Spoken Chinese*. Berkeley and Los Angeles, Cal.: University of California Press, 1965.
    The most comprehensive grammar of MSC in English.

M. A. K. Halliday, 'Grammatical Categories in Modern Chinese'. In *Transactions of the Philological Society*, 1956, pp. 177–224.
    An outline of the system of MSC grammar reflecting the approach characteristic for the recent development of the tradition established by J. R. Firth in British linguistics.

H. F. Simon, 'Two Substantival Complexes in Standard Chinese'. In *Bulletin of the School of Oriental and African Studies*, 1953, 2, pp. 327–355.

H. F. Simon, 'Some Remarks on the Structure of the Verb Complex in Standard Chinese'. In *Bulletin of the School of Oriental and African Studies*, 1958, 3, pp. 551–577.
    Descriptions of two types of MSC syntactic constructions using an approach similar to that of Halliday's article.

Lu Chih-wei, 'The Status of the Word in Chinese Linguistics'. In P. Ratchnevsky, Ed., *Beiträge zum Problem des Wortes im Chinesischen*. Berlin: Akademie-Verlag, 1960, pp. 34–47.
    A refreshing essay on the key problem of MSC grammar by one of the most outstanding contemporary Mainland Chinese linguists.

W. S-Y. Wang, 'Some Syntactic Rules in Mandarin'. In *Proceedings of the IX International Congress of Linguists* (*Cambridge, Mass., 1962*). The Hague: Mouton & Co., 1964, pp. 191–202.
    A brief outline of MSC syntax from the viewpoint of transformational grammar.

THE NORM

Studies in Chinese Communist Terminology. Berkeley, Cal.: University of California, 1956–.
    This excellent series is more than its title suggests: it contains items ranging from descriptions of sets of new MSC vocabulary elements to the translation of the first draft of a normative grammar of MSC which appeared in Mainland China in 1956. The series is the only existing source of information in English on new trends in MSC vocabulary and normative grammar.

C. F. Voegelin and F. M. Voegelin, Ed., 'Languages of the World: Sino–Tibetan' (Fascicle 1). In *Anthropological Linguistics*, vol. 6 (1964), no. 3, pp. 19–29.

Probably the clearest brief account of the nature of the traditional Chinese writing system in English. Much preferable to the various existing essays on the Chinese writing system contained in general books on script (such as D. Diringer's *Writing, Its Origin and Early History*. New York: Praeger, 1962) most of which tend to perpetuate myths about the system.

W. Simon, *How to Study and Write Chinese Characters*. London: Lund Humphries & Co., 1944. (Revised edition 1959.)

A textbook of the traditional Chinese writing system.

John DeFrancis, *Nationalism and Language Reform in China*. Princeton, N.J.: Princeton University Press, 1950.

A detailed essay on the development of the language norm and the reform of script in Modern China.

INDEX

196 Index

prefix (also see 'affix'), —bú-~bù-,
58, 60–61, 70–71, 86, 113; verbal,
143
Project on Linguistic Analysis, Ohio
State University, 183
prominence, point of, 40, 47
pronoun, 114, 117, 130–131
'Pronunciation Alphabet', see 'zhùyīn
zìmǔ'
proper name, 65
pǔtōnghuà, 164

Qū Qiūbái, 169
Quo, J. C., 185

-r, see 'suffix'
r-sound, 27
radical, a, 151–152
reconstruction, 22
redundancy, 110, 118, 142–143, 159
reduplication, 78–79
referent, nominal, 70, 76–77, 81, 130–
133, 137, 143–144, 176
reform of the writing system, see
'writing system'
regular alternation of stress, see
'stress'
representation, level of, 153
response, 92–93, 102
resultative verb, see 'verb'
retroflex, see 'consonant', 'vowel'
Revue Bibliographique de Sinologie,
183
rhyming, 48
rhythm, 46, 121–126, 128, 178,
rhythmical, —homogeneity, see
'homogeneity', —pattern, 40
Ricci, Matteo, 168
rising tone, see 'tone'
'Rites of [the state] Chou, The', see
'Zhōu lǐ'
River dialects, see 'dialects, Northern
Chinese'
Romance languages, see 'languages'
root, see 'morpheme'
root morpheme, see 'morpheme'
rote repetition, 96
rules, of the standard, 162 et seq.,
Russian, 79, 143–144

sandhi, 178; tone, 38–39, 41–42,
46–47

script, see 'writing system'
script reform, see 'writing system'
segmental, —constituent of intonation pattern, see 'intonation',
—features, 23 et seq., 35, 85, 92,
116, 121, 178, —ɪc of the syllable,
see 'syllable', —phoneme, see
'phoneme', —morpheme, see 'morpheme', —sentence, see 'sentence',
—structure, 35, 40–41, 116, 129,
—unit, 35–36
semi-marker, 119, 123
semivowel (also see 'vowel, onset of'),
32, 49–51, 178
sentence, 44–47, 56–59, 61, 81, 83,
93–95, 100–107, 109–110, 112–115,
117–120, 121 et seq., 178;
complete, 129–130, 132–133, 142;
complex, 129; equational, 130;
functive, 130; grammatical, 93,
101; incomplete, 128–129, 132–133;
pattern, 107–108; segmental, 94–
95; simple, 129–130; stative, 130;
structure of, 95; ungrammatical,
93, 101
Shan, 13
Shanghai, 16
Shansi, 16
Shantung, 16
Shaw, G. B., 156
Shensi, 16
shící, see 'word, full'
shízì, see 'word, full'
sibilance, see 'consonant'
Simon, H. F., 187
Simon, W., 12, 185, 188
simple word, see 'word'
Sino-Japanese war, 145, 164–165,
169
sinologue, 21, 53, 90
sinology, 50, 54
Sino-Tibetan languages, see 'languages'
slang, 20
slogan, political, 136–138, 160
'Some Remarks on the Structure of
the Verb Complex in Standard
Chinese', 187
'Some Syntactic Rules in Mandarin',
187
Sound and Symbol in Chinese, 186